TEACHING ROMANS

Volume 1

TEACHING
ROMANS
Volume 1

Unlocking Romans 1–8 for the Bible Teacher

CHRISTOPHER ASH

SERIES EDITORS: DAVID JACKMAN & ROBIN SYDSERFF

PTMEDIA

CHRISTIAN
FOCUS

Teaching Romans volume 2: Unlocking Romans 9–16 for the Bible Teacher is also available (ISBN 978-1-84550-456-4)

Copyright© Proclamation Trust Media 2009

ISBN 978-1-84550-455-7

10 9 8 7 6 5 4 3 2 1

Published in 2009

by
Christian Focus Publications Ltd.,
Geanies House, Fearn, Ross-shire,
IV20 1TW, Scotland, Great Britain
with
Proclamation Trust Media,
Willcox House, 140-148 Borough High Street,
London, SE1 1LB, Great Britain.
www.proctrust.org.uk

www.christianfocus.com

Cover design by Moose77.com
Printed in the U.S.A.

Contents

SERIES PREFACE

Whether you are a preacher, Bible study or small group leader, the Teach the Bible series will be an ideal companion. Few commentaries are written specifically with the preacher or Bible teacher in mind, and with the sermon or Bible study as the point of reference. The preacher or teacher, the sermon or talk, and the listener are the key 'drivers' in this series.

The books are purposefully practical, seeking to offer real help for those involved in teaching the Bible to others. The introductory chapters contain basic 'navigation' material to get you into the text of Romans: 'Getting our Bearings in Romans', 'Why Should We Preach and Teach Romans?' and 'Ideas for Preaching and Teaching a Series on Romans'.

This introductory material is followed by detailed work on the text, taking the preacher or Bible teacher through the various steps from text to sermon or Bible study. Volume 1 covers Romans 1–8. The companion volume 2 covers chapters 9–16.

Romans is a 'big' book in every sense! But it is a vitally important book for the Church in every generation. Teaching Romans is, therefore, an important contribution to the series. We are delighted that Christopher Ash, our friend and colleague at The Proclamation Trust, agreed to distil his many years of preaching and teaching Romans in these volumes. Christopher is first a preacher, but also a teacher of preachers. That rare combination brings rigour and accessibility, scholarship and application to his writing. We wholeheartedly commend the results of his labours to preachers and teachers of God's Word.

Our thanks to Zoë Moore, Sam Parkinson, Moira Anderson and Anne and George Sydserff for editorial assistance and, as ever, to the team at Christian Focus for their committed partnership in this project.

David Jackman and Robin Sydserff
Series Editors, London, October 2008

Author's Preface and Acknowledgements

On a work visit to Italy some years ago, I managed to set aside 24 hours to visit Florence as a tourist. As I studied the guidebook on the train, my heart sank as I realized just how much there was to see. There was enough for a month's continuous sightseeing. A young man joined me on the train. He was 'doing' the whole of Europe in a month and he asked me if there was much to see in Florence. With English understatement I dryly said there was probably enough to keep him occupied for a day. Romans needs to be approached as I approached Florence, with awe and wonder at the riches to be explored in it.

Few of us will have the chance to teach right through Romans. One aim of these two volumes is to help us teach parts of Romans with a better grasp of the whole, and especially in line with the purpose of the whole letter (see Chapter 2). My aim is to help us when we feel daunted. We know Romans is important. But it is big, it seems complicated, and we know that in places its interpretation has sparked controversy. If we have been puzzled by chapter 7, or by chapters 9–11, we are not the first to have struggled. So we wonder what hope we have of teaching it faithfully. I hope these volumes will help.

The difficulty with going into print about Romans is that I find I am constantly seeing new things in the letter, always developing my understanding. Although I teach it every year at Cornhill, I never teach it exactly the same way and keep realizing things I had not really grasped before. However carefully I have worked over the material, this book cannot avoid being a 'work in progress'. I hope it will be read as such.

Teaching Romans on the Cornhill Training Course year by year and preaching it in churches have been the most helpful influences in deepening my understanding. I am grateful to the Cornhill students for their thoughtful engagement, questions and comments. I am grateful to St. Andrew the Great, Cambridge, to All Saints, Little Shelford, to Emmanuel, Wimbledon, and to all the other churches who have generously invited me to preach from Romans. Although commentaries have their place, I often feel that real understanding only comes in the context of preaching in the local church. A number of my fellow ministers and others, in churches and at Proclamation Trust conferences, have helped me with encouragement and comments, including Mark Ashton, Ian Garrett, Jonathan Fletcher, William Taylor, Mark Lawrence, Ian Dobbie, Alistair Tresidder, Mark Meynell, Marcus Nodder, Alistair and Sarah Seabrook, Neil Robbie, Stephen Walton, and Stephen Moore. I owe much to my colleagues at The Proclamation Trust, especially David Jackman and Robin Sydserff, the series editors, and to Moira Anderson for checking the Bible references. As usual, my faithful wife Carolyn has cheerfully borne the brunt of my obsession with this letter during all sorts of times when she might have wished not to have to share me with the apostle Paul.

Christopher Ash
London
October 2008

How to Use This Book

After the introductory chapters, the main chapters on the text of Romans are structured as follows:

A. The main section in each chapter is entitled **'Attentive listening to the text'**. Beginning with the **context** and **structure** of the passage, we work through the text carefully. Since this is not a technical commentary, I have tried to steer a clear line through the main flow of the text. I have tried to cover the most important disputed options, but have not had space to defend each decision, or to refer to the secondary literature. I hope that, even if you disagree with my interpretation in places, the book will remain helpful.

B. After each section of text we turn **'From text to teaching'**. Here we stand back from the detail of the text and ask two questions. First, what is the central theme of this passage? We need to do this so that we do not miss the wood for the trees. Second, what is the purpose of this passage? Why did Paul write it, and why did God inspire him to write it? This will give us controls and pointers to the major directions in which the passage applies to us and our hearers. I have also added some '**Pointers to application**'. These are not written systematically, but I hope will stimulate thought.

C.   At the end of each chapter there are '**Suggestions for preaching and teaching the text**'. This includes suggestions for how to divide it up, ideas for possible sermon outlines, and some ideas for leading Bible studies. These are only suggestions. Preaching is never done in a vacuum. It depends crucially on the relationship between the preacher, with his personality, and the hearers, in their particular culture and circumstances. Different preachers express the same truths in different ways. Different groups of hearers need clarification on different points, and to be guarded against different misunderstandings. So, although I hope the suggestions may be helpful, no preacher will tackle a passage in exactly the same way, and no hearers will need the passage tackled in exactly the same way. This is especially true when it comes to pressing home the implications of the passage. Bible study questions are of two kinds: the first group get our noses in the text to make sure we have read it attentively; the second group are more open-ended and point the way to honest application.

A Note on Bible Translation

The main translation used is the New International Version (NIV). All translations make compromises so as to read smoothly in English. So from time to time I have given pointers to a more literal translation from the Greek. I have done this in three ways.

The main text of Romans has been printed in a smaller type than the main text and indented to show the logical flow of each passage. Also, to show where the Greek differs from the NIV the following indicators have been used:

1. Words added in square brackets in italics after a phrase in NIV are a more literal rendering. For example, in 1:5 [*to the obedience of faith*] is a more literal translation of NIV 'the obedience that comes from faith'.
2. Words put in parentheses are in the NIV but not in the Greek. (NIV has added them to make the translation more readable.)
3. Words added in italics are in the Greek but have been omitted by NIV.

In the main text, I have used NIV with these minor altera-
tions. In particular I have tried to draw attention to important logical connecting words ('for', 'therefore', etc.), and
highlight word echoes in the Greek, where Paul has used an
important word several times in the letter. With important
phrases such as 'works of the law', 'the obedience of faith', and
'the righteousness of God', I have tried to translate literally. In
3:21-26, I have simply replaced NIV by a more literal translation.

Bible references with no book stated are all from Romans.

SECTION ONE:

Introductory
Material

STRUCTURE OF ROMANS

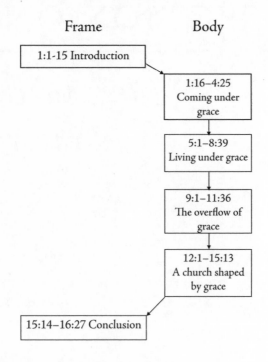

Frame   Body

1:1-15 Introduction

1:16–4:25
Coming under
grace

5:1–8:39
Living under grace

9:1–11:36
The overflow of
grace

12:1–15:13
A church shaped
by grace

15:14–16:27 Conclusion

I

Getting our Bearings in Romans

This chapter is to help the preacher get into Romans. It is not a suggestion for how to begin a teaching series. Indeed it would be better not to start a teaching series with the material in this chapter. Few things start a teaching series more dully than a long introduction about matters like the precise date of writing, and where Paul was writing from. There is a place for this careful scholarly work, but church Bible teaching is usually not it. The danger, apart from inducing boredom, is that our hearers get the impression that Bible reading cannot really begin until we have completed what feels like a rather dull jigsaw puzzle.

On the contrary, we need to show people that profitable Bible reading begins with careful Bible reading, reading the letter attentively as it stands. We want to show people that the youngest Christian can read Romans and profit by it. Of course we thank God for those who translate it reliably and for those who, as it were, take us by the hand and guide us through the letter and link it to other parts of Scripture. But the aim of scholars who do this is to put the Bible into the hands of the ordinary Christian reader. In this we are the heirs of the great Bible translators, whose aim was famously put by William Tyndale when he said to a smug cleric that before long he would make the ploughman know more of the Bible than the clergyman. In our Bible teaching we are to continue what Tyndale began, putting the Bible into the hands of those we teach so that they may read it for themselves and be blessed in their reading.

It is a useful exercise, before embarking on teaching Romans, to read the whole letter aloud (preferably more than once), making a note of indications which tell us either about the writer and his circumstances or about the readers and their church. This will help us get a feel for the letter as a whole. It doesn't matter very much exactly when Paul wrote it, or where he wrote it from. But it matters a great deal to know about the people to whom he wrote it, and what was going on with them, and therefore why he wrote it (which is the subject of the next chapter).

Where and when in Paul's ministry did he write Romans?

Having said this, it is not difficult to get a rough idea of where Romans fits in to Paul's life. In 15:19-23 he says he has preached the gospel 'from Jerusalem all the way around to Illyricum' (roughly modern-day Albania) and that 'there is no more place for me to work in these regions'. Presumably he has completed the three missionary journeys recorded in Acts, in which he has planted churches in much of modern-day Turkey, Greece and Macedonia. He also says (15:25) that he is about to take an aid collection to the Christians in Jerusalem. This is the journey recorded in Acts 20 and 21 (confirmed in Acts 24:17, where he says that this journey was 'to bring my people gifts for the poor').

It took quite a while (and significant expense) to write a letter the length of Romans. You had to employ someone actually to write what you had composed, and writing was laborious and slow. For Romans this scribe was Tertius ('who wrote down this letter' 16:22). Usually you composed a draft and then corrected it before the final version was written out, so it was not easy to do while travelling. Probably Paul wrote it during the three months he spent in Greece (Acts 20:2, 3). Most likely he was in Corinth, the capital of Achaia, a city Paul knew well. There are several hints in the letter that it was written from Corinth. In 16:1 Paul commends to them Phoebe, 'a servant of the church in Cenchreae' (the eastern port of Corinth); Phoebe may have carried the letter to Rome, since he asks them to 'receive her in the Lord' (16:2). In 16:23 he sends greetings from his host Gaius, who may be the Gaius Paul baptized in Corinth (1 Cor. 1:14), and also from Erastus, 'the city's director of public works' (c.f. 2 Tim. 4:20, where Erastus 'stayed in Corinth' presumably to do his job). So Paul probably used these three months in Corinth among friends as the stable base from which to write Romans.

We are therefore to picture Paul as an experienced missionary church-planter with 25 years or more of pastoral experience (which is important, as we shall see). Not only has he known Jesus Christ for many years, he also knows how people 'tick' and how churches work. He has the heart and head of an experienced pastor. In particular, he understands (as every pastor ought) how doctrine is applied by preaching to change churches.

What do we know about the churches in Rome?

Paul writes (1:7) 'To all in Rome who are loved by God and called to be saints', that is, to all the Christians in Rome. Probably there was more than one assembly. Certainly there was one in the house of Priscilla and Aquila (16:5). Paul has 'planned many times to come to you' (1:13) and indeed has been longing 'for many years to see you' (15:23), so these are not brand-new churches; they have a history, and this history is an important reason why he writes, as we shall see. Although Paul has not been to Rome, he knows a lot about them, as we can gather from the extraordinarily full and detailed list of greetings, the longest of all Paul's letters (16:1-16).

We know nothing about how the Christian faith came to Rome. In view of the principle of 15:20 it seems unlikely he would wish to 'muscle in' on churches founded by Peter, and so it seems likely that ordinary Christians such as merchants or civil servants brought the gospel to Rome on their travels.

The most important thing to know about the make-up of the churches in Rome is that they contained both Christians from a Jewish background and Christians from a Gentile background. Scholars discuss what sort of mix there might have been, and tend to think that there was probably a Gentile Christian majority. But clearly both were present. In 15:7 he tells them to 'accept (i.e. welcome) one another', and the context in 15:8-13 makes it clear that 'one another' here means Jewish Christians and Gentile Christians. In 2:17 he addressed the 'Jew' (presumably meaning the Christian Jew, since he is writing to Christians, 1:7). Likewise in 4:1 he calls Abraham literally 'our forefather according to the flesh', which would only be true for Jews. And in 11:13 he speaks explicitly to 'you Gentiles' (that is, Gentile Christians). As we work through the letter we shall see that this mix of Jew and Gentile is enormously important (e.g. 1:16; 2:9, 10; 3:29; 9:24; 10:12).

One other fact is relevant. In Acts 18:2 Luke tells us that Paul met the Jewish Christians Aquila and Priscilla in Corinth, because the emperor 'Claudius had ordered all the Jews to leave Rome'. This may be because of civil disorder caused by the preaching of Christ, as the Roman historian Suetonius hints. Probably Claudius expelled all the Jews, Christian and non-Christian alike (he would not have been interested in the difference) in about A.D. 49. Claudius' edict of expulsion would have lapsed on his death in A.D. 54. Many expelled Jews presumably returned after that; there was a flourishing Jewish community in Rome under his successor Nero (A.D. 54–68). By the time Paul writes Romans (perhaps about A.D. 57) Priscilla and Aquila are back in Rome (Rom. 16:3).

We are therefore to understand a church founded some years before as the gospel was brought to Rome by Christian merchants or civil servants. Presumably it began mostly with converts from Jewish or God-fearing backgrounds associated with the synagogue. The gospel spread to other Gentiles. Then the Jewish Christians were expelled from Rome for a few years, leaving the Gentile Christians in charge. But after Claudius' death they came back. It does not take much imagination to see the tensions this expulsion and return might have caused, and we shall return to it in the next chapter.

The big structure of Romans
(See the diagram p. 18)

Romans begins and ends with a Frame, sections at the start and end that are very specific about the sender, the recipients, the reason for writing, and so on. This Frame encloses the doctrinal and ethical Body of the letter. The Frame begins in 1:1-15 with the greeting (1:1-7) and a word about how and why Paul is longing to preach the gospel to them (1:8-15). It ends (15:14–16:27) with Paul explaining further why he has written, what are his hopes, and a long section of personal greetings.

We may divide the Body of the letter into four main parts. First, from 1:16–4:25 he expounds the gospel of justification by grace alone through faith alone (beginning with two 'manifesto' verses in 1:16, 17); I have called this 'Coming under grace'. Then in chapters 5–8 he builds on that foundation (5:1 'Therefore, since we have been justified through faith …') to teach about the Christian life, the life of the man or woman who has been justified by faith; I have called this 'Living under grace'. In chapters 9–11 he builds from the climax of chapter 8 to teach about the wise grace of God as it overflows from Jew to Gentile and then back again to Jew; I have called this 'The overflow of grace'. Finally, in 12:1–15:13 he appeals to them all by the mercies of God that he has expounded in the letter so far, to offer themselves as a living sacrifice, and teaches them what this will mean in their life as a church; I have called this 'A church shaped by grace'.

In many ways the most important question with which we must grapple as we teach Romans is how the Frame relates to the Body. The Frame is very important to help us grasp why Paul writes the letter, and therefore why he expounds the doctrines he does in the way he does. We shall explore this in the next chapter.

A word about the style of Romans

Romans is a logical letter. But it is not linear. It is sometimes thought that Paul's argument goes strictly from one point to the next. But it is not as simple as that. In particular it is worth being aware of his technique of 'trailing'. Just as a trailer will whet the appetite for an upcoming movie, so Paul will sometimes introduce a subject briefly in preparation for expanding on it later. Here are two examples:

1. In 6:13, 19 he tells his readers to 'offer' themselves to God to be used by God. He doesn't expand on this until chapter 12, which begins with the same command to 'offer' themselves to God (12:1).

2. A more sustained example is the ministry of the Spirit. Chapter 8 is the great place where he speaks fully about this ministry in the believer. But he has already anticipated this ministry in 2:29, 5:5, and 7:6 (and I think implicitly also in 2:6-15).

So when reading Romans do not assume that the argument is always strictly linear; watch out for the trailers.

2

WHY SHOULD WE PREACH AND TEACH ROMANS?

Why should we preach and teach Romans? You may think this is a silly question. We all know that Romans is one of the most important of all the New Testament letters (arguably the most important). So of course we need to preach it. No teaching programme would be complete without Romans. But in fact the question is precise and important. So let me put the question another way: what do we hope to achieve by preaching Romans?

The answer ought to be: we hope to achieve in our preaching what Paul sought to achieve by his writing. That is, we trust that the reasons why Paul wrote Romans are the reasons why God wants us to preach Romans. That when God carried Paul along by His Spirit to write Romans (c.f. 2 Pet. 1:21) the purpose in the mind of Paul was and is the purpose in the heart of God, and ought therefore to be the purpose in the mind and heart of the preacher today. So to ask, 'Why should we preach and teach Romans?' is to ask 'Why did Paul write Romans?'

This is a very important principle in all Bible teaching. We need to ask not only what a Bible book or passage contains, but why it was written. For what purpose, and to what end, did the writer put pen to paper? All Bible books were written to do something. Paul did not sit down one sunny afternoon with nothing much to do and say to himself, 'I think it would be nice to jot down some edifying Christian thoughts and send them to those friendly brothers and sisters in Rome; they might be interested.' To some extent, this is where this Teaching the Bible series hopes to help, by addressing the 'why' question more fully than commentaries tend to do. It is very important for preaching. An understanding of purpose changes preaching from the conveying of information (what the text says) to preaching with purpose and force (why the text says it).

So why does Paul write Romans? What are the reasons for Romans? Of course there are some incidental things he does, such as commend Phoebe to them (16:1f) and send lots of greetings (16:3ff). But these are extras that he takes the opportunity to do because he is writing; they are not the reason for writing.

Let us begin by considering two explanations which are inadequate, and then move to two more, both of which are true and which, when held together, give us the key to the reasons for Romans. These are introduced briefly now to steer us as we get into the letter. You will need to test them at every stage and in every section of the letter, to see if I have understood this aright.

1st Inadequate Reason:
Paul expounds his Systematic Theology because it's a good thing to do
Romans is sometimes read as a fairly general and comprehensive exposition of Paul's gospel, written for no particular

reason, except perhaps that Rome happens to be a very important city and it seems a good place to send it. It is the fruit of Paul's mature reflection on the gospel he has been preaching around the Mediterranean, the most balanced exposition of his gospel. There is some truth in this. We have seen (p. 20) that Paul has completed the three missionary journeys recorded in Acts; he writes with the benefit of mature reflection on his experience. For example, his exposition of the doctrines of justification by grace alone through faith alone is more measured and nuanced than when he expounded these same truths earlier in a more desperate situation in Galatians (though neither more nor less true!). These doctrines are life-changing and central to the gospel of Christ, what Luther called 'purest gospel' and one seventeenth-century Puritan 'the quintessence and perfection of saving doctrine'.

It is also true that from 1:18 through to 14:1 at least there is little or nothing that directly and explicitly links to the situation in Rome, by contrast, for example, to the way Paul responds to issues raised in correspondence from the church in Corinth (e.g. 1 Cor. 7:1). This sustained section of the letter without explicit reference to Rome leads some to suggest that what drives Paul is the internal logic of the gospel rather than anything specific to the church in Rome and their needs.

There are several problems with this. The biggest is that it involves letting the doctrinal and ethical Body of the letter float free of the enclosing Frame (pp. 23-24). We will not be able to relate the Frame to the Body in a convincing or coherent way.

But even if the Body is allowed to float free of the Frame, there is still the problem that it does not read as a comprehensive or balanced exposition of Paul's gospel. Most notably, it hardly mentions the return of Jesus

Christ, despite this being a very significant part of Paul's belief. The return of Christ is a core part of the gospel, and yet although Paul does mention it (in 13:11, 12), he chooses not to expand on it in this letter, because it is not the doctrine he needs to emphasize to this church at this time.

A third problem is that it is very difficult to make sense of chapters 9–11 if they are read as part of a systematic exposition of the logic of the gospel. This may be why these chapters tend to be under-emphasized in much of our preaching.

It is true that Romans is not so obviously and tightly tied to the situation into which it is written as, say, Galatians–it is written with less urgency. But while Romans lacks the desperate intensity of Galatians, it is still written with specific purposes. It is not just what Luther's successor Melanchthon called 'a compendium of Christian doctrine'.

2nd Inadequate Reason:
The apostle to the Gentiles preaches the gospel to the heart of the Gentile world

Again, there is truth in this. In 1:5 he says he has received from Jesus Christ a particular apostolic commission and grace 'for his name's sake … to call people from among all the Gentiles to the obedience that comes from faith [*the obedience of faith*].' And 'among all the nations' includes those in Rome (1:6). He comes back to this same 'obedience of faith' in the second last verse of the letter (16:26). In 1:9-15 he explains that he is eager to preach the gospel to them because he is eager to preach the gospel to everyone (v. 13 'the other Gentiles'). He wants to reap a harvest among them, and to encourage them by his faith, which he then expounds in the letter.

All this is true, and it moves us forward from the very general first explanation. It recognizes the significance of Rome at the heart of the Gentile world. But again it is too general. Why write this particular letter, expounding these doctrines in this way to this church at this time? And when he applies these doctrines to them in the letter, why apply them in the particular ways that he does? This explanation is still too general. While some things are worth saying to any church, Paul gives us two clear indicators of precise reasons why he wrote to this church.

1st Precise Reason:
He wants them to become mission partners in the gospel

In 15:14-33 Paul opens his heart to the Christians in Rome. After he has taken the collection money to Jerusalem he hopes to visit them en route for further mission in Spain. He hopes 'to have you assist me on my journey' (15:24). The verb translated 'assist … on my journey' is almost a technical term for giving practical and financial assistance. He wants them to be a missionary-sending and supporting church, including prayer and material and spiritual refreshment for his ministry (15:31, 32).

In order for Rome to become a gospel-eager partnership church, they must have confidence in Paul and learn the same passion for the gospel that he has. He tells them he is 'eager to preach the gospel also to you' (1:15) because he wants them to catch this same eagerness for the gospel to be preached to others.

So as we read Romans we need to ask, how will this exposition of the gospel promote a church who will be eager and passionate to see the gospel proclaimed to all?

2nd Precise Reason:
He wants them to live in harmony with one another

Throughout the letter we see indications that Paul is very concerned about harmony between Jews and Gentiles in the church. We see this almost whenever he applies his doctrines. For example in 3:27 his conclusion from the doctrine of justification by grace is the exclusion of boasting, because boasting disrupts harmony. In chapter 12 he is concerned to see the body working together in harmony (e.g. vv. 3-8, 10, 16). In 14:1–15:13 the 'strong' and the 'weak' reflect Jew/Gentile distinctions and his aim is that they accept and welcome one another as Christ has welcomed them (15:7). He wants them to pray for his journey taking a collection from Gentile churches to Jewish Christians in Jerusalem (15:22-33) and they will only do this if they understand deeply how the gospel unites Jew and Gentile in Christ. The Jew/Gentile issue runs right through the letter. Indeed over 60 per cent of all Paul's uses of the word 'law' (generally referring to the Law of Moses) occur in Romans (74 out of 121).

The social background of Claudius' expulsion of the Jews and their subsequent return (p. 23) makes perfect sense of all this. Probably the first senior members of the church in Rome were Jewish Christians. This is likely because they would have heard the gospel first ('first for the Jew' 1:16), they would have known the Scriptures better, and when the light dawned on them that Jesus of Nazareth is the Messiah, the Christ, all the pieces of the jigsaw would have fallen into place (as they did with Paul at his conversion). But for the Gentiles, the pieces of the jigsaw were not even there in the first place; they had to be taught the Scriptures and what the word 'Christ' means. So, to start with, we may imagine Jews with names like Joseph, the church secretary, and Simeon, the church treasurer, sharing a quiet pleasure in their positions as the obvious ones to run the church. Of course, with their privileged background, they were the natural ones to choose. And then disaster strikes—Claudius expels them. Someone has to take over—Gentiles with names like Linus and Julius fill their positions. Then the emperor Claudius dies; and Joseph and Simeon and the other Jewish Christians return, and perhaps expect to be reinstated to their positions of influence. Perhaps Linus and Julius have different ideas. The church in Rome would not naturally be a place of harmony and peace. Only the gospel of justification by grace could make it so.

So Paul expounds the gospel in Romans with the aim of bringing Jew and Gentile together in harmony in the church. And so as we read Romans we need to ask, how will this exposition of the gospel promote a church today who live together in love?

Although I think both these precise reasons run like threads through Romans, I think we may see a stronger emphasis on mission in the Frame of the letter, both in 1:1-15 and then in 15:14-33. And there is generally a stronger emphasis on the unity of the Jews and Gentiles in the church in the Doctrinal Body of the letter. This leads us to ask how the two precise reasons are connected.

Putting the precise reasons together:
The key to reading Romans

These two precise reasons immediately make Romans of great importance for every pastor. Most of the reasons pastors lie awake at night concern unity and/or mission. Sometimes it is an issue concerning the unity and harmony of the local church fellowship; sometimes it concerns the unity of a leadership team. At other times it is perplexity as to how to turn an introspective fellowship outwards to the needy world, not simply for growth (for every human society is concerned with survival), but for crossing barriers into other people groups, other cultures, reaching unlikely people with the barrier-breaking message of Christ. We are bound to be concerned with this, unless that is, we are content to have 'Jews' and 'Gentiles' enjoying happily homogeneous and separate churches.

But although these two concerns are high on any pastor's priority list, on the face of it they are different and separate. One is to do with evangelism and mission, looking outwards with zeal. The other is to do with unity and harmony, looking inwards to build a new society in the church. One is about eagerness, the other about harmony, one about partnership, the other about peace.

In fact the connection is profound, and could only be made by an apostle shaped by knowing the risen Lord through years of practical sharp-end Christian church-planting and pastoral ministry. Paul understands that the full gospel, which is the foundation of justification (chs. 1–4), the ministry of the Spirit in the life of the believer (chs. 5–8), and the wise sovereignty of God in conversion (chs. 9–11) is the key both to gospel partnership and to church harmony. Only a church deeply soaked in the gospel will live in harmony; only a church thoroughly taught the gospel will reach out with zeal.

The reason is that only the gospel humbles men and women to the level of the ground, so that human pride ceases to make divisions and the church ceases to be a club, but reaches out (from floor level, as it were) to fellow sinners in love. A 'church' that is not shaped by the gospel may well reach out to others. Of course it will be concerned with growth, as any society will be that is concerned with its survival. But the outreach will inevitably be focused on 'people like us' (whoever we may be). Only the gospel enables us to live together with people unlike us and to reach out across human barriers to people very different from us.

Every human society or community is by nature both introspective and unstable. It is introspective, because it is always more comfortable to be a club to which only 'people like us' belong. And it is unstable, because I in my pride will always want to be narrowing the definition of 'people like us', so that it becomes 'people like me'. Human pride leads to human strife which divides a society from within; and human pride leads to dividing walls of hostility which cut us off from the world outside. The gospel therefore needs to counteract both internal instability and external defensiveness. And it does both in exactly the same way, by humbling human pride.

There is no such thing as a church that just exists for evangelism, or a church that just focuses on building itself up in love. For only a church that lives in harmony under Christ can reach out effectively with zeal. Unless its members understand their status under grace they will be riven with rivalries and party spirit, always at one another's throats or biting behind one another's backs. And evangelism will disappear off the agenda.

The same is true the other way around. For only a church that reaches out with zeal can live in harmony. When a church ceases to reach out, they become practical unbelievers in the gospel of grace; and when they become practical unbelievers in grace reaching out, they become practical unbelievers in grace bringing harmony within. If I don't really believe that the offer of grace is for all outside the church, then I will not believe that it is for all inside the church. And as soon as I forget that, my relations within the church become marked by non-acceptance of those who are not like me. And so my lack of evangelistic zeal bounces back into divisions within the church.

As we read Romans, therefore, we shall be asking how this particular teaching of the gospel impacts on these two precise aims of the letter: evangelistic zeal and church harmony. I hope we shall see that the reasons why Paul writes the letter dovetail with the gospel as he expounds it in the letter. The logic of the gospel as Paul expounds it will press us, like them, out into the world, and at the same time build us up together in love.

To anticipate the argument of the letter, let me state in simple terms the doctrinal key both to unity and mission. It is to lift Jesus very high and bring you and me very low, or – to put it in more theological language – it is to magnify grace (which lifts Jesus high) and to emphasize faith (which brings me low, since it speaks of coming empty-handed to the Cross, 'nothing in my hand I bring …'). It is this Jesus-exalting, people-humbling gospel that Paul expounds in Romans.

We may set these two tightly linked purposes into the bigger framework of the glory of God. Paul's great aim in Romans is that God should be glorified, and in particular that the glory of His grace should be visible in the supernatural phenomenon of a united and missionary church. We may therefore take as a working hypothesis the following overall purpose statement for Romans.

The purpose of Romans
is the glory of God
seen in a united missionary church
humbled together under grace.

3

IDEAS FOR PREACHING AND
TEACHING A SERIES ON ROMANS

Planning a preaching or teaching series from Romans is usually subject to all sorts of timetabling constraints, for example, in the church or youth group diary. It is rare to have absolute control over how many weeks are available. It is also a matter of judgment as to what our hearers can cope with. Do they have the stamina for a long series, or would it be better to break it up into smaller chunks? Would it be easier to teach them longer passages from Romans, giving them the big sweep of the letter, or shorter passages in more detail? It is also to some extent a personal matter: what kind of series do we think we ourselves can prepare for and sustain?

There is a lot to be said for tackling Romans as part of a longer teaching programme and dividing it into teaching blocks. After one block, the programme can move to some contrasting part of Scripture, perhaps Old Testament, or working through a Gospel. Then, after a change, we can return to the next block of Romans ready to pick up the flow of the letter with freshness. I have suggested four blocks, following the structure of the letter as follows.

Block A (chapters 1–4):   Introduction + first section of
                              letter 'Coming under grace'

Block B (chapters 5–8):   Second section of letter 'Living
                              under grace'

Block C (chapters 9–11):   Third section of letter 'The over-
                              flow of grace'

Block D (chapters 12–16):   Fourth section of letter 'A church
                              shaped by grace' + conclusion

In general, longer passages help to show the flow and logic of the letter well, but are hard to teach with faithful attention to detail. If we teach the detail accurately, we may find we have very little time left for practical application. Shorter passages give us less explaining to do, so we can devote more time to application; but the danger is that we lose the big context and sweep of the letter.

There is also the question of whether a series will be taught by one person or by several members of a leadership team (and perhaps visiting speakers as well). It is easy to lose the continuity of a series by having too many different speakers, who may not know how the series is developing and may neglect some of the big themes as they are opened up by other speakers. Also, when one person is taking a series, that speaker can keep the overall balance by adjusting what is covered in one week in the light of what will be covered the next. It is not easy for a visiting speaker to be parachuted into a series that is already under way with its own momentum.

If the whole series cannot be taught by one person, there are strategies for keeping as much continuity as possible. For example:

1. Divide the series into blocks, each block being taught by one person. This means that that speaker can begin to build momentum and show the flow and continuity of the passages in their block.

2. A leadership team may decide to plan and preach a series in close cooperation. One team member may take the overall lead, planning the series and then briefing the others. Then, perhaps early in each week, the team can meet and the upcoming speaker give the proposed outline to the others for comment and discussion. This is time-consuming but can be a very effective training exercise in which less experienced speakers learn from those with more experience.

This chapter contains three suggestions. First, a medium-pace sweep through Romans, which can be divided into four blocks. Second, a slower sweep through Romans, similarly divided into four blocks, but with shorter passages. Third, some ideas for 'mini-series' from parts of Romans. These suggestions can be varied in many ways.

Medium-pace series (in four blocks)

A. *Coming under grace (1:1-4:25)*

(1)	1:1-17	Why be eager for the Christian good news
(2)	1:18-32	Why God is right to be angry
(3)	2:1-29	Why repentance really matters
(4)	3:1-20	Why we cannot save ourselves
(5)	3:21-26	Why God is right to declare wrongdoers right
(6)	3:27–4:25	Why boasting is excluded in the church

B. *Living under grace (5:1-8:39)*

(1)	5:1-21	Grace is stronger than sin
(2)	6:1-23	How sin's slavery is broken
(3)	7:1-25	Why moralism fails
(4)	8:1-17	Children of God
(5)	8:18-39	Safety and suffering

C. *The overflow of grace (9:1-11:36)*

(1)	9:1-29	Let God be God
(2)	9:30–10:13	The Saviour King
(3)	10:14-21	The word of Christ
(4)	11:1-10	The remnant
(5)	11:11-36	It's not the end of the story

D. *A church shaped by grace (12:1-16:27)*

(1)	12:1-21	The shape of genuine love
(2)	13:1-14	The reasons for genuine love
(3)	14:1-15:13	The cost of genuine love
(4)	15:14-33	Gospel partnership (1)
(5)	16:1-27	Gospel partnership (2)

Slower-pace series (in four blocks)

A. *Coming under grace (1:1-4:25)*

(1)	1:1-7	The everyone gospel
(2)	1:8-15	The eager preacher
(3)	1:16, 17	The saving righteousness of God
(4)	1:18-32	The anger of God
(5)	2:1-11	The patience of God
(6)	2:12-29	The need for a changed heart
(7)	3:1-8	God can save the world without me
(8)	3:9-20	Why we cannot save ourselves
(9)	3:21-26	Why God is right to rescue wrongdoers
(10)	3:27–4:12	Why boasting is excluded
(11)	4:13-25	The God of promise

B. *Living under grace (5:1-8:39)*

(1)	5:1-11	Peace with God
(2)	5:12-21	Why grace is stronger than sin
(3)	6:1-14	Dead to sin
(4)	6:15-23	Slaves of God
(5)	7:1-6	A destructive marriage ended
(6)	7:7-12	When the law on the wall meets sin in the heart
(7)	7:13-25	When the law in the heart meets sin in the heart
(8)	8:1-17	Children of God
(9)	8:17-30	Suffering and glory
(10)	8:31-39	Christian security

C. *The overflow of grace (9:1-11:36)*

(1)	9:1-5	The tragedy of the religious unbeliever
(2)	9:6-13	God makes Christians

(3) 9:14-29	God is more gracious than we think
(4) 9:30–10:4	Christ the King of all
(5) 10:4-13	Christ the Saviour for all
(6) 10:14-21	The word of Christ
(7) 11:1-10	The remnant
(8) 11:11-32	It's not the end of the story
(9) 11:33-36	To the praise of His marvellous grace

D. A church shaped by grace (12:1-16:27)

(1) 12:1-8	The serving of love
(2) 12:9-21	The shape of love
(3) 13:1-7	The submission of love
(4) 13:8-14	The reasons for love
(5) 14:1-12	Gospel welcome
(6) 14:13-23	Gospel love
(7) 15:1-13	Gospel glory
(8) 15:14-24	Gospel ambition
(9) 15:25-33	Gospel partnership
(10) 16:1-16, 21-23	Gospel qualities
(11) 16:17-20	Gospel watchfulness
(12) 16:25-27	The glory of God

Ideas for Mini-Series

These may be suitable in a context in which it is possible to give a short series of talks, such as a church weekend.

1:1-17 Promoting the gospel

(1) 1:1-7	Gospel fact
(2) 1:8-15	Gospel eagerness
(3) 1:16, 17	Gospel reason

1:18-32 Why God is right to be angry

(1)	1:18-20	What creation proves about God
(2)	1:18, 21-23	How humans respond to creation
(3)	1:18, 24-32	What a messed-up world proves about God

(We could insert a separate topical talk on the Bible and homosexual practice in this series.)

3:9-20 The anatomy of sin

(1)	3:9, 19, 20 with vv. 10-12	The empty heart
(2)	3:9, 19, 20 with vv. 13, 14	The bitter tongue
(3)	3:9, 19, 20 with vv. 15-18	The warlike way

5:1-11 Peace with God

(1)	5:1	Justification by grace alone
(2)	5:1, 2	Peace with God and standing in grace
(3)	5:3, 4	Suffering and where it leads
(4)	5:5-8	The double proof of the love of God
(5)	5:9-11	Full salvation

8:1-39 Suffering, safety and glory

(1)	8:1-8	Under new management
(2)	8:9-17	Children of God
(3)	8:17-27	The symphony of sighs
(4)	8:28-30	God and glory
(5)	8:31-39	No separation

9:1-29 Let God be God

(1)	9:1-5	The tragedy of the religious unbeliever
(2)	9:6-13	God makes Christians
(3)	9:14-29	God is more gracious than we think

12:1–13:14   *A church shaped by grace (1)*

(1) 12:1-8   The serving of love
(2) 12:9-21   The shape of love
(3) 13:1-7   The submission of love

(We could supplement 13:1-7 with some topical teaching on the attitude of the Christian to authority, with opportunity for questions to clarify the issues.)

(4) 13:8-14   The reasons for love

14:1–15:13 *A church shaped by grace (2)*

(1) 14:1-12   Gospel welcome
(2) 14:13-23   Gospel love
(3) 15:1-13   Gospel glory

15:14–16:27 *Gospel partnership*

(1) 15:14-24   Gospel ambition
(2) 15:25-33   Gospel partnership
(3) 16:1-16, 21-23   Gospel qualities
(4) 16:17-20   Gospel watchfulness
(5) 16:25-27   Gospel glory

SECTION TWO:

Coming Under Grace

Romans 1–4

4

INTRODUCTION TO ROMANS 1–4

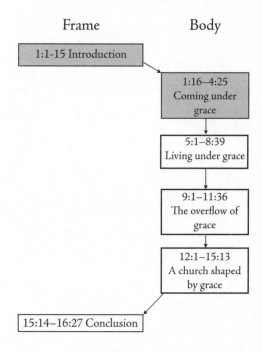

Frame	Body
1:1-15 Introduction	
	1:16–4:25 Coming under grace
	5:1–8:39 Living under grace
	9:1–11:36 The overflow of grace
	12:1–15:13 A church shaped by grace
15:14–16:27 Conclusion	

Chapters 1–4 contain the introductory part of the 'Frame' of the letter, in which Paul introduces himself and his gospel to his hearers (1:1-15). This flows directly into the first major block of the 'Body' of the letter, which I have called 'Coming under grace' (1:16–4:25). Its major theme is justification by grace alone received empty-handed by faith alone.

5

COMING UNDER GRACE
ROMANS 1:1-17

Think of the most non-Christian person you know, perhaps an ardent advocate of another religion, maybe an aggressive atheist, or an out and out seeker of pleasure. Now think of the most consistently Christian person you know, someone of integrity, zeal, Christ-like maturity and spiritual giftedness. What do these two have in common, apart from a shared humanity? Paul begins his letter with the answer to this question. It is an answer that is crucial to the health of the church and the blessing of the world.

Attentive listening to the text
Context and structure
Verses 1-15 are the opening part of the 'Frame' of the letter, which lead straight in to verses 16 and 17, the 'manifesto' which headlines the first doctrinal section.

The passage divides in three:

1.	vv. 1-7	Greeting
2.	vv. 8-15	Relationship
3.	vv. 16, 17	Manifesto

1 and 2 correspond to the first two parts of a standard Greek letter, in which you begin with a greeting ('From ..., to ..., greeting ...') and continue with something friendly about your relationship (vv. 8-15). Paul makes much more of this than a standard greeting; for him, it is like a hoarding at the entrance, or an overture before the play.

Working through the text

A. *The greeting (1:1-7): the everyone gospel*

Paul's readers would have been astonished by the theologically meaty way in which he introduces himself. Verses 1-6 are by far the longest of all Paul's introductions, not because he needs to tell them a lot about himself, but because he wants to introduce his gospel.

> [1]Paul,
>
>> a servant of Christ Jesus,
>> called to be an apostle,
>> and set apart for the gospel of God –

His focus here (unlike Galatians, for example) is not on his authority, but on his commission, to be 'an apostle ... set apart for the gospel of God'. Paul uses the words 'gospel' or 'preach the gospel' twelve times in Romans (1:1, 9, 15, 16; 2:16; 10:15, 16; 11:28; 15:16, 19, 20; 16:25). Seven of these are in his Frame, showing how important the gospel is to this letter. Paul wants to tell them about his gospel more than he wants to tell them about himself. It is as if he begins by saying, 'The only reason I want you to listen to me is because I want you to grasp the gospel of the Lord Jesus Christ.' So, while this is a greeting in its shape, it is Paul's headline teaching point in its substance.

> [2]the gospel he promised beforehand through his prophets in the Holy Scriptures

This is the gospel God 'promised beforehand through his prophets in the Holy Scriptures'. Here the 'prophets' are shorthand for all the Old Testament authors, including, for example, Moses (Deut. 34:10) and David (Acts 2:30).

1. The gospel cannot be understood from the New Testament alone, but needs the Old Testament as well (quoted a lot in Romans).

2. The Old Testament is only understood as fulfilled in Jesus Christ. Christ does not change the meaning of the Old Testament; rather he is the key to understanding what the Old Testament really means.

3. The Old Testament is fundamentally about the promise that 'Abraham and his offspring…would be heir of the world' (4:13, Paul's summary of Gen. 12:1-3; 15:5; 17:5, 6 etc). The gospel is God doing what he had promised to do, giving the government of the world to Abraham's offspring. When Paul speaks of 'the gospel…promised beforehand' he is not speaking of a random collection of predictions dotted through the Old Testament; he speaks of one coherent promise attested by the whole of the Old Testament.

> ³the gospel … regarding his Son,
> > who as to his human nature was a descendant of David,
> > ⁴and who through the Spirit of holiness
> > was declared with power to be the Son of God
> > [*was appointed the Son of God in power*]
> > > by his resurrection from the dead:
> Jesus Christ our Lord.

The fulfilment of promise leads in to verses 3 and 4, the heart of Paul's introduction. Notice how Jesus Christ brackets these verses. The gospel is 'regarding his Son … Jesus Christ our Lord.' Paul teaches four truths about Jesus:

1. He is God's Son, like Israel, corporately (Exod. 4:22, 'Israel is my firstborn son'), and the Davidic kings, representatively (2 Sam. 7:14, 'I will be his father, and he shall be my son').

2. Therefore it is no surprise that Jesus was 'as to his human nature … a descendant of David', the heir to David's throne.

3. The resurrection changed the state of Jesus. The literal meaning of verse 4 is that Jesus '*was appointed the Son of God in power* by his resurrection from the dead'. The word translated 'appointed' means something like 'crowned'. It is not just that the resurrection publicly showed us who Jesus had always been (NIV 'declared'); rather, at the resurrection the one who had always been Son of God was changed from being 'the Son of God in weakness' to being 'the Son of God in power'. The Holy Spirit, who is the executive arm of the Godhead on earth, raised him from a body of weakness to a resurrection body of power (c.f. Phil. 2:6-11). The resurrection has been called the turning point in the existence of the Son of God.

4. Consequently he is not only 'Jesus' (the man), but also 'Christ' (Messiah, anointed King), 'our Lord' (the ruler of all and heir of the world).

> [5]Through him and for his name's sake, we received grace and apostleship to call people from among all the Gentiles to the obedience that comes from faith. [6]And you also are among those who are called to belong to Jesus Christ.

> [... *Jesus Christ our Lord,*
> *⁵through whom we received grace and apostleship*
>   *to the obedience of faith*
>   *among all the Gentiles*
>   *for the sake of his name,*
>
>   *⁶among whom are you also*
>   *who are called of Jesus Christ.*]

It is helpful to have verses 5 and 6 in a more literal translation and order than NIV. Paul explains what the resurrection means for his job as an apostle. 'Jesus Christ our Lord' is the powerful agent 'through whom we' (Paul and his fellow apostles) 'have received grace and apostleship' (which means grace to do his job as an apostle). But what is the job of an apostle? Paul tells us the goal and scope of his apostleship and the deepest reason for it.

The goal of apostleship: the obedience of faith
His apostleship is 'to' (which means, 'aiming for') 'the obedience of faith.' Paul uses this important phrase right at the start here, and also in the second last verse of the letter (lit. 'to bring all nations *to the obedience of faith*' 16:26). What does this mean? **'The obedience of faith' means bowing the knee in trusting submission to Jesus the Lord, both at the start and all through the Christian life.**

One common understanding of 'the obedience of faith' is that 'faith' is the main thing, and obedience is the consequence of faith; first we believe, and then we obey (NIV 'the obedience *that comes from* faith' 1:5). True faith always results in obedience, but faith and obedience are distinct. This gives the impression that 'faith' is primary and 'obedience' secondary, a consequence of faith (albeit a necessary consequence). If this were so, we would expect that when Paul abbreviates the expression, he would always abbreviate it to 'faith' (if this is the primary meaning). In fact, he is quite likely to abbreviate it to 'obedience'. So, for example, he can rejoice that their *faith* is being reported all over the world' (1:8) and equally that 'Everyone has heard about your *obedience*' (16:19). He describes his ministry as bringing the Gentiles 'to obedience' (15:18), where we might have expected him to speak of bringing them to faith.

It is important to be clear that the basis on which we are justified before God is not our obedience. We shall see when we get to Romans 5 that, just as the disobedience of Adam made us all sinners, so we are made righteous not by our obedience but 'by the obedience of the one man', Jesus Christ (5:19). Theologians sometimes speak of Jesus' active obedience in his human life, obeying his Father every moment of the day and night (the actions of his life), and his 'passive' obedience on the cross, when he obeyed by submitting to suffering (his passion at the end of his life). Together, Jesus' life and death form one great act of obedience. It is through his obedience that we are justified. We are not justified by anything we have done, can do, or ever will do, but entirely by what Jesus did for us.

But having established the *basis* of our justification entirely in God's grace through Jesus, we still need to clarify the *nature* of saving faith. What does it mean to exercise saving faith in Jesus?

First, our *initial* repentance and faith is obedience to the command of God. In the gospel, God 'commands all people everywhere to repent' (Acts 17:30). To repent is therefore to obey God's command at the start of the Christian life. This is why the New Testament speaks of unbelievers as those who 'do not obey the gospel' (2 Thess. 1:8; Rom. 10:16 – where NIV 'accepted' is literally 'obeyed'). To believe is to obey the teaching of grace (6:17). We do not believe and then obey; we obey by believing. We give up trying to establish our own righteous status before God and surrender to his (9:31, 32; 10:3).

Second, *ongoing* faith means ongoing obedience. We do not obey at the start and then just content ourselves with believing after that. The Christian life consists of ongoing disobedience to sin's demands (6:12) and ongoing obedience to God (6:16), a glad slavery to righteousness (6:18). This obedience is expressed by practical submission to Christ's apostles and their teaching (2 Thess. 3:14; Phil. 2:12). Ongoing obedience is the outworking of our salvation (Phil. 2:12); it is not a subsequent thing, a consequence of faith; it is faith in its concrete expression. This is why James says: 'As the body without the spirit is dead, so faith without works is dead' (James 2:26). Our works (our actual obedience) are the life-giving breath that breathes life into what will otherwise be a dead 'faith' (that is, not a real faith at all).

Let us come back to my definition: **'The obedience of faith' means bowing the knee in trusting submission to Jesus the Lord, both at the start and all through the Christian life.** The words 'trusting submission' capture the nature and the benefits of faith. The nature of faith is submission, bowing the knee to the King. The benefits of faith are the benefits of coming under the gracious rule of this King, which is why this submission is a trusting submission. When we bow the knee to King Jesus, we entrust ourselves to his rule, trusting that under his lordship we will experience the blessings of his saving righteousness. We cannot come under his gracious protection without coming under his rule; there is no salvation without submission. We benefit from his rescue not just by believing that it is true, but by submitting to him.

The obedience of faith is therefore a trusting submission to Jesus the Lord, bowing the knee to him at the start (initial faith) and going on bowing the knee to him thereafter (continuing faith). The obedience of faith is an initial and an ongoing surrender.

'The obedience of faith' helps us rightly to understand both obedience and faith, which are two ways of speaking of the same thing. Authentic faith is both a receiving and a surrender, and it is followed by ongoing receiving and ongoing surrender. True faith in Christ consists in bowing the knee in trusting submission to him as Lord. This obedience is the goal of Paul's apostleship.

To see what the obedience of faith looks and feels like, in terms of delight in the law of God, see *Bible Delight* (Christian Focus/PT Media 2008 pp. 31-42).

The scope of apostleship: the whole world
Paul also tells us the scope of his apostleship, which is 'among all the Gentiles.' Because Jesus has been crowned King over all and heir of the promise to Abraham to inherit the world (4:13), it follows that the whole world is summoned to trusting submission to him. The gospel is 'the everyone gospel' because Jesus is 'the everyone Lord'. And therefore 'you also' (v. 6) are included. There is nothing special about Rome, however important they may think they are. Rome is just one more place where men and women are summoned to bow the knee to Jesus the Lord.

The deepest reason for apostleship: the glory of Jesus
Apostleship is 'for the sake of (Jesus') name'. When men and women bow the knee to him, the honour goes to Jesus alone. They are Christians not fundamentally because they decided to be (though they did), but because they

are 'called of Jesus Christ' (v. 6), which probably means not just 'called to belong to Jesus Christ' (NIV) but also 'called by Jesus Christ', since the usual meaning of 'call' in Romans is the sovereign call of God (e.g. 8:30).

> [7]To all in Rome who are loved by God and called to be saints:
>> Grace and peace to you from God our Father and from the Lord Jesus Christ.

He writes to 'all in Rome who are loved by God and called to be saints' (i.e. Christians, set apart by and for God). The love starts with God, the call comes from God, and the honour goes to God. He greets 'all' of them because he is concerned for their harmony.

It is on the basis of this great fact, the 'everyone gospel', that Paul goes on to speak of the kind of relationship he has with his readers.

B. Relationship (1:8-15): the eager preacher

> [8]First, I thank my God through Jesus Christ for all of you, because your faith is being reported all over the world. [9]God, whom I serve with my whole heart in preaching the gospel of his Son, is my witness how constantly I remember you [10]in my prayers at all times; and I pray that now at last by God's will the way may be opened for me to come to you.

> [11]I long to see you so that I may impart to you some spiritual gift [*grace gift*] to make you strong—[12]that is, that you and I may be mutually encouraged by each other's faith. [13]I do not want you to be unaware, brothers, that I planned many times to come to you (but have been prevented from doing so until now) in order that

I might have a harvest [*fruit*] among you, just as I have
had among the other Gentiles.

Just as Paul turned a conventional greeting into his first teaching point in verses 1-7, so now in verses 8-15 he turns a conventional expression of relationship into an opportunity to
develop this teaching point.

The tone changes from the proclamation of fact in verses 1-7,
to the expression of eager longing in verses 8-15. This section
is full of verbs expressing emotion and desire. He thanks God,
serves God wholeheartedly, prays constantly, longs to see them,
and has planned many times to come and see them. Above all,
he is 'eager to preach the gospel' to these Christians in Rome.
The key to this passage is to see how the fact proclaimed in
verses 1-7 leads to the eagerness of verses 8-15.

The theme of 'all' continues. He has spoken of 'all the
Gentiles' (v. 5), 'you also' (v. 6), 'all in Rome' (v. 7); now he
continues with 'all of you… all over the world' (v. 8), 'Greeks
and barbarians… wise and foolish' (v. 14), and 'also to you'
(v. 15). All sorts of people have submitted, in the obedience
of faith, to the 'everyone Lord' through the preaching of the
'everyone gospel'. Many more will do the same.

Notice also the emphasis on faith. Paul thanks God
'because your faith is being reported all over the world'
(v. 8). The sharing of faith leads to harmony and mutual
encouragement, whereas boasting of works divides. When
we speak of our works we puff ourselves up, we want people
to give glory to us, for our initiative, achievement or virtue.
This always leads to strife, as everyone knows from the
school playground onwards. But when we speak of our
faith, we proclaim the goodness of Jesus. Our faith is the
conclusive proof that we contribute nothing and God does

everything. The 'harvest [*fruit*]' Paul longs for is the work of God in changing lives to righteousness (as in Isa. 5:1-7), both by new conversions and by growth in godliness.

> [14]I am bound [*under obligation*]
>> both to Greeks and non-Greeks [*barbarians*],
>> both to the wise and the foolish.
> [15]That is why I am so eager to preach the gospel also to you who are at Rome.

In verse 14 he draws the logical step from 'the everyone Lord' and 'the everyone gospel' to the eager preacher. He is 'under obligation both to Greeks' (that is, educated people who speak Greek, just as educated people in medieval Europe would have spoken Latin) 'and barbarians' (an insulting onomatopoeic word, uneducated dimwits, who speak gobbledegook!). (Paul uses the same word 'barbarians' in 1 Cor. 14:11 of unintelligible speech.) He owes the gospel 'both to the wise' (that is, those who consider themselves clever, Greek-speakers) 'and the foolish' (that is, those considered stupid by clever people). The 'Greek' is put right with God in exactly the same way as the 'barbarian' (c.f. 1 Cor. 1:18–2:5). Each of them comes empty-handed (that is, with faith) or they do not come at all.

Why is Paul 'under obligation'? The metaphor of a monetary debt doesn't capture the urgency. It is like a city being conquered by a new king, who entrusts to the herald the proclamation of his victory and the offer of his pardon. The herald therefore owes it to all the citizens to tell them urgently. If he does not, they will incur the anger of the new king by not bowing the knee to him and accepting his pardon. This urgency makes Paul 'eager to preach the gospel also to you who are at Rome' (v. 15).

C. Reason (1:16, 17): the righteousness of God

Paul now leads straight in to the headline manifesto which sets the agenda to the end of chapter 4.

> [16]**For** I am not ashamed of the gospel,
>> **because** it is the power of God for the salvation of everyone who believes:
>> first for the Jew, then for the Gentile [*Greek*].

> [17]**For** in the gospel a righteousness from God
> [*the righteousness of God*] is revealed,
>> a righteousness that is by faith from first to last
>> [*from faith to faith*],
>>> just as it is written: 'The righteous will live by faith.' (Hab. 2:4)

Notice the three connecting words ('For … because … For …', all the same word in Greek).

Why am I eager to preach the gospel to you (v. 15)? *Because* I am not ashamed of the gospel. He is eager because he is not ashamed (c.f. 2 Tim. 1:8). The fear of shame will make us less than eager to preach the gospel, even if we know we ought to do it ('under obligation' v. 14). To be 'ashamed' includes having a subjective sense of shame (feeling ashamed). But the main Bible meaning is objective: to be ashamed is to be publicly disgraced, to be shown to be in the wrong. No doubt Paul sometimes feels the weakness of the gospel in the eyes of the world (c.f. 1 Cor. 1:18). But he is confident that in the last day he will not be held up to shame as one who has preached something untrue and ineffective.

Why am I not ashamed of the gospel? *Because* it is the power of God to rescue. He is not ashamed because the gospel is not weak (though it may seem so). Every human being God rescues, he will rescue by the gospel of Jesus.

No one anywhere or at any time (including before Christ) will have been rescued in any other way. Paul will devote 1:18–3:20 to proving this controversial assertion.

'Salvation' refers not to becoming a Christian, but to the final rescue at the end of the Christian life. Christians have already been justified, but will not be fully saved until the end (5:9, 10). 'Salvation is nearer to us now than when we first believed' (13:11). The gospel is God's instrument not only to make us Christian in the first place, but also to keep us Christian to the end. This is another reason why he is eager to preach the gospel to the *Christians*.

The emphasis is that it is God's power to rescue 'everyone who believes ... first ... the Jew, then ... the Gentile.' This continues the theme of 'all' or 'everyone' we have seen in verses 1-15. Paul again uses the expression 'everyone who believes' in 3:22; 4:11 and 10:4 (and c.f. 10:11). In the missionary journeys in Acts they went 'first to the Jew'. But the gospel that saves the Jew is the same gospel as that which saves the Gentile. Neither contributes anything of their own, except the sin from which they need to be rescued. We do not even contribute our faith, for faith itself is a gift from God.

But the big question is this: why is the gospel God's power to rescue all who believe? This is the climax of the manifesto: 'For in the gospel *the righteousness of God* is revealed, a righteousness that is by faith from first to last [*from faith to faith*], just as it is written: "The righteous will live by faith"'(Hab. 2:4).

Let us unpack the four parts of verse 17.

1. What is 'the righteousness of God'?
2. What does it mean for it to be 'revealed' in the gospel?
3. Why is it 'from faith to faith'?
4. How does the Old Testament quotation help us understand it?

1.   What is 'the righteousness of God'?

This important expression is used eight times in Romans (1:17; 3:5, 21, 22, 25, 26; 10:3a, 3b) and once elsewhere in Paul's letters (2 Cor. 5:21). It covers three important elements: who God is, what he does, and how he does it.

1.   It is an attribute of God's character, 'God's righteousness' (a possessive genitive). In himself, he is just, true, utterly fair, consistent, glorious and holy. His 'righteousness' is the utter rightness of his character, right to the core of his glorious being.

2.   It is an activity of God's person, 'the righteousness shown by God' (a subjective genitive), not a static quality but a dynamic activity, God 'doing the right thing', especially by keeping his promises. Righteousness is God reaching out to rescue people, as he said he would do. It is therefore an expression of his power to save (as here in v. 16). We see this meaning clearly in the Old Testament, for example, in Ps. 98:2, 3a, where his 'salvation', his 'righteousness', his 'love' (that is, covenant steadfast love), and his 'faithfulness' (that is, to his promises), all stand in parallel and mean much the same thing (c.f. 1 Sam. 12:7 where Samuel speaks literally of 'the righteousness of the LORD for you and your fathers.') God's righteousness is his saving activity.

3.   It is a free gift of God to the believer, a status of right relationship with God freely conferred by grace, 'a righteousness from God' (an objective genitive, as conveyed in NIV). This meaning is explicit in Phil. 3:9 where it is literally 'a righteousness *from* God.' This status is a legal (forensic) declaration. It concerns an instantaneous change in status before God and not inner moral transformation (for which we must wait until later in the letter).

In summary, we may take 'the righteousness of God' to mean his activity in reaching out to rescue all who trust in Christ by giving them, as an undeserved gift, a right status before him. In other words, it is the doctrine of justification by grace alone received by faith alone.

2. *What does it mean for the righteousness of God to be 'revealed' in the gospel?*

God did not begin rescuing people after Jesus came. He began with Adam's son Abel (Heb. 11:4). Whenever he rescued anyone, he did it 100 per cent by grace, and they received it 100 per cent by faith (and 0 per cent by their own merit). What the gospel did was to show clearly why and how he does it. A useful analogy (attributed to Augustine) is that the Old Testament is like a fully-furnished but darkened room. All the 'furniture' of God's rescue is present, but it is only perceived dimly and in shadow. The gospel turns the light on so that we say, 'Ah, now I can see what God has been doing and how he has been doing it!' We shall grasp this more clearly when we get to 3:21-26. In the gospel the righteousness of God 'is being revealed', a present continuous tense, meaning an ongoing activity. Everywhere the gospel is preached, a light is shone on God's rescue work.

3. *Why is the righteousness of God 'from faith to faith'?*

This expression seems to be an emphatic way of saying that the righteousness of God is only appropriated by those who come empty-handed (which is what faith means) and rely 100 per cent on his grace. Justification (the legal declaration of righteousness) is given by grace alone and received by faith alone.

4. *How does the Old Testament quotation help us understand
    the righteousness of God?*

Paul quotes from Habakkuk 2:4 (quoted also in Gal. 3:11
and Heb. 10:38). It is worth looking up in its context, since
the New Testament writers never make a text that meant
one thing mean something contradictory. They bring out the
full meaning that the Old Testament text originally had. In
Habakkuk 2 the believer waits for the appointed time when
God's promises will be fulfilled. Fulfilment seems slow, but
it will come (Hab. 2:3); what God has promised, he will do.
There are two possible responses, then as now. Some will be
'puffed up' (v. 4a) with a proud self-sufficiency that thinks
it can cope on its own. By contrast, 'the righteous' (that is,
those who believe the promises) 'will live by his faith.' His
believing the promise will both bring him into right relation
with God (the main emphasis in Romans), and also keep
him in right relation (the emphasis in Heb. 10:38). So faith
is taking God at his word. The opposite of faith is pride.
Either I wait for God to rescue me, or I think I can rescue
myself.

From text to teaching
Getting the message clear: the theme

In verses 1-7 Paul has begun with a great fact. By his resurrection Jesus has been crowned as King, the heir of the promises
to Abraham, Israel, and David. He is the Christ, to whom all
nations owe the obedience of faith. So the gospel is for all. This
is why Paul is apostle to all nations.

In verses 8-15, because Paul knows that Jesus has been made
Lord of all, he understands that the gospel of Jesus must go to
all. This is why he is eager to preach. Notice that he is eager to
preach to the *Christians* in Rome. We might expect him to be
eager to preach to the unbelievers in Rome, and no doubt he is

(if his visits to other cities are anything to go by). But he doesn't ask them to organise evangelistic meetings in the Forum and invite their friends. His first aim is to preach the gospel to the Christians, because he knows this will build up a church in harmony and missionary zeal. As the gospel changes them, so they will reach out humbly and eagerly to others.

Verses 16 and 17 explain Paul's eagerness to preach the gospel. He is eager because he knows it is powerful, and so he won't be disgraced by it in the end. The reason it is powerful to save anyone who believes, is that believing is not a human achievement. If God only saved those who achieved something, belonged to some group, had some knowledge, or enjoyed some privilege, then the gospel would only be useful to save those qualified for it. But because it reveals God's saving arm of 100 per cent grace, it can reach to save anyone without distinction who grasps that rescue.

Getting the purpose clear: the aim

In verses 1-7 Paul wants his readers to understand that the resurrection has crowned Jesus King of every human being without exception. In a pluralist world which is suspicious of any claim to absolute authority, we proclaim that all authority has been given to Jesus. No human being is exempt from the obligation to submit to him. This is a deeply counter-cultural message, which the world will consider divisive. The trouble with absolute claims to truth is that they lead to strife, they say. This is true. And yet the irony is that the authority of Jesus is the only message that can unite human beings. It is the only message that can humble us together at the feet of the one who died for us and then conquered death. Paul headlines it to the church in Rome, because only the exalted Jesus will bring about a humbled and therefore harmonious church, and also a missionary church (the two great aims of the letter).

I take it that Paul's aim in communicating his eagerness in verses 8-15 is so that they too will begin to share that gospel zeal. There is a difference between understanding the truth of verses 1-7 and having the gospel eagerness of verses 8-15 coursing through our veins. This is the challenge to the preacher, so to pray and so to preach this passage that people do not go away just with full notebooks, agreeing with what we have said. Our longing must be that they go away determined for the gospel to be preached and heard.

There is a natural link here with Paul's longing that the church in Rome will partner him in getting the gospel to Spain (15:24). He lifts Jesus high that we may grasp that he is Lord of all, and therefore that we should be eager for all to hear and bow the knee with the obedience of faith.

We might suggest therefore that our aim in preaching or teaching vv. 1-17 could be stated as follows: be eager for all to hear the gospel for all. Begin to share Paul's eagerness to have Jesus preached to all. A sermon that leaves people saying, 'I think I get it now' has fallen short of the aim. We want people to go away not only with clarity in their heads, but fire in their hearts.

Incidentally, it would be a mistake to aim that our hearers will all want to preach the gospel as Paul did, for not all are called to the public preaching of the gospel. Instead we should pray for a shared eagerness in our churches that the gospel should be preached and heard. This will include eagerness that each of us individually will speak words of testimony to Christ in the workplace or neighbourhood. But it will also include all the other ways in which we can support the preaching of the gospel (financial support, prayer, etc). Only a church deeply convinced that Jesus is great and we are small will have this eagerness.

Pointers to application

+ Understand that the gospel centres on a person. It is not an '-ism' and it is not do's and don'ts.

+ Grasp that we need to read the Old Testament to understand Jesus.

+ Understand that the resurrection crowns Jesus the Lord of all human beings without exception: not just certain races, not just clever or educated people, not just people in some countries. Think about unlikely people in our families, workplaces, neighbourhoods, people of other religions, atheists. He is Lord of them all. Engage with the corrosive challenge of the pluralist agendas that would confine Jesus to the private sphere of 'values' rather than the public realm of 'facts'.

+ Grasp that 'faith' does not mean 'believing something to be true' but is shorthand for 'the obedience of faith' which means trusting submission to Jesus.

+ Long for the name of Jesus to be honoured as all kinds of people all over the world bow the knee to him.

+ Experience how the sharing of our faith (rather than boasting about our works) encourages and unites, and apply this to our conversations: how much are we talking about ourselves, and how much are we singing and speaking the praises of Jesus?

+ Address the challenge of being ashamed of the gospel because:

    1. we fear it isn't true. The resurrection proves that it is true.

    2. we worry it isn't relevant to some people. The resurrection proves it is relevant for everybody.

3. we are not sure it is powerful, because it seems such a weak and pathetic message. And yet it is the way God has chosen to save those he saves.

+ Feel our obligation to take the gospel to every human being. If we do not seek to do this, we are treating people as if they were sub-human (since we are not under obligation to preach the gospel to cats and dogs).

+ Be eager for gospel partnership:

1. in prayer for non-Christians and for other gospel workers.

2. in our own courageous testimony to Jesus.

3. in working together in evangelism, helping one another build friendships with non-Christians and share the gospel of Jesus with them.

4. in financial partnership with those needing support in gospel work.

5. for some, being gifted, equipped and supported for public preaching.

6. in practical support for gospel work, e.g. cooking for an enquirers course.

7. in inviting non-Christians to events where they will hear the gospel of Jesus.

+ To grasp that Christianity is a rescue religion. It is about salvation, not about becoming more knowledgeable, respectable, secure or feeling good about ourselves.

+ We Christians ought never to tire of hearing the gospel.

+ Whet our appetites to pay close attention to the letter that follows.

Suggestions for preaching and teaching the text

A. One sermon on 1:1-17

Our teaching points will most naturally follow the three-fold structure of the passage. We might lead in with the theme of gospel eagerness and what it looks like in individuals and a church. Then we might make our main points as follows:

1. Introducing the fact: Everyone needs to hear that Jesus is King of everyone (1:1-7). Keep a clear focus on this central point.

2. Motivating for the desire: Therefore we should be eager for all to hear that Jesus is King (1:8-15). Build from the fact of verses 1-7 to the eagerness of verses 8-15.

3. Teaching the reason: God uses this message to rescue anyone who believes (1:16, 17).

A simpler wording for these teaching points might be:

1. Jesus is King (vv. 1-7);
2. ... and must be proclaimed (vv. 8-15);
3. ... because this is how God rescues (vv. 16, 17).

B. Three sermons on 1:1-17

We could preach this as a three-sermon series, so long as we make the connections clear between one passage and the next.

Sermon 1 (1:1-7) Jesus the King

This first sermon is preached primarily for understanding, that we grasp the significance of this great, and central, fact.

We might lead in on the theme of the scandal of this claim in a pluralist culture. Our teaching points might be:

1. God promises that a man will govern the world (vv. 1, 2).
2. God crowns Jesus to be this man by raising him from the dead (vv. 3, 4).
3. Jesus is honoured when people all over the world bow the knee to him ('the obedience of faith') (vv. 5, 6).

Sermon 2 (1:8-15)

What does a 'gospel-eager' church look like in practice? We might begin by painting this picture and contrasting it with a church that is theoretically evangelical but actually 'gospel-indifferent'. Our teaching points might be:

1. Christian faith in some encourages faith in others, because faith levels us and can therefore unify unlikely people (vv. 8-13). This can be applied to the blessings of non-homogeneous churches and cross-cultural mission partnerships.
2. God has entrusted the gospel to us to give to all without distinction (v. 14). Here the point is our obligation to be churches that are 'gospel-eager'.
3. And so we should be eager for the gospel to be preached and heard (v. 15).

Sermon 3 (1:16, 17)

We might lead in with the scandal that the gospel of Christ is the only way any human being can be rescued by God. Our teaching points might be along the following lines:

1. The gospel of Jesus Christ is God's power to rescue (v. 16a) – and so we can be eager for the gospel without fear of being ashamed.
2. The gospel is God's power to rescue all (without distinction) who come empty-handed (and only those who come empty-handed) (v. 16b)…
3. …because God only rescues those who come empty-handed (and never the proud) (v. 17).

Leading a Bible study
To clarify understanding
1. What did God promise in the Old Testament (v. 2) and how do verses 3 and 4 clarify this (c.f. 4:13)?
2. What did the resurrection do for Jesus (v. 4)? (i.e. What is the significance of the resurrection, what does the resurrection mean?)
3. What was the aim of Paul's job as an apostle (v. 5)?
4. For what reasons does Paul want to visit the church in Rome (vv. 8-15)?
5. Why is Paul not ashamed of the gospel (v. 16)?
6. Why is the gospel God's power to rescue anybody who believes (v. 17)?

To encourage honest response
1. Why is it hard to say that Jesus is King of all the world, in the workplace, school, neighbourhood, etc? What are we worried about, if we say this?
2. How do verses 1-7 help us to do this? (i.e. in what ways do the truths of these verses help us engage honestly with pluralist friends?)
3. Why is it encouraging to see lives changed by faith, in people who are different from us? How can we

promote this kind of mutual encouragement in our church, in mission partnerships, etc?

4. How can we be a church that works together in gospel eagerness in our neighbourhood?

5. How does the truth of verses 16 and 17 promote harmony between different kinds of people in our church fellowship?

6

COMING UNDER GRACE
ROMANS 1:18-32

A student asked me once, 'What if someone goes through life just trying to be good?' It sounded so reasonable. How could I be so narrow as to suggest that God could be displeased with someone who was so 'nice'? And what about those who have never heard of Christ? Isn't it unfair of God to be angry with them? How often are those questions voiced! The image of the 'noble savage' and the idea of original innocence are never far below the surface of objections to Christianity. The passage we are about to consider proves that God is furious even with those who have never heard of Christ; and he is absolutely right to be furious. If this is true, we need to pay very careful attention to what Paul teaches.

Attentive listening to the text
Context and structure
In 1:1-7 Paul insists that God rescues all who believe and bow the knee in trusting submission to Jesus. But he rescues only those who believe, and no one else. This is a staggering claim, and it is being 'revealed' as the gospel is preached (v. 17).

But why can there be no other way? Paul sets out to prove it. Verse 18 is tied to verse17 by the connecting word 'For' (omitted in NIV). What follows is the proof of verse 17. In teaching 1:18-32 it is important to bear in mind that this is just the first stage of the proof. This passage does not stand on its own.

1:18-32 has a clear logical structure. First, Paul states the charge against every human being by nature. Then he proves it, in four stages.

A. The charge is stated (v. 18)
B. The charge is proved (vv. 19-32):
    a)   What God has done (vv. 19, 20);
    b)   What people have done (vv. 21-23);
    c)   What God has done (vv. 24-31);
    d)   What people have done (v. 32).

Working through the text
A. *The charge is stated (v. 18)*

> [18]*For* the wrath of God is being revealed from heaven against all the godlessness and wickedness of men [*people*] who suppress the truth by their wickedness...

Why is God's saving righteousness revealed only to those who come empty-handed with faith (v. 17)? Answer: because God is very angry with everyone else in the world. The 'wrath of God' means his hot, settled, just, personal fury against sinners. This is worse than just saying that bad actions have bad consequences. There are three parts to Paul's charge:

1.   God's wrath 'is being revealed' (present tense). Paul is not yet speaking of the final judgment (see 2:5). The righteousness of God is being revealed as the gospel is preached (v. 17). The wrath of God is being revealed in human society.

2. It is being revealed 'against all the godlessness' (rebellion against God, perhaps corresponding to the first four commandments) 'and wickedness' (treating other people wrongly, commandments 5-10) 'of people'. That is to say, against everything except 'the obedience of faith' (1:5). God is very angry with everyone except those who bow the knee to Jesus.

3. God is right to be angry because 'people…suppress the truth by their wickedness.' We know we do what we ought not to do.

B. *The charge is proved (1) What God has done (vv. 19, 20)*

[19]…since what may be known about God is plain to them,

  because God has made it plain to them.
  [20]For since the creation of the world
    God's invisible qualities—his eternal power
    and divine nature—
      have been clearly seen,
      being understood from what has been made,
        so that men [*people*] are without excuse.

To show that we 'suppress the truth,' Paul must first establish that we know the truth, for we cannot be guilty of suppressing a truth we never knew. So what does everybody know? Answer: that there is a creator God. 'What may be known about God' (that is, without a Bible) 'is plain to them, because God has made it plain to them.' And he has done this by 'what has been made,' because creation is covered in his fingerprints. This is why science is worthwhile, since there is no point doing science unless there is an order to be discerned (which is why so much of modern science has its roots in Christian soil).

God is invisible (John 1:18; 4:24; Col. 1:15; 1 Tim. 1:17). But his invisible 'godness', 'his eternal power and divine nature' has been made visible in 'what has been made.' The rain and harvests witness to his existence (Acts 14:15-17), the stars declare his glory (Ps. 19:1), all the earth is full of his footprints, his echoes, the marks of his existence and presence, his 'glory' (which is the outward visible shining of his invisible being) (Isa. 6:3).

Theologians speak of 'natural theology,' meaning what may be known about God without a Bible. That is right. But they are wrong if they suggest that 'natural theology' can rescue us. For the point of these verses is, 'that people are without excuse.' Creation reveals only enough of God to make me inexcusably guilty for not worshipping him.

C.   *The charge is proved (2) What people have done (vv. 21-23)*

> [21]For although they knew God,
> they neither glorified him as God
> nor gave thanks to him,
>> but their thinking became futile
>> and their foolish hearts were darkened.
>> [22]Although they claimed to be wise, they became fools
>> [23]and exchanged the glory of the immortal God
>> for images made to look like mortal man and
>> birds and animals and reptiles.

What do we do with the revelation God gives in creation? Answer: although we 'knew God' (that is, knew enough to know we ought to worship him), we do not worship him as we ought. The proper response to the knowledge of God through creation is to glorify him as God and give thanks to him (that is, recognize that we owe him everything). Grumblers are practical unbelievers. Gratitude is a fundamental mark of the obedience of faith.

At the heart of the human condition Paul diagnoses a terrible exchange. They 'exchanged the glory of the immortal God for images…' The glory of God is the outward shining of his invisible being. Human beings were meant to shine as God-like creatures (Gen. 1:26). When we look at a human, we are meant to be able to say, 'Ah! Now I can see what God is like.' The reason we lack this glory (3:23) is that by nature we direct our affections and energies downwards, to created people, projects or principles (all of which are idols) rather than upwards to the Creator. The result is that we can no longer think straight ('their thinking became futile… claiming to be wise, they became fools') or desire or choose right ('their foolish hearts were darkened').

We may represent this exchange by the following diagrams:

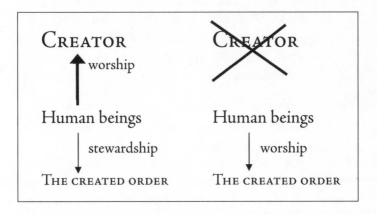

D.   *The charge is proved (3) What God has done (vv. 24-31)*

[24]Therefore **God gave them over** in the sinful desires of their hearts to sexual impurity for the degrading of their bodies with one another. [25]They exchanged the truth of God for a lie, and worshipped and served created things rather than the Creator—who is forever praised. Amen.

> [26]Because of this, **God gave them over** to shameful lusts. Even their women exchanged natural relations for unnatural ones.
>
> [27]In the same way the men also abandoned natural relations with women and were inflamed with lust for one another. Men committed indecent acts with other men, and received in themselves the due penalty for their perversion [*error*].

[28]Furthermore, since they did not think it worthwhile to retain the knowledge of God, *God* **gave them over** to a depraved mind, to do what ought not to be done.

> [29]They have become filled with every kind of wickedness, evil, greed and depravity. They are full of envy, murder, strife, deceit and malice. They are gossips, [30]slanderers, God-haters, insolent, arrogant and boastful; they invent ways of doing evil; they disobey their parents; [31]they are senseless, faithless, heartless, ruthless.

The third stage of Paul's proof is God's response. Three times he says, 'God gave them over' (vv. 24, 26, 28) to the consequence of disordered worship, which is disordered desire. God is the subject of the main verbs here: 'God gave them over.' The behaviours Paul describes are not the root problem, but the result of the 'exchange' of verse 23. Because we do not love God, all our loves become disordered. When we suppress the truth (v. 18) and exchange the truth for a lie (v. 25), God hands us over to disordered desire in other areas of life.

But why does Paul take homosexual desire as his leading example (in vv. 24-27)? We feel uneasy because Paul seems to make a minority group his prime target for disapproval.

We need to be clear that he is speaking of all homosexual desire and practice. He is not just speaking of the Greek practice of sex between men and boys, since he speaks of lesbianism as well. Nor is he speaking of those who are 'naturally' heterosexual behaving 'unnaturally' by homosexual acts, since the word translated 'natural' refers not to what is subjectively 'natural for me', but to how God made the world (creation order).

There would seem to be two reasons why Paul begins with this disorder. The first is that it graphically illustrates an 'exchange' between order and disorder. He picks up the word 'exchange' from verses 23 and 25, and uses it in verse 26 of lesbian desire. Same-sex erotic desire is one of the clearest expressions of disordered affection. But we must remember that this is not the root of sin; it is but one example of a sin that is a consequence of the fundamental sin, which is idolatry. Further, we cannot draw a one-to-one equation between individual idolatry and individual homosexual desire (c.f. John 9:1ff in another context). Paul's point is that the very existence of these desires in society is an evidence (among others) of God's handing us over to the consequences of our idolatry.

All the other examples in the list (vv. 29-31) also illustrate disordered desire. All are the result of disordered worship.

The second reason Paul begins with this is that homosexuality was supremely the Gentile sin. When the Jew looked at the Gentile world one of the things that most horrified him and most made him happy to be a Jew was the appalling practice of homosexuality. Popular religious writings railed against Gentile homosexuality as proof of the moral superiority of the Jews. The Jewish Christian hearing verses 24-27 would have been cheering

Paul on. We shall see how Paul responds, in chapter 2. At this stage it is worth noting that in Psalm 106:20 and Jeremiah 2:11 the same language of 'exchanged glory' is used of Israel. So the Jew who knows his Scriptures will not be so complacent.

Paul's main point is that the moral chaos of the world is the visible evidence here and now of the wrath of God. The wrath of God is revealed by moral chaos. It has been said that the history of the world is the judgment of the world. 'Look at a messed-up world,' Paul says, 'and you will see that God is angry.' This is clearly not the world as it was meant to be. God's anger is revealed in present degradation and not (yet) in future condemnation.

E.   *The charge is proved (4) What people have done (v. 32)*

> [32] Although they know God's righteous decree that those who do such things deserve death, they not only continue to do these very things but also approve of those who practise them.

Paul's punchline is that not only do they do what they know they ought not to do (the list of vv. 29-31), they create a society in which these things are accepted and approved. They want others to approve of them, and so they approve of others when they behave like this. Every time I condone behaviour in others, I make it easier to do it myself, because I create a climate of public opinion in which this is acceptable. All this raises my sin to a new level of seriousness. No longer is it a guilty secret of which I am ashamed; now it is a brazen rebellion against God (c.f. Isa. 3:9). This shows a set purpose and fixed preference for sin.

From text to teaching

Getting the message clear: the theme

Paul's theme is that disordered desires reveal the just anger of God against disordered worship. The invisible God has made enough of his god-ness visible through creation, so that we ought to honour him. We suppress this truth and choose to worship people or projects other than God. We are guilty and God is right to be angry. We know he is angry because of the moral chaos of a messed-up world. The 'noble savage' does not exist. All are guilty and under the just fury of the Creator.

Getting the purpose clear: the aim

Paul is aiming to prove that God rescues only the believer; there really is no other way. These verses prove that God is rightly furious with every human being except those who live 'the obedience of faith.' But Paul also knows that we have well-developed strategies for applying this passage to *other people*. This is the 'tabloid mentality' that loves to read about the bad behaviour of others because it makes me feel better about myself. So when I read verse 32 my response is to say, 'Well, that is certainly not *me*. I don't approve at all of that terrible behaviour. Not me. I look down my nose and thank God I am not like them' (c.f. Luke 18:11).

In preaching this passage we must pray for a deep conviction in ourselves and our hearers that each of us individually and inescapably is by nature under the righteous fury of God and utterly without excuse. God really is very, very angry with us. And only 'the obedience of faith' offers any way of escape. We want people to go away deeply convinced that there is absolutely no alternative way of escape.

Only a church of men and women humbled under this sober truth will properly appreciate the wonder of grace, live in harmony with one another, and reach out with humble urgency to a needy world, because we know that Christ is our only hope.

Pointers to application

+   Expose the excuses we make: poor parenting, dysfunctional families, ways in which we have been victims, school bullying, financial pressures, chronic health problems, being badly treated by an 'ex', never having been well taught the Bible, living in the wrong part of the world… and press home that we are each one of us really and objectively guilty before God, and without excuse.

+   Expose how our ingratitude reveals our misdirected worship, the ways in which we think the world (or God?) owes us a living, comfort, health, success.

+   Expose idolatry, when we make a person (e.g. in a relationship), a career, comfort, security, some project, perhaps even a charitable enterprise, the goal of life to which we devote our time, money, energy and affections. It's a good test to ask, 'What or who, if taken away from us, would make life feel like hell?' That is our idol.

+   Expose our determination to be masters/mistresses of our own lives.

+   Expose disordered desire, using examples that show that the world is out of order as a result of human decisions. For example, statistics show that charitable giving is in inverse proportion to wealth (the richer we are, the smaller proportion we give).

+   Speak with great care about homosexuality, being constantly aware of the pain as well as the evil of these desires. We need to make it clear that all homosexual desire is an example of disordered desire; that this is but one terrible result of the fundamental human sin of idolatry; that an individual who experiences these desires is no more exceptionally evil than is someone born blind; and to point those mastered by these terrible desires to the rescue of God offered to all in Christ. Take great care not to speak as a Pharisee condemning the sins of others, if we ourselves have not been mastered by these desires. Remember verses 29-31!

+ Look at our heroes, the men and women we admire and talk about. Why do we admire them? Is it sometimes that their ungodly behaviour makes us feel better about our own ungodly behaviour? (After all, 'everybody does it').

+ Apply this to our attitudes:
a)   to our fellow Christians. We are all alike without excuse, all on the same level (and always will be), all undeserving of grace (and always will be),
b)   to those not yet Christian. Reach out to them with humility (for we are by nature no better than they) and yet with urgency, not allowing our evan-gelistic zeal to be blunted by any shallow optimism.

+ Anticipate the self-righteous objection with which chapter 2 will begin.

+ Anticipate and include some of the gospel, for the benefit of those who may not be there to hear the rest of the series!

Suggestions for preaching and teaching the text

It is probably best to preach this as one sermon, leading in to the remainder of Paul's argument to the end of chapter 4 (or at least to 3:20).

A. *One sermon on 1:18-32*
Possible beginnings would include:

1. 'God is furiously angry with everyone who does not bow the knee to Jesus Christ. Furiously angry, even if someone has never heard of Jesus. Does that sound extreme? I'm sure it does. But sometimes it is necessary to shock in order to save (as, for example, some anti-smoking or drink-driving posters do).'
2. 'Christianity is all very well for those who like that kind of thing, and I'm sure it works for you. But I don't really *need it*.'
3. 'I know so many really *good* people who are not Christians. Are you really saying they are in danger?'

We need to set the context and it would probably be good to read the passage from verse 16, including the connecting 'for' at the start of verse 18.

Teaching points might be as follows:

1. God is very angry with everyone except the believer (v. 18 with v. 17).
2. God is right to be angry with everyone except the believer because we have no excuse for not worshipping God (vv. 19-23).

> Point 2 could be subdivided into:
>
> a) Creation shows us there is a God to whom we owe everything (vv. 19, 20).
>
> b) But we choose to devote our desires and energies to our own projects and people (vv. 21-23). That is, we suppress the truth by misdirected worship.

We are preaching against 'I didn't know' righteousness. (In chapter 2 we will preach against another substitute, 'I'm not as bad as you' righteousness.)

3.   Moral chaos proves God is angry with everyone except the believer (vv. 24-31).

> (It will be important to focus on Paul's central point, and not to let people think that this is primarily about homosexuality. It may be wise to have a separate teaching meeting about sex).

4.   Our choice of heroes proves that God is right to be angry with everyone except the believer (v. 32).

> Press home Paul's punchline by looking at our choices of heroes and our desire to be affirmed in wrong behaviour.

Conclusion. Each of us is without excuse. And therefore we must take the one way of rescue, God's saving righteousness offered to us in Christ (v. 17). In the church we are all equal under grace. And we ought to be eager for others to hear the only message that can rescue them.

B. A short series from 1:18-32
It would be possible to develop Paul's argument in more detail with a short series, under the overall headline of verse 18. We might divide it as follows:

Sermon 1. What creation proves about God (vv. 18-20)
Here we teach what the created order does (and does not) show about God, to make the point that all people everywhere are without excuse for not seeking God.

Sermon 2. How humans respond to creation (vv. 18, 21-23)
This is an opportunity to teach what idolatry is, and where idolatry leads. Idolatry is the exchange of the worship of the Creator for the worship of created projects or people. Idolatry leads to the loss of glory (i.e. godlikeness), to confused thinking, to people who think they are clever while actually being fools.

Sermon 3. What a messed-up world proves about God (vv. 18, 24-32)
We look carefully at the evidence for a world which is not as it ought to be. In particular we examine the theme of disordered desires (not only sexual, but also the list of vv. 29-31) and the decline of a society into a place where disorder becomes normal (v. 32).

In all these, it is vital to remember that the argument continues straight in to the start of chapter 2.

Leading a Bible study
To clarify understanding
1. What does creation show (vv18-20)?
2. Why is God right to be angry with everyone (vv. 18, 21-23)?
3. How does God respond to our refusal to give thanks to him (vv. 24-31)?
4. What does Paul teach about homosexual desires and how do they illustrate his main point (vv. 24-27)?
5. What is Paul's main point in vv. 24-31?
6. How does v. 32 make things even worse?

To encourage honest response
1. When I look at the world God has made, what conclusions do I draw? What conclusions do the makers of 'nature programmes' draw? What conclusions do scientists draw? What conclusions ought we to draw?
2. Examine my own life against the gratitude test of v21. How does my ingratitude expose my heart?
3. In what ways are my desires out of order? That is, what do I want that I know I ought not to want, and what do I not want that I know I ought to want? (An opportunity for honest self-examination against Paul's examples in vv. 24-31).

4. How do my 'out of order' desires show up my 'out of order' heart?
5. In what ways do I want others (including my fellow church members) to think my ungodly behaviour is acceptable and understandable?
6. In the light of this passage, how ought we to look at others (including, for example, homosexual people)?

7

Coming Under Grace

Romans 2

'Dear Paul,

I have just read the second half of Romans chapter 1. I congratulate you on a vigorous, refreshing exposé of evil. I agree with you that it is disgusting when people not only behave badly but actually approve of bad behaviour. It did me good to read your chapter. You will be glad to know that I for one do not for a moment *'approve* of those who practise' (v. 32) these terrible things. On the contrary, I recognise them for the evils they are and agree that such people are 'without excuse' (v. 20). I look forward to chapter 2.

Yours sincerely, …'

Attentive listening to the text

Context and structure

The section 'Coming under grace' began like this:

| 1:16, 17 | Paul's manifesto: God does the right thing by rescuing all believers, but only believers. |
| 1:18-32 | It has to be only believers, because God is rightly angry with everyone else. |

Chapter 2 continues the argument, because Paul knows that many of his hearers will not be convicted of their need of Christ by 1:18-32. Like the imaginary letter-writer at the start of this chapter, they will simply be feeling good about themselves.

2:1-29 divides naturally into verses 1-11 and 12-29. The argument may be broken down and summarized as follows:

2:1-11
God will judge me by the same standards as everyone else.

2:1-3	Every time I condemn someone else, I condemn myself before God.
2:4, 5	God doesn't punish me straight away, to give me time to repent.
2:6-11	There are no exceptions to the fairness of God, so I really must repent.

2:12-29
The only way to be right with God is to do what God wants.

2:12-13	Only those who do what God wants will be right with God.
2:14-16	This includes the least privileged when their hearts are changed…
2:17-24	…but it excludes the most privileged when their hearts are not changed.
2:25-29	This heart-change comes only from the Spirit of God.

Working through the text

A. *Every time I condemn someone else, I condemn myself before God (2:1-3)*

> ¹You, therefore, have no excuse [*are without excuse*], you who pass judgment on someone else,
>> for at whatever point you judge the other, you are condemning yourself,
>>> because you who pass judgment do the same things.
>
> ²Now we know that God's judgment against those who do such things is based on truth.
>
> ³So when you, a mere man [*person*], pass judgment on them and yet do the same things,
>> do you think you will escape God's judgment?

'You, *therefore* …'. follows straight on from 1:18-32. In 1:32 he has condemned those who 'approve' of evil behaviour. But he knows that the religious people in the church do not approve; they 'pass (disapproving) judgment' on these wicked people. So, what of these religious people? Are they in the right with God because they disapprove of evil? Not at all! They are right to disapprove. But they are terribly mistaken if they think their disapproval puts them in the clear.

We move now from 'I didn't know' righteousness (1:18-32) into 'I'm not as bad as you' righteousness. The argument is simple and complete. We 'know that God's judgment against those who do such things is based on truth' (that is, fair and right, in line with his 'righteousness' 1:17). We all agree about that. So the issue is what we '*do*,' not what we approve or disapprove. If I do something while passing judgment on that kind of thing, agreeing that God will judge it, then I am self-condemned. By my

disapproval, I simply add my own voice to God's in passing judgment on myself! 'Do you realise you have scored
a spectacular own goal?' asks Paul.

I cannot escape. If I disapprove, I condemn myself.
If I become wishy-washy and say it'll be alright if I 'do
not judge' (misunderstanding Matt. 7:1), then I am still
condemned, because I am now lined up with those condemned in 1:32. It is like a nightmare in which every
escape is blocked. Both the irreligious and the religious
come under the same verdict, 'without excuse' (1:20;
2:1, the same word).

When Paul speaks of doing 'the same things' or 'such
things' he does not mean that every religious person commits in detail every sin committed by the irreligious. For
example, few, if any, Jews practised homosexuality (condemned in 1:26-28). Paul probably refers to the more general list of 1:29-31. Besides, a heart is shown to be sinful
by its desires as well as its actions (Matt. 5:21-48), and by
breaking any part of God's law (James 2:10). Whatever
my individual sins, my actions reveal a heart of Sin.

Paul ends verse 3 by asking, '... do you think you will
escape God's judgement?' The answer ought to be, 'No, of
course I don't,' unless I think God will make an exception
for me, that I have (in terms of the game *Monopoly*)
a 'Get out of jail free' card. This is exactly what the Jew
supposed, by being a member of the covenant people.
And it is just what many in Christian churches suppose.
We want to answer, 'Yes, I do think I will escape, because
I call myself a Christian, I've been baptized, I try to lead
a respectable life, I know my Bible.' Paul says the answer
is, 'No', and proves it in verses 4-11.

B. *God doesn't punish me straight away, to give me time to repent (2:4, 5)*

⁴Or do you show contempt for [*presume on*] the riches of
his kindness, tolerance [*forbearance*] and patience,

not realizing that God's kindness leads you toward
repentance?

⁵But because of your stubbornness and your unrepentant
heart,

you are storing up wrath against yourself for the day
of God's wrath,

when his righteous judgment will be revealed.

I may think I'm alright because when I sin God does
not immediately punish me. I experience no immediate
adverse effects and so I suppose I am in God's 'good books'
despite not repenting. Every day I experience 'his kindness,
forbearance and patience.' And so I suppose I can go on in
hypocrisy, condemning evildoers while doing evil. I live in
what has been called 'cheap grace,' which is not real grace at
all. My 'faith' is not 'the obedience of faith' (1:5; 16:26) but
a counterfeit faith. I begin to 'presume' on the grace of God.
I need to grasp that every time he doesn't punish me, his
kindness is meant to lead me 'toward repentance.'

Verse 5 makes it clear that Paul is speaking not of imper-
fection but of persistent impenitence. Wrath comes not on
those who sin, but on those who sin and habitually will not
repent ('your stubbornness and your unrepentant heart').
We must not misunderstand this – as those with sensitive
consciences are likely to do – to mean that my security is only
as strong as my most recent repentance, or that every time
I sin, I place myself in danger of hell until I repent (because
I fear that if I die with any unconfessed sin I will be condemned). That misunderstanding would be clean contrary

to the gospel of grace which Paul expounds so wonderfully in this letter (especially 8:28-39). Paul is not condemning shaky discipleship, but complacent and persistent hypocrisy, the pseudo-discipleship that thinks the need for repentance ended with my 'conversion'. What Paul wants to expose is not the life that sometimes falls into sin (and therefore needs repentance as an ongoing discipline), but rather the hard and impenitent heart that systematically will not repent. Paul speaks not to the penitent heart that lacks assurance, but to the impenitent heart that has a false assurance. To them, his warning echoes John the Baptist and the Lord Jesus himself (Matt. 3:7-10; 21:28-32). The 'wrath' that is shown partially and provisionally in present moral chaos (1:24-32) will one day be poured out in terrible fullness, 'on the day of God's wrath, when his righteous judgment will be revealed.' On that day we shall see that God has no favourites.

C. *There are no exceptions to the fairness of God, so I really must repent (2:6-11)*

> [6]God [*who*] 'will give to each person according to what he has done' (Ps. 62:12).

A   [7]To those who
>   by persistence [*patient endurance*] in doing good
>   seek glory, honour and immortality,
>   he will give eternal life.

B   [8]But for those who
>   are self-seeking and who reject [*do not obey*] the
>   truth and follow evil,
>   there will be wrath and anger.

A   [9]There will be trouble and distress
>   for every human being who does evil:
>   first for the Jew, then for the Gentile;

B   ¹⁰but glory, honour and peace
          for everyone who does good:
               first for the Jew, then for the Gentile.

¹¹For God does not show favouritism.

The idea that God has favourites is deep-rooted. Paul devotes verses 6-11 to confounding it. Verse 6 follows closely on verse 5, and reads literally, 'on the day of the wrath and revelation of the righteous judgment of God who 'will give to each person …"

This carefully-structured section begins and ends with Paul's main point. In verse 6 he quotes Psalm 62:12. God 'will give to each person according to what he has done.' In verse 11 he says the same thing, 'God does not show favouritism.' God is fair. He makes no exceptions. This is consistently taught in both Old Testament and New Testament. It is part of the righteousness of God' and it is not altered by the New Covenant. See, for example, Ecclesiastes 12:14; Isaiah 3:10f; Jeremiah 17:10; Hosea 12:2; Matthew 7:21;Matthew 16:27;Matthew 25:31-46;John 5:28f; 2 Corinthians 5:10; 2 Corinthians 11:15b; Galatians 6:7-9; Ephesians 6:8; Colossians 3:24f; 2 Timothy 4:14; 1 Peter 1:17; Revelation 2:23; Revelation 20:12f; Revelation 22:12.

To make his case comprehensively, Paul gives both sides twice, in an ABBA format. Everyone is in one of these two groups. Each group includes some religious and some irreligious people (note the repetition of 'first for the Jew, then for the Gentile'). The most fundamental division of the human race is not between Jew and Gentile, but between group A and group B.

But who are they? Some think that because group B are sinners, group A cannot really exist (since all are sinners, 3:23). But it is more likely that group B are unbelievers and group A are believers. There are six reasons for thinking this:

1. Paul describes each group in exactly the same style. He does not say, 'If anyone actually did seek glory etc, then God would have given them eternal life (but, by implication, nobody does).' The style suggests two groups of people who exist.

2. Group B are described as not obeying the truth (v. 8), which is the description of an unbeliever rather than just any old sinner (c.f. 2 Thess. 1:8). To be disobedient to the truth is the opposite of 'the obedience of faith' (1:5; 16:26).

3. The context in verses 4, 5 is not 'sin versus sinlessness', but 'repentance versus hard and impenitent hearts'. This suggests that group A are not sinless but penitent (that is, believers).

4. Group A are described not by their moral achievement (sinlessness) but by the direction of their life, a seeking with *patient endurance* (the same word is used of believers in 5:3, 4, NIV 'perseverance', in 8:25 NIV 'patiently', and in 15:4 NIV 'endurance'). When verse 10 says they 'do good,' it must therefore mean what is described in verse 7, a direction of life rather than moral perfection.

5. The rewards promised to group A are 'eternal life' (v. 7), 'glory, honour and peace' (v. 10), which are the destiny of believers (e.g. 8:18).

6. When we come to verse 27 these people who 'obey the law' will condemn you who ... are a law-breaker.' If nobody 'obeys the law' (in this sense), then there won't be much condemnation and Paul's point is pointless!

For all these reasons, it makes more sense to take the contrast here to be between believers and unbelievers. This is one of Paul's 'trailers' in which he speaks briefly of something on which he will expand later (especially in ch. 8).

What does it mean for the believer to be judged 'according to what he has done' (v. 6)? This cannot mean that we will get what we deserve, for then none would be saved. Nor can it mean that our deeds need to reach a certain standard before we die; nor that our assurance rests even 1 per cent on what we do or will ever do, for it always rests 100 per cent on the obedience of Christ (5:19 'the obedience of the one man'). It means that our works are the public evidence of our faith. In the Last Judgment the full disclosure of our lives will accurately prove whether or not we are real believers. It will be no use in court to say that mentally I believed or verbally I professed faith in Christ. That will cut no ice. The only evidence will be a changed direction of life. Without that evidence we shall be condemned as frauds. And so we are saved entirely by God's grace, but judged entirely by our works; for true grace is always grace which works by changing the heart (c.f. 1 Cor. 15:10).

If this is true, then I really must repent. This is the force of Paul's argument. I, who have such well-developed strategies for avoiding repentance, really must repent.

D. Only those who do what God wants will be right with God (2:12, 13)

> [12]All who sin apart from the law
>> will also perish apart from the law,
> and all who sin under the law
>> will be judged by the law.

> [13]For it is not those who hear the law
>> who are righteous in God's sight,
> but it is those who obey the law
>> who will be declared righteous.

For the first time in the letter, Paul speaks of 'the law,' that is, the Law of Moses. So 'apart from law' refers to Gentiles and 'under the law' to Jews. The key to verses 12-29 is to see that Paul is comparing two competing ways of dividing the human race. One is 'Jew and Gentile,' the outward distinction between religious privilege, Bible knowledge, moral respectability on the one hand, and the absence of those privileges on the other. The other is inward, those whose hearts are changed by grace, and those whose hearts are hard and disobedient. We may picture this by a simple grid.

		OUTWARD	
		Jew	Gentile
	Faith	OK	?
INWARD			
	Disobedience	?	Not OK

Presumably Jewish believers are OK, for they score positive on both axes. By the same token Gentile unbelievers are not OK, for they fail on both counts. But what of Jewish unbelievers? Does their Jewishness (religion) trump their unbelief? And what of the Gentile believer? Does faith make up for the absence of Jewishness (religion)? Similar questions must be asked in every church today.

In verses 12 and 13 Paul states the principle which will govern verses 12-29. Outward religious privilege or achievement cannot make us right with God; only the obedience of faith can do this. 'All who sin apart from the law will also perish apart from the law'; Gentiles do not need the Bible to make them guilty before God (as Paul has proved in 1:18-32). But also, 'all who sin under the law' (i.e. as Jews) 'will be judged by the law.' Knowing and having the law will not protect those who don't obey it, because (v. 13) 'it is not those who hear the law' (that is, hear without obeying, the Jewish unbeliever) 'who are righteous in God's sight, but it is those who obey the law who will be declared righteous.' To be 'declared righteous' (or 'justified') means for God to declare that we are in right relationship with him. Justification is the opposite of condemnation (5:16).

What does justification mean?

Declared to be in the wrong = CONDEMNED	Declared to be in the right = JUSTIFIED

Who are these 'who obey the law'? The answer is either (a) nobody, or (b) the believer. If we think there is nobody in group A (vv. 6-11), then nobody obeys the law. But we have seen that it is more likely that group A are believers. Since Paul speaks of these people being 'justified' (and justification is always and only by faith), it seems more likely that Paul speaks of believers 'obeying the law' in some sense. They do this imperfectly but genuinely, because their direction of life has changed from disobedience to 'the obedience of faith' and they are now seeking for glory (v. 7). These are those who prove their genuine faith by hearing and doing (James 1:22-25).

Paul now takes the two hard cases from our grid, and considers each in turn. First (probably), the Gentile believer.

E.   *This includes the least privileged when their hearts are changed ... (2:14-16)*

14(Indeed, when Gentiles, who do not have the law, do by nature things required by the law, they are a law for themselves, even though they do not have the law, 15since they show that the requirements of the law are written

on their hearts, their consciences also bearing witness, and their thoughts now accusing, now even defending them.)[1]
[16]This will take place on the day when God will judge men's secrets through Jesus Christ, as my gospel declares.

This is a difficult passage. We may first dismiss two wrong understandings.

1. It cannot mean that some Gentiles have a good nature (a kind of 'original virtue') and are put right with God apart from Christ (c.f. 3:22-24).

2. It is unlikely that Paul is speaking of Gentiles who have not heard of Christ but who somehow prove by their good lives that they would have believed if they had heard. There is no encouragement elsewhere in Scripture for this eccentric idea. Besides, it is hard to see why Paul would have been so keen to go to Spain (15:24), if the good people of Spain would be saved anyway.

Paul may be speaking of non-Christian Gentiles who yet have some sense of right and wrong (from their consciences). What is more, they sometimes do the right thing. Not every unbeliever is a murderer or adulterer. And when they do the right thing this shows that 'the requirements of the law' (right and wrong) are somehow 'written on their hearts.' Usually they have a bad conscience ('their thoughts now accusing …') but from time to time a good conscience ('… now even defending them'). But they are not saved by these conflicting thoughts. NIV understands verses 14, 15 this way by putting them in brackets, and implying that verse 16 ('This will take place …') refers back to verse 13

---

1. These parentheses are original to NIV.

('… be declared righteous'); on Judgment Day those who obey the law will be declared righteous.

While this is a possible solution to a difficult passage, there are three reasons why it may not be correct.

1. By having to put verses 14, 15 in brackets it arbitrarily breaks the flow of the text. Verse 14 begins with 'For' which ought to connect it with verse 13. And verse 15 flows straight into verse 16 in the Greek.

2. The reference to 'written on their hearts' would seem to be an echo of the New Covenant language of Jeremiah 31:33, an echo supported by Paul's reference to the work of the Spirit in verse 29.

3. If these are Gentile Christians, we have a coherent structure to the argument, beginning with Gentile believers (vv. 14-16) and going on to Jewish unbelievers (vv. 17-24).

One difficulty with these being Gentile believers is that Paul speaks of them 'doing *by nature* things required by the law'; and yet believers do not do this 'by nature' but by grace. The solution may perhaps be found if we translate literally as below.

> *14For when Gentiles,*
>> *who do not have the law by nature,*
>>> *do the things of the law,*
>>>> *they – not having the law – are a law in themselves.*

> *15They show that the work of the law is written on their hearts,*
>> *their conscience testifying with them,*
>> *and their conflicting thoughts accusing or even defending*

>> *16in the day when God judges the secrets of people,*
>>> *according to my gospel through Jesus Christ.*

There is no punctuation in the Greek, and it is possible to take 'by nature' as a description of the Gentiles rather than as a description of what they do. They 'do not have the law by nature,' that is, by their 'nature' as Gentiles. Paul uses the same word 'by nature' to describe the Jew in Galatians 2:15 (NIV 'Jews by birth').

So Paul says, '13 …it is those who obey the law who will be declared righteous,' because '14 when Gentiles, who do not have the law by nature (i.e. their nature as Gentiles) do the things of the law' (i.e. their lives are turned around to begin to go God's way), then 'they—not having the law (in a formal sense, i.e. not being Jews)—are a law in themselves' (that is, they have internalised the true law, by the work of the Spirit at their conversion). And so, '15 they show that the work of the law (what God really wants) is written on their hearts (by the Spirit, at their conversion), 'their conscience testifying with them, and their conflicting thoughts accusing or even defending, in the day when God judges…' That is to say, some of these Gentiles who profess conversion to Christ will be shown in the Last Day to be the real thing (but others may not).

If this is right, Paul is supporting verse 13b ('those who obey the law will be declared righteous') by showing that Gentile Christians do just this, in spite of not having the Law of Moses. In spite of lacking all the privileges of the Jew, their hearts are changed and they really begin to go God's way.

The next section is less difficult. Paul moves from the least privileged to the most privileged, from the Gentile to the Jew.

F. ... but it excludes the most privileged when their hearts are not changed (2:17-24)

[17]Now you,
>   if you call yourself a Jew;
>   if you rely on the law
>   and brag about your relationship to God;
>   [18]if you know his will
>   and approve of what is superior
>>   because you are instructed by the law;

[19] if you are convinced that you are
>   a guide for the blind,
>   a light for those who are in the dark,
>   [20]an instructor of the foolish,
>   a teacher of infants,
>>   because you have in the law the embodiment
>>   of knowledge and truth—

[21]you, then, who teach others, do you not teach yourself?
>   You who preach against stealing, do you steal?
>   [22]You who say that people should not commit
>   adultery, do you commit adultery?
>   You who abhor idols, do you rob temples?
>   [23]You who brag about the law, do you dishonour God by
>   breaking the law?
>>   [24]As it is written: 'God's name is blasphemed among
>>   the Gentiles because of you.' (Isa. 52:5)

We must remember that some described here were – and still are today – within the visible church. The elder brother of Luke 15 is alive and well and living in most churches; he may be reading or even writing this book.

Paul begins with the privileges of the Jew (vv. 17, 18). He trusts that because he is a Jew and has the Law of Moses (i.e. is a member of the covenant people, outwardly), he has a relationship with God and knows right and wrong. What is more, he approves good things, unlike the terrible people of 1:32. Indeed, he sits in superior judgment on those bad people.

And therefore (vv. 19, 20) he is able to instruct others. In the Scriptures he really does have 'the embodiment of knowledge and truth' (c.f. 9:4, 5). So he can guide the blind, bring light to those in darkness (as the Lord's servant does in Isa. 49:6), instruct the ignorant (foolish), and teach those who know nothing ('infants'). All this is wonderfully true because he knows his Bible.

But does he do his Bible? That—as we have seen repeatedly—is the question. He teaches others, but does he teach himself? Paul gives three examples of inconsistency, the first two of which are easy to understand. He preaches against stealing (the eighth commandment), and yet he steals, albeit perhaps in clever and less obvious ways. His heart is grasping and he lives for himself. He says adultery is wrong (the seventh commandment), and yet he is not faithful in marriage, whether it be by the lustful look (Matt. 5:27, 28), or perhaps by divorcing his wife so that he can find a better one (Matt. 5:31, 32). We cannot be sure what Paul meant by his third example about robbing temples. But the principle is clear: inconsistency between what we know and approve, and what we do, dishonours God (v. 23).

In fact a professing Christian who is not genuine is worse than someone who doesn't claim to be a Christian at all. This is the force of the quote from Isaiah 52:5. The rest of the world looks at God's people in exile. They know it is punishment for sin. They conclude that Israel's god isn't much of a god ('God's name is blasphemed among the

Gentiles') since even his people don't honour his standards. Just so today: irreligious unbelievers look at religious unbelievers and conclude that the god they claim to follow isn't much of a god.

G. *This heart-change comes only from the Spirit of God (2:25-29)*

25Circumcision has value if you observe the law,
but if you break the law, you have become as though you had not been circumcised.

26If those who are not circumcised keep the law's requirements,
> will they not be regarded as though they were circumcised?

27The one who is not circumcised physically and yet obeys the law
> will condemn you who,
>> even though you have the written code and circumcision, are a lawbreaker.

28A man is not a Jew if he is only one outwardly,
> nor is circumcision merely outward and physical.

29No, a man is a Jew if he is one inwardly;
> and circumcision is circumcision of the heart,
>> by the Spirit,
>> not by the written code.
Such a man's praise is not from men, but from God.

Paul sums up the chapter by restating his principle and making it even clearer. Although Abraham was circumcised (in Gen. 17) long before the Law of Moses was given (Exod. 20), 'circumcision' became a shorthand for 'being a Jew, having the law (i.e. belonging to the people whose men are circumcised)'. (Paul uses the same shorthand in 4:9-12.)

What is the point of being a Jew (c.f. 3:1)? Answer: much if you obey the law, but nothing if you don't (v. 25). To be a Jewish believer is better than to be a Gentile believer, for you have a head start in the life of discipleship; you know your Bible, you have all the pieces of the jigsaw, as Paul had before his conversion. All that is needed is for those pieces to fall into place with Jesus Christ at the centre.

But to be a Jewish unbeliever is worse than nothing, for the symbolism of your outward circumcision is nullified by your uncircumcised heart (v. 25). Indeed (v. 27), just as the seeking Queen of Sheba and the penitent people of Nineveh will condemn the unbeliever (Matt. 12:41, 42), so the Gentile convert will condemn the Jewish unbeliever because, in spite of all his privileges, he kept a hard and stubborn heart. There is no such thing as 'handshake righteousness', a righteousness that comes from 'shaking hands' with the right people, belonging to the right group.

This passage makes it clear that to 'observe the law' (v. 25), to 'keep the law's requirements' (v. 26), to 'obey the law' (v. 27) all mean being converted and receiving the gift of the Spirit (v. 29). They do not refer here to sinless perfection, but to real Christianity. Paul contrasts 'the Spirit' to 'the written code' (lit. 'the letter'). For the unconverted, the law of God remains outside, a true but dead letter. For the converted, those same moral truths come inside by the Spirit and change the heart, so that the converted heart is concerned above all not with what people think ('praise … from men') but with what God thinks and approves ('praise … from God', c.f. John 5:44).

So the question is not, 'Is the law good or bad?' The question is, 'Is the law inside or outside my heart?'

From text to teaching
Getting the message clear: the theme

Romans 2 supports the manifesto message of 1:16, 17—the saving righteousness of God is revealed to anyone who bows the knee with the obedience of faith, but to no-one else. In 1:18-32 Paul proves that the irreligious, including those who know nothing of the Bible, are guilty before God. Now in chapter 2 he turns his focus onto the religious person. Probably this was all addressed to the Jew, but in principle it is for anyone who disapproves of the bad behaviours of 1:18-32. The central theme of the chapter is the absolute necessity of real repentance and faith.

In verses 1-5 Paul proves that the self-righteous person is self-condemned and must therefore repent. He supports this in verses 6-11 by spelling out comprehensively that the righteousness of God involves absolute fairness, with no exceptions. All people will be judged by what they have done. That measure will reveal whether they are real believers. So the burden of verses 1-11 is that my correct disapproval of evil points emphatically to my urgent need to live a life of repentance and faith.

In some ways the second main section of the chapter (vv. 12-29) goes over the same ground, but now specifically with reference to the Law of Moses. The distinctive emphasis in these verses is on the need for a changed heart (vv. 15, 29) and the possibility of this changed heart only by the Spirit of God. God's true people are not marked by outward markers like circumcision or Bible knowledge, but by obedience from the heart by the Spirit, who writes the law on the heart.

Getting the purpose clear: the aim

For preaching today, we need to think how to translate the categories of 'Jew' and 'circumcision'. In many of our contexts, the original groups of Jewish and Gentile Christians are not very relevant (because, sadly, there are so few Jewish Christians in most of our churches). But it does not take much thought to understand how the mindset of religious privilege occurs in every church. The church member from a Christian family, who has been brought up to know his Bible, who has perhaps some status in his church by association with significant people, who has been to the 'right' church as a student, whose lifestyle has been outwardly pretty respectable, whose life has perhaps been fairly straightforward, may be tempted to think he is just a bit superior to the new Christian who is clueless about his Bible, doesn't know anybody who matters, has never been to a well-known church, and whose life is still pretty much a moral mess. In these terms there are plenty of 'Jews' and 'Gentiles' in all our churches.

At one level Paul's aim is simple. He wants to close off the escape hatch by which the morally upright person tries to evade the fact that he or she can be right with God only and 100 per cent by free, unmerited grace, received empty-handed by faith. This is so offensive to human pride that in every church evasions of grace spring up like weeds in a springtime garden. Paul understands the deceitful attractiveness of a complacent false assurance and wants to expose it for the dangerous sham that it is.

Our general aim, like Paul's, must therefore be that we and our hearers be deeply and urgently moved to practical repentance today. We must understand that the only alternative to a life of repentance is an ever-growing debt of wrath to be poured out on the Last Day (v. 5).

Verses 12-29 move us beyond this to grasp and cry for the urgent necessity of a changed heart by the Spirit of God.

Evangelicals have traditionally been those who have insisted on heart-conversion. This passage forcefully supports that insistence.

We need also to ask how this aim relates to Paul's overall aims in writing the whole letter (chapter B). How will chapter 2 promote a church living together in harmony? A church of self-righteous Pharisaical 'Christians' (or Luke 15 older brothers) will always be split by rivalries. We will be measuring ourselves by our perceived morality, and looking down on those who seem to us to be worse than ourselves. Daily repentance by every member of a church is the precondition for harmony within the church.

How does chapter 2 contribute to a missionary church? The moment we adopt the tabloid mentality of just being horrified by the terrible world around, we inevitably pull up the drawbridge to keep that terrible world out (little realizing that we also trap the same world inside our church). Only sinners with hearts changed by grace alone will have the heart and humility to reach out to unforgiven sinners.

Pointers to application

+ Take some time to think about behaviours we are *right to condemn*. Make sure we understand we are right to disapprove of these behaviours, because they are wrong.

+ Give thought to how we can carefully, accurately and specifically expose hypocrisy, ways in which we show that by nature our hearts are no better than those who do these terrible things.

+ Give examples that show how our intolerance of the bad behaviour of others is matched only by our leniency towards ourselves. To take a small example, in a marriage, if my wife mislays the car keys I get angry, but if I mislay them I expect her to be sympathetic and supportive. Or when someone speaks unkindly or misleadingly about me behind my back, I become very angry. I turn the offence over and over in my mind. I write eloquent mental letters about how disgracefully they have behaved. But if I do the same about someone else, it's just that I'm tired or stressed; it's not really my fault.

+ Consider some particular examples of sin that are not punished immediately – perhaps fiddling our business expenses, looking at internet pornography, exaggerating to puff ourselves up or put others down. Press home that every time God does *not* immediately punish us, he is leading us to repentance.

+ Open up what it means to live a life whose direction and aims are those of verse 7.

+ '...do you not teach yourself?' (v. 21) How do we hear Scripture, just to increase our head knowledge or to change our lives?

+ Cry day by day for a deep, growing and lasting work of the Spirit of God in our lives and hearts.

+ Apply this to how we view our fellow believers, so that we do not begin to think we are on a higher level than any of them.

+ Apply this to how we view non-Christians, not as those on a lower spiritual level than us, but as sinners just like us in desperate need of grace.

Suggestions for preaching and teaching the text

A. *One sermon on the whole chapter*

We might begin with summing up 1:18-32 and responding with the self-righteous letter with which this chapter began. Our teaching points will need to focus on the most central parts of the argument. We might choose:

1. Repentance is essential, because it is the only way to be acceptable to God (vv. 1-11).

2. Repentance is only possible with a heart changed by God's Spirit (vv. 12-29).

So I must come empty-handed to God and plead for his Spirit.

B. *Dividing the chapter into two sermons*

Sermon 1 (2:1-11)

As above, we could begin with the self-righteous letter. Or we might start with a gossiping group, of Christians or others ('Did you hear what X did/said …?' 'I think that's *disgraceful …*').

Our teaching points might be:

1. Every time I condemn bad behaviour in others, I condemn myself (vv. 1-3).

2. Every time I am not punished immediately, God is giving me time to turn around (vv. 4, 5).

3. So I must turn my life around, because only the turned-around life will be accepted in the Judgment (vv. 6-11).

Sermon 2 (2:12-29)

We might begin by saying that every church contains real Christians and pretend Christians, or by using some illustrations of appearance not corresponding to reality.

This might be impressive appearance masking empty reality, such as a veneer. Or it might be unimpressive appearance hiding a great reality (in Britain, the very ordinary-looking Victoria Cross makes this point).

Our teaching points might be:

1. Outward religious privilege cannot determine eternal destiny (vv. 12, 13).
2. The least privileged will be saved when their hearts are changed (vv. 14-16) – assuming my interpretation is correct.
3. The most privileged will not be saved unless their hearts are changed (vv. 17-24) (or 'Knowledge about God is a wonderful thing, but it is not enough').
4. Only a heart-change by the Spirit of God can bring us into the people of God (vv. 25-29).

C. *Two sermons from 2:1-11*
We might divide verses 1-11 into two sermons with teaching points as follows:

Sermon 1 (2:1-5)
1. Every time I condemn someone else I condemn myself before God (vv. 1-3).
2. Every time I am not punished immediately, God is giving me time to turn round (v. 4).
3. If I persist in not turning round, I store up more of God's right anger for the last day (v. 5).

Sermon 2 (2:6-11)
1. Overall truth: the only evidence accepted at the final judgment will be the full story of our lives (our works).

2. For believers, these works will be the public evidence of faith and will show:

   a) The *aim* of the believer's life (glory, honour, immortality).

   b) The *nature* of the believer's life (patient perseverance in doing good).

   c) The *rewards* of the believer's life (eternal life).

3. Likewise for unbelievers, these works will show the *aim* (self), the *nature* (disobedience to truth, as in 1:20), and the *reward* (trouble and distress) of the unbelieving life.

Leading a Bible study on Romans 2
To clarify understanding

1. Why does condemning bad behaviour in others condemn me too (vv. 1-3)?

2. What is the reason why God does not punish impenitent people immediately (v. 4)?

3. What is really happening to the persistently impenitent during their lives (v. 5)?

4. What is the overall principle of verses 6-11?

5. How are the two groups described in verses 7-10 and what does this tell us about them?

6. How are non-Christians and Christians described in verses 12, 13?

7. It is best if the leader explains clearly the two options for verses 14-16, rather than the group pooling their ignorance!

8. How is the Jew described in verses 17-20?

9. What happens when professing Christians are not real Christians (vv. 21-24)?

10. What change is needed to bring someone into the real people of God (vv. 25-29)?

To encourage honest response
1. In what ways are we like the 'Jew' of Romans 2 in our responses to the rest of the world?
2. How can we stir up one another to the urgent need for daily repentance?
3. What indicators (litmus tests) are there in our lives that reveal whether we are those in verses 7, 10 or those in verses 8, 9?
4. How is Bible knowledge both a valuable and yet a dangerous thing to have? How can we grow in Bible knowledge while avoiding the dangers of hypocrisy?
5. How will the message of Romans 2 make our church a place of harmony?
6. And how will it drive us out in humble evangelism?

8

Coming Under Grace

Romans 3:1-20

Nothing I can do can stop God being very angry with me. And quite rightly so. It doesn't matter how good a life I manage to lead, how well I know my Bible, how zealous I am about church, how wonderful a Christian family or friends I may have, the right thing for God to do is to be very angry with me. It would be quite wrong of God not to be angry with me.

This sounds outrageous. But it is true. And until we grasp this, we will never fully appreciate the wonder of the gospel of Jesus Christ.

Attentive listening to the text
Context and structure
So far in the section 'Coming under grace' the argument has run as follows:

1:16, 17 Paul's manifesto: God does the right thing by rescuing all believers, but only believers.

1:18-32 It has to be only believers, because God is rightly angry with everyone else.

2:1-29   'Everyone else' includes the self-righteous religious person,
          who urgently needs to repent and cry for a work of the Spirit
          to change their heart.

At the end of chapter 2 Paul says very provocative things
about being a Jew. A Jew who 'breaks the law' might as well
be uncircumcised (2:25). The true people of God are defined
not by outward membership, but by a changed heart by the
Spirit (2:28, 29). This naturally raises the question, 'What's
the point of the outward Jewish things, then? If they can
so easily be nullified, why are they there at all?' In a similar
way today, people might ask, 'What is the point of being
a member of a church, being baptized, Bible knowledge,
living a moral life, if none of these things are guaranteed to
do me any good?'

3:1-20 consists of two sections which begin with the
same question.

1. 3:1-8 (v. 1 'What advantage, then, is there in being
    a Jew ...?'). This section follows very closely from
    chapter 2 and concludes that part of the argument.
2. 3:9-20 (v. 9 'Are we (Jews) any better off?'). This section
    ties together 1:18-32 with 2:1-3:8 and rounds off the
    whole argument begun in 1:18. This prepares us for the
    pivotal section 3:21-26.

Working through the text
A. *God shows his righteousness by punishing the religious unbeliever (just as much as he does by rescuing the believer) (3:1-8)*

> [1]What advantage, then, is there in being a Jew, or what
> value is there in circumcision?

> [2]Much in every way! First of all, they have been entrusted
> with the very words of God.

³What if some did not have faith [*what if some were unfaithful*]?

Will their lack of faith [*their unfaith*] nullify God's faithfulness [*God's faith*]?

⁴Not at all! Let God be true, and [*though*] every man a liar.

> As it is written:
>> 'So that you may be proved right [*justified*] when you speak
>> and prevail when you judge [*when you are judged*]'
>> (Ps. 51:4)

⁵But if our unrighteousness brings out God's righteousness [*the righteousness of God*] more clearly, what shall we say?

> That God is unjust [*unrighteous*] in bringing his wrath on us?

> (I am using a human argument.)

>> ⁶Certainly not! If that were so, how could God judge the world?

⁷(Someone might argue,)

'If my falsehood enhances God's truthfulness and so increases his glory,

> why am I still condemned as a sinner?'

⁸Why not say—as we are being slanderously reported as saying and as some claim that we say—

> 'Let us do evil that good may result'?

> Their condemnation is deserved.

Verse 1 responds to the negative things Paul has said about the outward privileges of the Jew (in 2:25-29) by asking the same thing in two parallel ways: 'What advantage … is there in being a Jew, or what value is there in circumcision?'

(Circumcision is shorthand for the privileges of being a Jew.) Paul's first answer (v. 2) is that it's a wonderful thing to be a Jew. When he says, 'First of all ...' Paul may be beginning a list (one of Paul's 'trailers,' not continued until 9:4, 5!), or he may be saying, 'Supremely, above all, the privilege of being entrusted with the actual words of God.' This is what the Jew has claimed in 2:18-20, and Paul agrees. It's a wonderful thing to have a Bible.

Specifically, Paul seems to have in mind not just 'what God has said' in general, but 'the promises God made to Abraham.' It is a wonderful thing to know what God has promised the world through Abraham's family (Gen. 12:1-3 etc, summed up in Rom. 4:13 to be 'heir of the world'). The words used of God are 'faithfulness' (v. 3), 'true' (v. 4), 'proved right' (v. 4), 'righteousness' (v. 5), and 'truthfulness' (v. 7). All these mean that he does what he says he will do.

The big question is this: can God keep his covenant promises and pour out wrath on his covenant people at the same time? On the one hand, God's promises are certain; he must do what he says he will do, Abraham's seed must inherit the world. But, on the other hand, God's promises are also *conditional* on Abraham's family keeping their side of the Covenant, being faithful. So how can a conditional promise be certain? What if his people don't keep their side of it?' What if some did not have faith?' Verse 3 means, 'What if some were unfaithful to the Covenant, not loyal to the Lord, not loving him with all their heart (Deut. 6:4, 5)?'

Notice that 'faith' has never been just 'believing something to be true' (c.f. James 2:19). 'Faith' means 'loyalty, keeping faith'. So 'God's faith' means his loyalty to his people, and their 'faith' means their loyalty to him. This is why our faith is called 'the obedience of faith' (1:5; 16:26). For example,

when Moses describes the people's refusal to enter the land
after the spies report, he describes this refusal both as disobedience (Deut. 1:26 'you *rebelled against the command* …')
and as unbelief (Deut. 1:32 'you did not *trust* in the LORD
your God'). The obedience of faith means to believe the
promises and therefore to obey the commands of God.

So Paul rephrases the question in a way that points to
the answer: 'Will their unfaith nullify God's faith?' (v. 3b)
Of course not! Never mind '*some*' being unfaithful (v. 3);
even if '*every* man' were 'a liar' (i.e. untrue to the Covenant),
God would still be 'true' to his promise (v. 4).

To support this Paul quotes David in Psalm 51. After his
adultery with Bathsheba, David admits his guilt (Ps. 51:4a
'Against you, you only, have I sinned…') and admits that
God is right to pour out wrath on him (v. 4b 'so that you
may be proved right (*justified*, *shown to be in the right*) when
you speak' (that is, speak in wrath) 'and prevail when you
are judged' (that is, God will come out vindicated in the
courtroom when his wrathful actions are challenged).

In short, David admits that 'the righteousness of God' is
shown not only in blessing his people when they are faithful,
but also in cursing them when they are not (c.f. Neh. 9:32, 33.)
The complacent nominal member of the people of God
(whom Paul has been addressing in chapter 2) would do well
to remember that.

In verses 5 and 6, and then in verses 7 and 8, Paul mentions
an absurd idea. If I am unjust, false to the Covenant, and God
is just and true to the Covenant when he punishes me, then
you might say that my badness has brought God's goodness
more clearly into the open. And since the result was glory to
God (his righteous character being seen), it seems a bit unfair

to condemn me for it! The body language of the objector is like the footballer holding up his hands in disbelief when the referee penalizes him ('What, *me*? Referee!'). Paul says this is 'a human argument,' by which he means 'a load of nonsense!' When the Jew argues that God can't punish him, he is denying that God can judge *anybody* (v. 6), including those terrible people in 1:18-32 (and he wouldn't want to deny that!). In verse 7 he repeats the absurd idea, and then in verse 8 says it amounts to saying the end justifies the means ('Let us do evil that good may result'). He dismisses this out of hand. People who say God is wrong to condemn them are precisely the people who deserve to be condemned.

The nominal Jew of chapter 2 thinks the certainty of the promise trumps its conditionality, and therefore he is safe however he behaves. This is illustrated by the false assurance of those to whom Jeremiah preached his famous 'Temple sermon' (Jer. 7). They trusted they were safe because they were in 'the temple of the Lord, the temple of the Lord, the temple of the Lord' (Jer. 7:4). After all, they might have reasoned, if God destroys us, where will the children of Abraham be to inherit the world? How wrong they were! At the heart of false assurance lies the presumption that God fulfils his promises without his people's loyal response. They thought that if they had the promises (I have been baptized, I know my Bible, I belong to a church, etc) they would be safe, even if their hearts are not changed.

Paul has more to say about this in chapters 4, and 9–11. Here he just shows that God can quite fairly punish his people. Later he will show that, in the words of John the

Baptist, God is well able to 'raise up children for Abraham' however he wants (Matt. 3:9).

B. By nature, every human being without exception is under the power of sin (3:9-20)

Verses 9-20 begin with a rhetorical question in verse 9 and end with a conclusion in verses 19, 20. In between are three structured collections of Old Testament quotations.

Summary statement: all human beings by nature are trapped under the power of sin (v. 9).

> ⁹What shall we conclude then? Are we any better? Not at all!
>> *For* we have already made the charge that Jews and Gentiles alike
>>> are all under sin.

Paul begins to sum up the argument. His aim from 1:16, 17 has been to prove that God's rescue comes always and only to those who contribute nothing of their own (i.e. to faith). This is because God is rightly very angry with everyone else (1:18). He has considered two kinds of people. In 1:18-32 there are bad people who approve bad behaviour (1:32). His readers will agree that these people deserve to be condemned. From 2:1-3:8 he proves that those who disapprove of bad behaviour are just as guilty.

Paul repeats the question of verse 1: 'Are we' (that is, in the original context, 'we Jews') 'any better?' Paul is not asking whether people who know their Bibles are morally better, but whether they are 'better off', whether their Bible knowledge is worth anything. Bible knowledge is a wonderful privilege (v. 2) but it cannot change the heart. Why? '*For we* have already made the charge that Jews and Gentiles alike are all under sin.' The reason the saving righteousness of God comes to 'everyone who believes' (and only those who believe) '... first ... the Jew, then ... the Gentile' (1:16, 17) is that 'Jews and Gentiles alike are all under sin.'

For the first time in Romans, Paul speaks of sin as a slave-master: until we are rescued by Christ, we are under the power of sin, which enslaves us (as Paul explains in chapter 6). Why do people 'suppress the truth by their wickedness' (1:18)? Because they are 'under sin'. Why do people not only do evil but approve of evildoers (1:32)? Because they are 'under sin'. Why do religious people sit in judgment on evildoers while doing evil themselves (2:1)? Because they are 'under sin'. Therefore we cannot save ourselves. God is very angry with us and he is right to be angry. And there is nothing we can do about it, because we are 'under sin'.

Paul now supports this with three sections of Old Testament quotations. His aim is to prove that, 'Jews and Gentiles alike are all under sin.'

First section: Slavery to Sin means every heart by nature turns away from God (vv. 10-12)

> [10]As it is written:
>   'There is no-one righteous, not even one;
>   [11]there is no-one who understands,
>   *there is* no-one who seeks God.
>
>   [12]All have turned away,
>   they have together become worthless;
>   there is no one who does good [*kindness*], not even one.' (from Ps. 14:1-3)

Paul starts with two sets of three lines, adapted from the Greek translation of Psalm 14:1-3. When we look carefully at the whole of Psalm 14 we notice four features of this adapted quotation:

1. In his extract, 8 times Paul emphasizes universality. Four lines begin, 'There is no-one'; two lines end, 'not even one'; and in lines 4 and 5 he includes 'all' and 'together'. What he says applies to 'Jews and Gentiles *alike*' (v. 9).

2. Psalm 14 itself makes clear that there is only one kind of exception. Within Israel there is 'the company of the righteous' (v. 5), those 'poor' (c.f. Luke 6:20) for whom 'the LORD is their refuge' (v. 6). There is a true 'Israel' within nominal Israel for whom 'salvation' will come (v. 7). These people are righteous by faith (since there has never been any other righteousness before God). Paul's point is that every human being without exception is *by nature* under sin; they can only be justified by grace.

3. Plenty (perhaps most) of the 'fools' of whom the psalmist speaks (v. 1) come from within Israel. These are not just the distant Gentiles, but those in the land 'who devour my people' (v. 4).

4. The focus is on the direction of the heart. Do they 'seek God' or 'turn away'? This echoes the distinction between those who '*seek* glory, honour and immortality' and those who 'are self-*seek*ing' (2:7). No human beings seek God until their hearts are changed by grace. (And so by nature we will not 'do kindness'; the same word is used of God in 2:4. The heart that turns from God leads to the life that isn't kind like God.)

Second section: Rotten hearts speak with bitter tongues (vv. 13, 14)

> [13]'Their throats are open graves; their tongues practise
> deceit.'   (Ps. 5:9)
>
> 'The poison of vipers is on their lips.'   (Ps. 140:3)
>
> [14]'Their mouths are full of cursing and bitterness.'(Ps. 10:7)

The next two pairs come from three more psalms, and move
the focus from the heart to the tongue (perhaps a progress
from 'throats' to 'tongues,' 'lips' and 'mouths'). Out of the
heart the mouth speaks. Hearts that turn away from the
'kindness' of God lead to words that deceive, poison, curse
and spread bitterness (c.f. James 3:1-12). A bitter tongue is
evidence of a self-seeking heart.

As with Psalm 14, so here, there is one exception only. The
only people who do not speak like this are 'righteous' by faith;
they take refuge in the Lord and love his name (Ps. 5:11); they
cry for mercy and say, 'You are my God… my strong deliverer'
(Ps. 140:6, 7); they are 'the righteous' who 'will praise your
name' and long for his saving 'righteousness' (Ps. 140:12, 13).
And, as in Psalm 14, the wicked people are often to be found
within Israel (e.g. Ps. 140:11 'established in the land'). So 'Jews
and Gentiles alike are under sin'. No tongue speaks kindness
unless it is changed by the kindness of God.

Third section: Bitter tongues destroy human community
(vv. 15-18)

> [15]'Their feet are swift to shed blood;
> [16]ruin and misery mark their ways,
> [17]and the way of peace they do not know.'
>
>   (shortened from Isa. 59:7, 8)
>
> [18]'There is no fear of God before their eyes.'   (Ps. 36:1)

A self-seeking heart (vv. 10-12) leads to a bitter tongue (vv. 13, 14), and a bitter tongue creates strife (vv. 15-17). The focus is on a direction of life ('feet … ways … the way …') that destroys harmony. In the context of Isaiah 59:1-20 the righteous remnant within Israel are oppressed by unbelievers within the nominal people of God. The *religious* unbeliever causes most problems in the people of God.

Summing it all up, from Psalm 36, 'There is no fear of God before their eyes' (that is, the eyes of the wicked). (The words 'there is no …' echo 'there is no-one …' in vv. 10-12). By nature no one fears God (which is what Paul had asserted back in 1:18). The only people who do fear God are those 'both high and low' (c.f. Jew and Gentile) who 'find refuge in the shadow of your wings', 'who know you' and who are 'upright in heart' (Ps. 36:7, 10).

So the point of all these quotations is that apart from the saving righteousness of God there are only self-seeking hearts, bitter tongues and strife. No human community can survive the unconverted heart. This is just as true amongst religious people who know their Bibles as it is in the rotten world outside: 'Jews and Gentiles alike are under sin'.

Conclusion: the Bible exposes all this, but just knowing it won't do us any good (vv. 19, 20)

> [19]Now we know that whatever the law says,
> > it says to those who are under the law,
> > > so that every mouth may be silenced
> > > and the whole world held accountable to God.

> [20]Therefore no-one will be declared righteous [*justified*]
> > in his sight (c.f. Ps. 143:2b)
> > > by observing the law [*by works of the law*];

> rather [*since*] through the law we become
> conscious of sin.

Paul's aim is that 'every mouth may be silenced and the whole world held accountable to God'. The defendant has nothing to say in his defence. There is no more protesting, 'It wasn't my fault, if only you had lived in my dysfunctional family, I'm just a victim, I've tried my best, I'm better than many other people….' and so on. We admit that God was right to be furiously angry with us all.

We think the harder task is to persuade the person who has never heard of Christ to admit this. Paul knows better. He understands the older brother of Luke 15, because he used to be one. Paul's biggest challenge is to silence the pro-testing mouths of respectable people who know their Bible, who cannot really accept that God is right to be angry with *them*. In vv. 10-18 he has quoted the Scriptures ('whatever the law says', taking 'law' here in its wider sense of all Old Testament Scripture). These condemning verses speak 'to those who are under the law' (that is, the Jews). They do not simply condemn the nasty sinner 'over there'; they condemn the nominal Jew whose heart has not been changed by the Spirit (2:25-29). So these Scriptures silence the protesting mouths of the self-righteous and make sure that on 'the day of God's wrath' the whole world will admit God was right to condemn (2:5).

Paul concludes (v. 20), 'Therefore no-one' (echoing 'there is no-one' in vv. 10-12) 'will be justified in his sight by works of the law, since through the law we become conscious of sin.' Paul uses the important expression 'works of the law' for the first time in Romans.

Works of the law

Paul uses this phrase six times, twice in Romans 3 (3:20, 28) and four times in Galatians (2:16; 3:2, 5, 10). To try to be right with God 'by works of the law' is not the same as the believer who seeks glory, honour and immortality (2:7); who 'obeys the law' (2:13); who is a true Jew by observing the law and keeping the law's requirements (2:25, 26); and who, by obeying the heart of the law, will condemn the nominal Jew whose heart has not been changed (2:27).

To try to be right with God ('be justified') 'by works' means by human initiative. It is to deny that God is angry with me *and I cannot do anything about it*. It is the opposite of 'by faith', which means coming empty-handed to God for his undeserved rescue. To try to do this 'by works *of the law*' (that is, the Law of Moses) means to try to do this in specifically Jewish ways ('works' with a Jewish flavour), by what we might call Bible knowledge, religious privilege, or our own moral achievement in obedience to the Ten Commandments.

It is much deeper than just the things a Jew did to mark him out from the Gentiles (male circumcision, kosher food, and Sabbaths). Certainly to trust in these Jewish distinctives or 'boundary markers' would be no good. But 'works of the law' is deeper than this. In Galatians 3:10 Paul says that those who rely on 'works of the law' are 'under a curse', the covenant curse of Deuteronomy 27:26. This curse in Deuteronomy comes on anyone who is not loyal to the covenant God (c.f. Deut. 6:4, 5), whose heart is stubborn and turns away (Deut. 9:6). It comes on those with unchanged (uncircumcised) hearts (Deut. 10:16; 30:6). It is about heart faithfulness to the true God. Not one of us shows this faithfulness by nature. And so reliance on 'works of the law' is the opposite of faith in Jesus Christ (3:28; Gal. 2:16) and of receiving the Spirit by faith (Gal. 3:2, 5).

The reason 'works of the law' cannot put us right with God is that while Bible knowledge is a wonderful thing (3:2) it cannot change the heart. All it does is make us 'conscious of sin'. It shows us the rottenness of our hearts; but it cannot make rotten hearts clean.

The words, 'no-one will be justified in his sight' are from Psalm 143:2b. In this Psalm, David cries out 'for mercy' and for the Lord's 'faithfulness and righteousness' to 'come to my relief' (v. 1). He knows he deserves to be brought 'into judgment' because 'no-one living is righteous before you' (v. 2). He knows the Lord is right to be angry with him and he cannot do anything about it. He has no righteousness of his own, and so he prays for 'your righteousness' to bring him out of trouble (v. 11). He longs for the saving 'righteousness of God' to be revealed to him (1:16, 17). In other words, he longs for the promised Christ, in whom all the promises of God are confirmed (2 Cor. 1:20). David does not seek to be justified 'by works of the law' but by the saving righteousness of God revealed in Christ.

From text to teaching

Getting the message clear: the theme

Verses 1-8 round off the argument of chapter 2. The complacent member of the covenant people thinks he is safe because God is committed to fulfil his promises. He thinks he is safe without need for repentance. He thinks God could not possibly destroy him - it wouldn't be right. Paul says it would be quite right for God to reject me. He can keep his promises without including me (as David admits in Ps. 51).

Verses 9-20 conclude the whole argument of 1:18-3:20. They prove why the positive statement of 1:16, 17 is true. God's saving righteousness comes only by grace to those who come empty-handed. This is the only way, because by nature every human being is trapped under sin. This includes the person who knows the Bible. The Bible exposes this, but it cannot cure it.

Getting the purpose clear: the aim

The aim of verses 1-8 is to seal the last corner of the escape hatch for the impenitent religious person. Our aim must be the same. We need to persuade ourselves and our hearers that God can perfectly fairly be angry with us, and 'being a Christian' (outwardly) is no protection.

The conclusion from verses 9-20 is that I must abandon all trust in anything I can do to put myself right with God. There is no other way but to trust his saving righteousness in Christ. Why does Paul include the Old Testament quotes? Why not go straight from verse 9 to verse 19? He wants to expose the terrible anatomy of sin, so that we do not just admit it in a shallow way but feel it deeply. He wants each of us – including (indeed especially) the religious person – to be speechless with guilt and shame before God (v. 19). He wants us to feel in anticipation that final Judgment scene, that without Christ we will have nothing to say in our defence. Our aim and prayer in preaching must be that we and our hearers really feel that no amount of Bible knowledge, no long-term church membership, no baptism, no taking part in the Lord's Supper, no moral respectability, will count at the Judgment. Our rotten hearts, bitter words and hostile deeds will prove that we are right-ly condemned. We want the law to do its preliminary painful work, to make us 'conscious of sin' (3:20).

Only this deep conviction will humble us together under grace and enable us to live in harmony. Only this deep despair without Christ will drive us out in mission to a Christless world.

Pointers to application

+ (vv. 1-8) Expose how we who are professing Christians begin to think God won't punish us because we are baptized, take the Lord's Supper, are members of churches, know our Bibles, or associate with 'the right people.'

+ (vv. 1-8) Look at the shallow thought, 'It's alright to sin because Jesus died for me' and expose the cheap idea of grace that lies behind it.

+ Work hard to show, with examples, how we experience being, 'under sin' (v. 9). Take examples such as patterns of selfish behaviour in marriage, greedy habits with money, lazy patterns of life, habits of caring a lot about image, addictive 'little' surrenders to lustful thoughts and looks, and how impossibly hard we find it actually to *break* any of these destructive patterns of life.

+ (vv. 10-12) Undermine the shallow idea that there are 'good people' out there who do not need Christ. 'What if someone went through life just trying to be good?' asked the student. The answer is, 'What if?! No one ever did or does or can. Because we are under the power of sin.'

+ (vv. 13, 14) Expose the evil that comes out of our mouths by nature, how our words destroy relationships (e.g. things said in a broken marriage and never forgotten), how we spin and twist truth (exaggerating, puffing ourselves up, doing others down), how our words can be a poison that spreads gossip in a workplace, how our words of grumbling show a bitter and ungrateful heart.

+ (vv. 15-17) Move from words to actions and show how what we do (or don't do) brings harm to others ('shed blood'), causes people's lives to spiral down ('ruin and misery') and destroys harmony in a family, school, workplace, neighbourhood ('the way of peace they do not know').

+ (v. 19) Preach and pray so that both we and our hearers can *feel* ourselves speechless with shame, with nothing – absolutely nothing – to say in our defence in the presence of God. Imagine that terrible scene on Judgment Day and what it will feel like to have not even a whisper of self-justification, of extenuating circumstance, of excuse.

+ (v. 20) Preach the detail of the law of God (especially the Ten Commandments) so that 'we become conscious of sin' in all its horror.

+ (v. 20) Help us really to grasp that nothing we can say or do can help at all. We are trapped 'under sin' and must cry for the saving righteousness of God. There is no other hope.

Suggestions for preaching and teaching the text

It is best to teach these verses in two sections.

A.   Two Sermons on 3:1-20

Sermon 1 (3:1-8)

We might begin by playing devil's advocate and stating as convincingly as we can the objection. We might put it as a logical sequence:

1. God has promised that Abraham's family will inherit the world, and God always keeps his promises.
2. I am part of Abraham's family.
3. So I am bound to inherit the world, whatever I do.
4. And therefore all this talk of my needing to live a life of repentance is ultimately just preacher's bluff. I'm sure it would be good if I did. But it cannot be really necessary.

Our teaching points might be along the following lines:

1. It is wonderful to know what God has promised the world (vv. 1, 2).
2. But knowing this doesn't guarantee that I will be a part of it. God can keep his promise while leaving me outside (vv. 3-8).

    So I must repent!

Sermon 2 (3:9-20)

We might begin as this chapter began, by stating upfront and provocatively that God is very angry with you and me, he is right to be very angry, and nothing we can do will stop him being very angry.

Our teaching points might be:

1. We are all by nature trapped under the power of sin (v. 9).
2. Sin's slavery shows itself in:
    a) ... hearts that turn from God (vv. 10-12);
    b) ... tongues that are hostile to truth (vv. 13, 14);
    c) ... actions that cause strife (vv. 15-18).
3. The Bible exposes this, but just knowing it won't do us any good (vv. 19, 20).

In conclusion, press home our terrible helplessness before God, and then anticipate the wonder of the gospel Paul has trailed in 1:16, 17 and will expound in 3:21-26.

B. A series from 3:9-20 on the anatomy of sin

We might preach a three-sermon series, taking each of the Old Testament quotations in turn, with time to look at them in their Old Testament contexts and in the context of verses 9, 19, 20, with the aim of exposing sin in all its horror.

A. The empty heart (vv. 10-12)
B. The bitter tongue (vv. 13, 14)
C. The warlike way (vv. 15-18)

Leading a Bible study on 3:1-20
To clarify understanding

1. What advantage was there in being a Jew (vv. 1, 2)?

2. How do verses 3-8 show us the advantage the unconverted Jew *thought* he had? That is, why did he think the faithfulness of God guaranteed that he would be safe even if he didn't repent?

3. How does what David says in Psalm 51 undermine this false assurance (v. 4)?

4. How does Paul prove that God could perfectly fairly reject the Jew who will not repent (vv. 3-8)?

5. How does Paul sum up his argument from 1:18-3:8 (v. 9)?

6. How does the quotation from Psalm 14 back this up (vv. 10-12)?

7. How do the quotations from Psalms 5, 140, 10 develop this (vv. 13, 14)?

8.   How do the final quotations from Isaiah 59 and Psalm 36 complete his argument (vv. 15-18)?

9.   How do these Scriptures make sure no one will be able to protest their innocence on Judgment Day (v. 19)?

10. What does the Bible do, and what can it not do (v. 20)?

To encourage honest response

1.   How do 'Christian people' persuade ourselves it would not be fair for God to be angry with us, even if we will not repent (applying vv. 1-8)?

2.   Look at the Old Testament quotations in turn (in their Old Testament contexts). Relate them honestly to our hearts, lips and lives, as we are by nature.

3.   Pray for a deeper conviction of sin, and for a stronger understanding that we cannot save ourselves.

9

COMING UNDER GRACE
ROMANS 3:21-26

How much does it matter that God is fair? How much does it matter that God forgives? Both matter a very great deal. Take the second question. Which Christian has not stood at a graveside trusting that a loved one is forgiven and safe in Jesus? There is not much that matters more, than to be sure of that.

But what of the first question? How much does it matter that God is fair? What if God's forgiveness came at the expense of his fairness? What if he could only forgive by having favourites or by winking at wrong? It would matter desperately. The moral fabric of the universe would tear in pieces if God were not fair. From the football crowd watching a referee's dodgy decision, to workers watching an incompetent colleague promoted, we are hard-wired with an instinctive sense that fairness matters. How relieved we are when justice triumphs, and how outraged when an election is rigged, a criminal escapes or a wrong is never righted. We need to know that God cannot be mocked (Gal. 6:7) and that he does not do what he tells human judges never to do, that is, to pervert justice (e.g. Prov. 17:15).

But if God is fair, how can he forgive? How can the judge of all the earth (Gen. 18:25) forgive those who, by their own admission, are guilty? By what possible system of justice can this happen?

Attentive listening to the text

Context and structure

We now reach the turning point of the section 'Coming under grace.' This section takes us back to Paul's manifesto in 1:16, 17 and begins to unpack it. The structure of the argument may be summarized as follows:

1:16, 17	God rescues all believers, but only believers.
1:18-32	This is because he is rightly angry with everyone else,
2:1-3:8	*including* people who have Bibles (religious insiders).
3:9-20	So religious insiders and irreligious outsiders are all by nature under sin, and therefore under his righteous wrath (and having a Bible just makes us see this all the more clearly).

Having established this negative truth, Paul now moves to answer the question, 'How is the righteousness of God revealed in the gospel of Christ?' There is a close parallel between 1:17 and 3:21.

1:17 … in the gospel	the righteousness of God	is revealed …
3:21 But now	the righteousness of God …	has been made known …

Working through the text

Translation issues

Unfortunately there are several places where the NIV disguises the literal reading. So we will work from a more literal translation, as follows.

²¹But now, apart from law,

> **the righteousness of God** has been manifested,
>> to which the law and the prophets testify,

²²**the righteousness of God**

> through the faith of Jesus Christ [or 'through faith in Jesus Christ'] for all who believe.

> For there is no distinction,
> ²³for all sinned and lack the glory of God,

²⁴being **'righteoused'** freely by his grace through the redemption that is in Christ Jesus,

> ²⁵whom God put forward as a propitiation
>> through faith [or 'through faithfulness']
>> by his blood,

to demonstrate **his righteousness**, (i.e. 'the righteousness of God')

> because of the passing over of former sins,
>> in the forbearance of God,

²⁶to demonstrate **his righteousness** (i.e. 'the righteousness of God')

> in the present time,
>> so that he might be **righteous**
>> and the **'righteouser'** of the one based on the faith of Jesus [or 'the one who has faith in Jesus'].

Significant translation points include:

1. Four times Paul refers to the righteousness of God (vv. 21, 22, 25, 26). This is the theme of the paragraph, referring back to 1:17. NIV disguises this by translating the first two 'a righteousness from God' and the second pair 'his justice'.

2. The phrase that reads literally 'the faith of Jesus Christ' (v. 22) may mean 'the faithfulness (covenant loyalty) of Jesus Christ' or it may mean 'faith (i.e. our faith) in Jesus Christ'. Similarly in verse 25 'through faith' may mean

that Jesus made propitiation 'through his faithfulness to God', or it may mean that we appropriate the benefits of his sacrifice by our faith in him. Likewise in verse 26, 'the one based on the faith of Jesus' may mean, 'the one whose standing before God rests on the faithfulness of Jesus (to God)', or it may mean, 'the one who has faith in Jesus'.

3. The end of verse 22 reads literally, '*For* there is no distinction …'

4. In verse 24 NIV 'the redemption that came by Christ Jesus' is literally, 'the redemption that is *in Christ Jesus*,' that is, the redemption that comes from being vitally united to Christ Jesus through faith.

5. In verse 25 NIV 'through faith in his blood' suggests we are to put our trust 'in his blood'. While this is true, it is more likely that both the phrase 'through faith' and the phrase 'by his blood' describe Jesus' sacrifice of propitiation (hence ESV 'a propitiation by his blood'). It was by his blood that he made propitiation.

6. I have invented the word 'righteoused' to mean 'declare righteous'. I have used this instead of 'justify' to emphasize that the same group of words are used throughout this paragraph. These words may be translated by 'just', 'justice', 'justify', 'justification', and equally by 'righteous', 'righteousness', 'declare righteous', in English.

Three key points

Before we launch into the detail, it is worth noting three points. The first is that the central idea of the paragraph is 'the righteousness of God' (vv. 21, 22, 25, 26) (see comments on 1:17 on pp. 64-65). This central theme reminds us that the paragraph is about God before it is about us.

The second point to note is that it is about a public revelation of the righteousness of God. We see this in five places:

1. In verse 21 'the righteousness of God has been *manifested*' (as in 1:17 'revealed').

2. The law and the prophets *testify* to it (v. 21). So we have here the clear revelation of something attested in type and shadow in the Old Testament.

3. In verse 25 God '*put forward*' Christ, in a public display.

4. In verse 25 God did this to '*demonstrate*' his righteousness.

5. This is repeated in verse 26.

In gospel preaching something that has always been true becomes crystal clear for all to see. The gospel does not introduce a new kind of righteousness that was not available before Christ; it shows clearly why the righteousness that put Abraham, David and others right before God was indeed a 'right' kind of righteousness (i.e. that God had been right to do it that way!).

The third, and most important, point is that all this comes entirely and only from Jesus Christ. It comes 'through the faith of Jesus Christ' (v. 22); the redemption is 'in Christ Jesus' (v. 24); it comes by his 'propitiation' (v. 25); and it comes to 'the one based on the faith of Jesus' (v. 26). None of God's past actions, and none of the Old Testament promises, make any logical sense apart from Jesus Christ and him crucified.

The paragraph divides into four:

A. *The witnesses. The saving righteousness of God is taught in the Old Testament and more clearly taught in the gospel (v. 21)*

Paul has just proved that no-one will be justified, declared righteous ('righteoused') in God's sight 'by works of the law', since the law makes us 'conscious of sin' (3:20). And yet now, in the gospel (1:17) the saving righteousness of God 'has been manifested.'

Negatively, this is 'apart from law'. That is to say, the law on its own does not provide a means by which we can get right with God. If the Jew thought that the Law of Moses was there to provide a ladder which he could climb by his own initiative, his own moral effort, his own religious knowledge and privilege, to get himself right with God, he had misunderstood the purpose of the law (as we shall see in 9:30–10:4). The law had a temporary purpose (Gal. 3:15–4:7) but that purpose was never to provide an alternative way to get right with God.

Positively, however, 'the law' (of Moses) 'and the prophets' (who were preachers of the Covenant) bear witness to the righteousness of God that was to be clearly revealed in the gospel of Jesus Christ. Anyone who read the Old Testament aright would have understood that Moses preached Christ (c.f. John 5:46). Whenever a Jew believed the promises of God he believed, in principle, in the Christ who would fulfil those promises (2 Cor. 1:20). The promises preached the gospel to Abraham (Gal. 3:8). The problem arose when they trusted the law without the promise, the commandments without the Christ to come, the statutes without the Saviour who fulfilled them.

B. *The recipients. The saving righteousness of God comes only from Jesus Christ to those who bow the knee to him (vv. 22, 23)*

1. This righteousness comes:

    a. 'through the faith of Jesus Christ' or
    b. 'through faith in Jesus Christ'.

    Translation (a) would mean that God's saving righteousness comes 'through' (by the agency of) 'the faith' (i.e. covenant faithfulness) 'of Jesus Christ'. None of us is loyal, faithful, to God by nature. But Jesus was. And by his faithfulness as our substitute on our behalf, we can be put right with God.

Translation (b) means we receive this righteousness by bowing the knee to Jesus with the obedience of faith.

Both translations are possible and have meanings that are valid.

2.   This righteousness comes 'for all who believe' (that is, believe in Jesus). If translation (b) above is right, then the emphasis here is on the word 'all' ('for *all* who believe').

3.   The reason it has to be 'for all who *believe*' (and in no other way) is that 'there is no distinction' between human beings, 'for all have sinned …' This sums up 1:18–3:20. Rescue comes only to empty-handed faith.

4.   Because we sinned we 'lack the glory of God'. The word 'lack' is better than 'fall short of'. The idea is not that we have failed to reach God's 100 per cent pass-mark (though we have), but that by exchanging the worship of God for worship of human people or projects (idols), we lost our glory as God-like creatures (1:23). We were meant to shine with the glory of God, so that when someone looked at us they could say, 'Ah, now I see what God is like.' We forfeited that privilege, we lack that glory (to put it mildly). The believer earnestly seeks the restoration of that glory (2:7; 8:18 'the glory that will be revealed in us'). We know it will be restored because one human being does not lack that glory (as Heb. 2:6-10 expounds Ps. 8). Because of his faithfulness and obedience those who are 'in Christ' will one day shine with that same glory.

C. *The source. The saving righteousness of God comes only from
    the death of Jesus Christ as our propitiation (vv. 24, 25a)*

All who believe are 'righteoused', 'declared righteous', 'justified',
put in right relation with God by God's declaration. God
declares here and now for every believer that he or she will
be vindicated in the final Judgment. This is not a moral
change in us (which happens later and gradually), but an
absolute and immediate change of legal status. It does not
depend on our reaching any standard. It is given 'freely by
his grace'. It comes by 100 per cent grace and therefore 0 per
cent our works.

This legal declaration of righteousness achieves 'the
redemption that is in Christ Jesus' so that all who are united
with Christ by faith are 'redeemed', set free from slavery
to sin. Those 'under sin' (3:9), who could do nothing to
save themselves, are brought out of sin's kingdom by the
Redeemer's outstretched arm, just as the people of Israel
were taken out of Egypt at the Exodus.

But how is this possible? Paul speaks of what happens and
of the deep reason why it happens. What happens is redemption. The deep reason why it happens is 'propitiation' (NIV 'sacrifice of atonement'). A propitiation is a sacrifice which takes
away wrath—a 'wrath-quencher', which satisfies God's anger.
The sacrifice on the cross was the perfect 'satisfaction' of the
wrath of God. (The translators of the Revised Standard Version substituted the weaker impersonal word 'expiation' which
means a sacrifice which takes away sin.)

So it is not just that 'God hates the sin but loves the sinner.'
God hates *the sinner* and his wrath rests upon him. If God
loved me but just didn't like some of the things I did, then
the lesser sacrifice of expiation would be sufficient. But God
hates *me* as a guilty rebel. He is very angry with me, and right

to be angry. It is from this awful truth that the gospel of Jesus rescues me. The paradox of the gospel is that, as Luther put it, 'God loved us even as he hated us.' We must not soften God's wrath. For, if we soften God's wrath, we diminish his justice, and we minimise the sacrifice of the cross.

Notice that '*God* put forward' Jesus. Jesus is not an innocent third-party intervening between a vengeful God and sinners; he is God himself taking upon God the self-substitution that pays the penalty we deserve.

Paul says God put Jesus forward as a propitiation:

1. 'through faith.' This may mean 'through the faithfulness of Jesus' who, in his obedience even to death on the cross, proved himself utterly faithful and loyal to God. And only because of his obedience, both in life and in death, can his propitiatory sacrifice be acceptable to God.
2. 'by his blood.' Jesus' 'blood' means his life given up by violent death on the cross.

D. The Proof. This revealed righteousness of God proves that God is right to rescue guilty people (vv. 25b, 26)

The cross demonstrates, manifests, publicly proves, that God has always been right to rescue the guilty when they repent and trust in the promise of the Saviour. It proves that God is fair to forgive.

In verse 25 'the passing over of former sins, in the forbearance of God' is a problem without the cross. Like the angel of death at the Passover, God had 'passed over' the homes on whose doorposts was the blood of the lamb. Believers of every age have not been punished for their sins. From Abraham onwards, people like the adulterer and murderer King David have been justified ('righteoused') by faith. The word 'forbearance' is translated 'tolerance' in 2:4, where Paul spoke of 'the riches of God's kindness, tolerance and patience' (c.f. 2 Pet. 3:9). It is the quality in God that was intended to move us to repentance (2:4).

But it is a problem, because it suggests a judge who is slack about his work, who ought to punish, but for some reason doesn't. How can he be 'righteous' if he is at the same time the one who 'righteouses' (declares righteous) adulterers and murderers? The propitiatory death of Jesus proves God is right to declare righteous all who are covered by that sacrifice. Paul calls these (literally) 'the one based on the faith of Jesus'. This may mean 'the one who has faith in Jesus' (as NIV), or it may mean 'the one whose legal status comes from being united to Jesus, the one who is counted as faithful because Jesus was faithful'.

And so 'in the present time' of gospel proclamation we can see clearly that God is both just and the one who justifies, that he is fair to forgive all who are in Jesus. We see this because on the cross God himself, in Jesus, substituted himself for the sinner. And so the justice of God is satisfied and the mercy of God is complete. In the words of the old children's chorus, 'At the cross of Jesus, pardon is complete. Love and justice mingle, truth and mercy meet.'

From text to teaching
Getting the message clear: the theme
It is easy for the preacher to get lost in the riches of this dense paragraph. Doctrines tumble over one another calling for our attention. It is doctrinal caviar! At the heart of the passage lies this truth: *God is right to rescue sinners because he has punished sinners at the cross.* He has not just punished sin; in Jesus he has punished every sinner who is

united with Jesus by faith. He not only punished my sin; he punished *me*. And so, because he punished me, he does the right thing when he declares me righteous in Jesus. It would be hard to exaggerate the wonder of this truth.

Getting the purpose clear: the aim
The big danger in preaching this paragraph is that we treat it as if it were about us, when it is about God. It is not centrally about 'me and my salvation', but rather about 'God and his reputation'. It is the proof that when God *justifies* men and women by faith in Jesus, he does something *just*. This God-centredness is a problem for preachers, for we think people will pay more attention if the message is centred on human beings. We think that verses 25b, 26 are a rather nice, philosophically tidy extra at the end. It is deeper than that. And so in preaching we need to feel the urgency and universe-threatening seriousness of the questions with which we began the chapter.

How much does it matter that God is fair?
How much does it matter that God forgives?

We preach for understanding of the gravity of the problem, and therefore for a sense of wonder and gratitude for the majesty of the solution. We and our hearers ought to go home singing if we have even begun to understand what Paul teaches here. There is no exhortation; we preach for understanding and the response of wonder and praise.

Pointers to application

+ Avoid slipping into standard exhortation and challenge, which are not the point of this passage.
+ Give examples on different scales to show how much

it really matters to us that God is fair (ranging from little examples like the referee in sport, through bigger ones like unfairness in the workplace, up to unpunished crime, war crimes, genocide). Make sure we feel the importance of justice in the universe.

+ Pray that we will therefore *feel* the terrible danger we are in, because we want and need justice and yet we ourselves must be punished by justice.

+ Debunk the wishy-washy idea that it is God's job to forgive. Perhaps illustrate this from the famous quotation of the eighteenth century Empress Catherine of Russia: 'I shall be an autocrat: that is my trade. And the good Lord will forgive me: that is his' (C'est son metier). Or the poet W.H.Auden: 'I like to commit crimes. God likes to forgive them. Really the world is admirably arranged.' Show that God's 'job' is justice.

+ Preach so that we really understand propitiation, that God himself took the wrath of God against sinners upon God himself, in Jesus. (And make sure we understand this is not immoral, because Jesus was not an innocent third-party).

+ Make it clear that faith is not a 'work' of human merit smuggled in the back door. Faith is not something we do, for which we can take credit. Perhaps use the old analogy of our faith as a cheap metal ring with a clasp, the clasp holding a priceless jewel, who is Christ with all his merits. The value is not in our faith (as in 'I envy you your faith') but in the Christ to whom we cling by faith.

+ Make sure we understand that grace is not a 'top up' to bring our valuable but not quite adequate righteousness up to scratch (as it were, God making up the deficiency).

Grace is God providing, by Jesus' death, 100 per cent of the righteousness we need.

+ Preach and pray that we will *feel* the wonder and rightness of justification and go home singing.

Suggestions for preaching and teaching the text

Unless we want to do some detailed exposition of doctrines, we will probably expound this passage in one sermon.

One sermon on 3:21-25

We need to begin (perhaps as at the start of this chapter) making sure our hearers understand the gravity of the problem.

Our teaching points might follow the four stages of the paragraph as we have seen above:

1. The witnesses. The saving righteousness of God is taught in the Old Testament and more clearly taught in the gospel (v. 21).

2. The recipients. The saving righteousness of God comes only from Jesus Christ to those who bow the knee to him (vv. 22, 23).

3. The source. The saving righteousness of God comes only from the death of Jesus Christ as our propitiation (vv. 24, 25a).

4. The proof. This revealed righteousness of God proves that God is right to rescue guilty people (vv. 25b, 26).

Alternatively, we might simplify this as follows:

1. God puts people right with him only through Jesus (vv. 21-23). We cannot put ourselves right ('apart from law') and there is no other way except by Jesus;

2. ...because only Jesus paid the penalty for sinners (vv. 24, 25a). We expound the foundation (propitiation) and the result (redemption);

3. ... and this proves God is fair to forgive (vv. 25b, 26).

Leading a Bible study on 3:21-26

It will be helpful for the group to have a copy of the literal translation, and some explanation of it (from the section on 'Translation issues' above).

To clarify understanding

1. What is Paul's main point in 1:16, 17? How is this echoed at the start of 3:21?

2. How does Paul prove in 1:18-3:20 that there is nothing we can do to stop God being angry with us?

3. What is the central theme of this paragraph, and how does Paul show this by saying it four times?

4. In what five places does Paul tell us he is speaking of an old truth that is now more clearly *revealed* in the gospel?

5. What can the law not do (3:20, 21) and what does the whole Old Testament do (3:21)?

6. Why is trust in Jesus the only way to be rescued (vv. 22, 23)?

7. What does it mean to 'lack the glory of God' (see also 1:23; 2:7; 8:18)?

8. What does the death of Jesus achieve for us (v. 24)?

9. How does it achieve this (v. 25a)?

10. What does the sacrifice of Jesus on the cross prove about God (vv. 25b, 26)?

To encourage honest response

1. Consider carefully how much it matters for the universe that God is fair.

2. Restate the meaning of the cross in your own words, and spend time responding in adoration, love and praise.

10

Coming Under Grace
Romans 3:27–4:25

Let me introduce you to Mr X. Mr X has not really grasped that he is put right with God 100 per cent by grace (justification by grace alone through faith alone). Mr X is rather aware of his own religious privileges—that he and God go back some way together, that he comes from a Christian family, that he has been going to church for years and has an honoured place on the church council, that he knows his Bible, has been baptized and takes part in the Lord's Supper. What is more, his life is pretty much 'together', morally upright. Indeed, he is a pillar of the church.

Because he thinks about all this, two things happen. On the one hand, Mr X can't help but notice that he is on a higher spiritual level than some of the new Christians in his church. Some of their lives are rather a mess and they don't know their Bibles very well. Mr X can't help boasting a bit, at least privately to himself. On the other hand, paradoxically, Mr X is always a bit insecure. Because he bases his good standing with God partly on his own achievements and privileges, he can't help being a bit anxious. There are deeds, words, and certainly thoughts in his life which he would not want projected on the screen at the church council meeting. And so, alongside his boasting, he is never quite comfortable in his own spiritual skin.

Then there is Mrs Y, who thinks more of what she has done for the church than about what Jesus has done for her. Indeed Mr X and Mrs Y are part of a large spiritual family and they have cousins in every church. What happens to a church with Mr X's and Mrs Y's families in membership?

Attentive listening to the text
Context and structure
The structure of the section 'Coming under grace' is as follows, up to 3:26.

1:16, 17	God rescues all believers, but only believers.
1:18-32	This is because he is rightly angry with everyone else,
2:1-3:8	*including* people who have Bibles (religious insiders).
3:9-20	So religious insiders and irreligious outsiders are all by nature under sin.
3:21-26	God is right to rescue sinners because he has punished sinners at the cross.

From 1:16–3:26 Paul has expounded the doctrine of justification by grace alone through faith alone. From 3:27–4:25 he explores the pastoral implications of this for the life of the believer and the life of a church. This section is the antidote to Mr X and Mrs Y.

In 3:27–4:25 the first part of Paul's argument (3:27–4:12) addresses Mr X's first problem, his boasting. The second part (4:13-25) addresses his need for assurance and shows that assurance is only possible when we rest 100 per cent on grace.

Pastoral implication A: no boasting (3:27–4:12)

3:27, 28   The implication is stated: no boasting.

This is followed by 4 supporting arguments and expansions:

1) 3:29-31   One God means one means of justification.

2) 4:1-5   Abraham was justified by grace alone.

3) 4:6-8   All Old Testament believers were justified by grace alone.

4) 4:9-12   Abraham was justified by grace alone so that he would be the spiritual father of one united church.

Pastoral implication B: full assurance (4:13-25)

13-17a   The promise of God: 'What God says, God does …'

17b-22   The God of promise: '… because he can raise the dead'.

23-25   Conclusion and application to us.

Working through the text
Pastoral implication A: no boasting (3:27–4:12)
The implication is stated: no boasting (3:27, 28)

²⁷Where, then, is boasting? It is excluded.

On what principle?   On that of observing the law?   No, but on that of faith.

[*By what law?*   *Of works?*   *No, but by the law of faith.*]

²⁸For we maintain that a man is justified by faith   apart from
                                                          observing the law.

                                                       [*apart from
                                                      works of the law.*]

Why has Paul spent so long closing off all alternatives to justification by grace alone received by faith alone? He stated this doctrine briefly in 1:16, 17 and then spent all of 1:18–3:20 showing the futility of alternative ways of getting right with God. Then in 3:21-26 he expounded the doctrine itself. This whole section from 3:27–4:25 continues to centre on this doctrine; the words 'faith' and 'believe' occur 21 times in these 30 verses; if we add in the words 'justify', 'righteousness', 'unbelief', 'grace' and 'works/work' we get a total of 41 occurrences.

But why such a massive emphasis on faith? The answer is that he wants the church in Rome to live together in harmony. And he knows that only this doctrine can unite a church, because only this doctrine humbles every human being to level zero. And so the major conclusion he draws from the doctrine is: 'Where, then, is boasting? It is excluded.' Boasting asks the questions, 'What makes me cheer? What makes me cheerful? What brings a spring to my step and a sparkle to my eyes?' Is it that I am well thought of in the church, that I know my Bible better than others (and perhaps have a role teaching them), that I come from a Christian family, that I am respectable, that I am baptized and take the Lord's Supper? If I understand the doctrine of Romans 1:16-3:26 then I will grasp that all such boasting is out of order. The only boasting that is now in order is not in what I have done for him, but in what he has done for me (5:2, 11; c.f. Gal. 6:14, 'May I never boast except in the cross of our Lord Jesus Christ').

This applies to the Jew of Romans and to all of Mr X's and Mrs Y's cousins in every church. We shall see in chapter 11 that it humbles the Gentile Christian just as much as it humbles the Jewish Christian. Boasting is the religion of Cain (Gen. 4) who was angry when his sacrifice wasn't accepted, because (like Mrs Y) he reckoned he had done a lot for God and God owed him one. It is the religion of the older brother in Luke 15. (This doctrine also excludes all other kinds of human boasting, for example in human wisdom, c.f. 1 Cor. 1:19-31; 3:21; 4:7).

How is boasting excluded? 'By what law?' Although NIV translates 'law' here as 'principle,' it is more likely that the word still refers to the Law of Moses (as it generally does). We may paraphrase verse 27b as follows:

> 'By what understanding of the Law of Moses is boasting excluded? By the law understood as 'works of the law', as a means of getting right with God? No, that would be a misunderstanding. The Law of Moses was never intended to get anyone right with God by their own effort or privilege. On the contrary, we must understand it as 'the law of faith' which means the law understood as pointing to faith in the Christ to come (as v. 21b shows).'

Paul emphasizes this again in verse 28: 'For', the reason this proper understanding of the law excludes boasting is that, 'we maintain that a man is justified by faith apart from works of the law,' that is, apart from this wrong human-centred understanding of the law. The aim of the law of God is not to make religious insiders feel better about themselves, but to move us all to repentance and faith, humbled under grace together.

Paul now piles up four supporting arguments to press home the truth and implications of this humbling doctrine.

Supporting argument 1: One God means one means of justification (3:29-31)

> [29]Is God the God of Jews only? Is he not the God of Gentiles too?
> Yes, of Gentiles too, [30]since there is only one God [*God is one*],
>> who will justify the circumcised by faith
>> and the uncircumcised through (that same) faith.
>
> [31]Do we, then, nullify the law by this faith? Not at all!
>> Rather, we uphold [*establish*] the law.

Paul begins his first argument with an easy Sunday school question. Is God the God of any particular group within humanity, perhaps just of his chosen people? No, of course not, because we all know that 'God is one' (echoing Deut. 6:4), the one and only God of all the world. That he is 'one' means not just that he is the 'only one' (NIV) but that he possesses absolute integrity and consistency. He is the one who holds the moral order of the universe together. And therefore when he justifies (does the right thing by declaring the sinner righteous in Christ), he does so in one consistent way (with no favourites, 2:6, 11), by 100 per cent grace. This is his way for 'everyone who believes' (1:16). This principle does not make the Law of Moses pointless ('nullify the law'); rather it 'establishes' the law and fulfils its fundamental purpose, which was always to move people to faith in the promised Christ (3:20b). When we bow the knee to Christ, we do what the law always wanted us to do.

This argument is simple and profound. The moment I behave like Mr X, I become a practical pluralist. I replace the one God by some little tribal 'godlet' who has special rules for me and my in-group. Every divided church of first and second-class Christians, and every introverted 'ghetto' church, is a church of practical pluralists (or even polytheists)! The one God of all the world unites a church under his one means of justification, and drives that church out into his one world. For this reason boasting is excluded.

Supporting argument 2: Abraham was justified by grace alone (4:1-5)

¹What then shall we say that Abraham, our forefather *according to the flesh*, discovered in this matter?

²If, in fact, Abraham was justified by works, he had something to boast about
—but not before God.

³What does the Scripture say? 'Abraham believed God, and it was credited [*counted*] to him as [*for*] righteousness.' (Gen. 15:6)

⁴Now when a man works,
     his wages are not credited [*counted*] to him as a gift
     [*according to grace*],
     but as an obligation.
⁵However, to the man who does not work but trusts God
     who justifies the wicked,
     his faith is credited [*counted*] as [*for*] righteousness.

Paul's second argument is from Abraham. 'After all,' says an objector, 'Abraham was a good and obedient man. God even says that Abraham 'kept ... my laws' (Gen. 26:5). So the reason God declared Abraham in the right (justified him) was that he did the works of the law. It will be the same with us. Sure, we believe in grace. But we too must play our part.

Paul disagrees. 'Let's see,' he says (v. 1). 'Let's find out what Abraham discovered about this.' (He calls Abraham, 'our forefather according to the flesh,' which suggests he is addressing the Jewish Christian – and in our terms the spiritual family of Mr X and Mrs Y). Paul agrees that, 'If, in fact, Abraham was justified by works, he had (i.e. would have had) something to boast about (c.f. 3:27) – but not before God (which means, not at all, not in reality).' We know Abraham had no cause to boast because of the Scripture Paul quotes and expounds in this chapter (and also in Gal. 3): 'Abraham believed God, and it was counted to him for righteousness' (Gen. 15:6).

Note three things about this verse:

1. Abraham did not just 'have faith' as a kind of abstract quality (as society speaks of 'people of faith' today). No, Abraham believed the covenant promise of God, that he would have countless offspring who would inherit the world (Gen. 15:5; c.f. 4:13). That is, in principle, he believed in the Christ to come, in whom all the promises of God would be fulfilled (2 Cor. 1:20). He believed God would do what he said he would do.

2. Abraham's faith 'was *counted* to him'. The word 'counted' (NIV 'credited') means reckoned or imputed (from the Latin word meaning the same). It occurs in verses 3, 4, 5, 6, 8, 9, 10, 11, 22, 23 and 24. It speaks of the legal decision of God to count righteousness to Abraham, rather as a sum of money might be credited to an account. It concerns a change of status rather than a change of character. When God credited righteousness to Abraham, he did so in an instant. Any change in Abraham's character came gradually and subsequently.

3. When the verse says that Abraham's faith 'was *counted* to
    him for righteousness' this does not mean that Abraham
    and God did a swap: Abraham generously offered God
    his faith and in return for his faith God gave Abraham
    righteousness! That would turn 'faith' into a human
    'work'. No, it means that faith is the channel by which the
    undeserved righteousness of God is credited to a sinner.

NOT a swap:

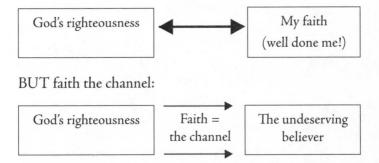

BUT faith the channel:

In verse 4 Paul uses a simple analogy from everyday life.
A worker does not write to his employer when he gets his
pay to say, 'Thank you for your generous grace in paying me.'
That would be absurd, for he has earned it! 'His wages are
counted to him' not 'according to grace' (undeserved) but 'as
an obligation' (earned). What happened to Abraham (v. 5)
is that 'to the man who does not work' (that is – not the
lazy man! – but the man who does not try to get right with
God by 'works of the law'), 'but trusts God who justifies
the wicked' (c.f. 3:26) 'his faith is *counted for* righteousness.'
Human-centred boastful 'work' is quite different from 'the
obedience of faith' 1:5; 16:26. Not to 'work' here means
to abandon all hope that anything I do or possess can
contribute anything at all to my status before God.

Abraham was not a good man; he was 'wicked'; he knew he was wicked; and he trusted 'God who justifies the wicked.' (So when we read in Gen. 26:5 that Abraham kept the law, this means he did what the law fundamentally wanted him to do, which was to believe the God of promise. His obedience was 'the obedience of faith'.)

So for this second reason boasting is excluded.

Supporting argument 3: All Old Testament believers were justified by grace alone (4:6-8)

> ⁶David says the same thing when he speaks of the blessedness of the man to whom God credits [*counts*] righteousness apart from works:
>
> ⁷'Blessed are they whose transgressions are forgiven, whose sins are covered.
>
> ⁸Blessed is the man whose sin the Lord will never count against him.' (Ps. 32:1, 2)

What happened to Abraham was not unique. It set the pattern for every Old Testament believer to be justified by grace alone. David speaks of this blessing in Psalm 32:1, 2. Notice how Paul picks up the word 'count' from verses 3 and 5, repeats it in verse 6 and quotes a psalm that uses it. All through the Old Testament, God did not impute the believer's sin against him, but rather 'covered' it and forgave. We know from 3:21-26 that he was right to do this, because the sinner was punished in the propitiation sacrifice of Jesus on the cross. And because the believer's sin is not counted against him, God is able to 'count righteousness' to him 'apart from works' (v. 6). There is a great exchange.

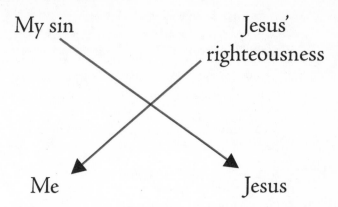

My sin   Jesus'
                          righteousness

Me   Jesus

This is called the doctrine of 'imputed righteousness': because of the cross, God counts or credits (imputes) the righteousness of Jesus to the believer, because the sin of the believer was counted (imputed) to Jesus on the cross. Other verses that contribute to building up the full picture of this exchange include 1 Cor. 1:30; 1 Cor. 15:3; 2 Cor. 5:19-21; and Phil. 3:8, 9.

Because this 100 per cent grace is how every true member of a church is right with God, it utterly excludes boasting.

Supporting argument 4: Abraham was justified by grace alone so that he would be the spiritual father of one united church (4:9-12)

9*So* is this blessedness only for the circumcised, or also for the uncircumcised?

We have been saying that 'Abraham's faith was credited to him as righteousness.' (Gen. 15:6)

10Under what circumstances was it credited [*counted*]? Was it after he was circumcised, or before? It was not after, but before!

> [11]And he received the sign of circumcision,
>> a seal of the righteousness that he had by faith while
>> he was still uncircumcised.
>
> So then, he is [*The purpose was to make him*]
>> the father of all who believe but have not been
>> circumcised,
>>> in order that righteousness might be credited
>>> [*counted*] to them.
>
> [12]And he is also [*And the purpose was also to make him*]
>> the father of the circumcised
>>> who not only are circumcised
>>> but who also walk in the footsteps of the faith
>>> that our father Abraham had before he was
>>> circumcised.

The Jew might object that David's blessing is only for the Jew. After all, David was circumcised! Paul needs to prove again that this is the only way God has ever put anyone right with himself, and that this is the humbling message to be offered to the whole world. So he asks whether the blessing of imputed righteousness (and non-imputed sin) is 'only for the circumcised, or also for the uncircumcised' (v. 9). He comes back to the main text he is expounding, Gen. 15:6, and asks what seems to us a pretty obscure question: did this counting of righteousness happen to Abraham before or after he was circumcised? (v. 10). Easy question for those who have been to Jewish 'Saturday school'! Righteousness is credited in Genesis 15, but Abraham is not circumcised until Genesis 17.

But what's the point of asking this? It seems like the stuff of pointless Sunday School quizzes. What does it matter? Paul reminds them that circumcision was 'a seal of the righteousness that he had by faith while he was

still uncircumcised' ('a sign of the covenant' Gen. 17:11).
That is to say, imputed righteousness came first, and circumcision confirmed (sealed) a status already granted
(as the seal on an envelope was the outward sign of the
authenticity of the letter that had already been placed
inside). Although the Law of Moses didn't come until
hundreds of years later, 'circumcision' came to stand as
a shorthand for all that the law meant by way of response
to God. So, in a symbolic and foreshadowing way, the
sequence of Genesis 15 before Genesis 17 indicates that
God puts anyone right with him by faith, whether or
not they come under the Law of Moses. In a manner of
speaking, Abraham was justified by faith while he was
still a Gentile!

Paul says this is important, and was deliberate. 'The
purpose (of doing it this way round) was to make him the
(spiritual) father' of two groups of people. (NIV disguises
this language of purpose, which is important here).

1. He is the spiritual father 'of all who believe but have
   not been circumcised' (i.e. Gentile Christians), 'in order
   that righteousness might be *counted* to them' (i.e. they
   might receive imputed righteousness and be justified by
   grace alone),

and

2. he is also 'the (spiritual) father of the circumcised'
   (i.e. Jews), so long as they are 'not only … circumcised
   but … also walk in the footsteps of the faith' of Abraham,
   that is to say, they are Jewish *Christians*.

So Abraham is not the father of unbelieving Jews (c.f.
Luke 3:8; John 8:39)—nor for that matter of Muslims—
but he is the father of all, Jew or Gentile, who believe in

Jesus Christ and are justified entirely by grace and by no merit of their own. He is the father of one united church.

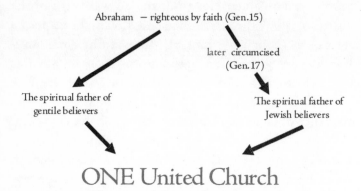

Abraham — righteous by faith (Gen.15)

later circumcised
(Gen. 17)

The spiritual father of
gentile believers

The spiritual father of
Jewish believers

ONE United Church

If I understand this, I will not boast. Paul comes back to an argument similar to his first one in 3:29-31. Just as the one God guarantees one way to be right with him (and has no favourites), so there is one father of the one united people of God, each of whom is put right with God entirely by grace.

Pastoral implication B: full assurance (4:13-25)

Before we get into the detail of verses 13-25, note five guiding points:

1. **The theme of these verses is the promise of God.** Paul's gospel was 'promised beforehand' (1:2). Now he focuses on this promise in verse 13 ('...received the promise'), verse 14 ('... the promise is worthless'), verse 16 ('... the promise comes by faith ...'), verse 20 ('...regarding the promise of God') and verse 21 ('...to do what he had promised'). The idea of the promise is also present in verse 17 (where a promise verse from Genesis is quoted) and again in verse 18 ('... as it had been said to him ...').

2. **The content of the promise** is amazingly summed up in
    verse 13 as 'to be heir of the world'! This is what it means to
    be 'father of many nations' (vv. 17, 18). This sums up all the
    promise verses in Genesis from Genesis 12:1-3 onwards,
    including the promise Abraham believed in Genesis 15:5, 6
    (c.f. Gen. 17:5, 6; 22:17 etc). Abraham's offspring will rule
    the world, and therefore do what humankind was origi-
    nally meant to do (Gen. 1:26-28) before our first ancestors
    rebelled. Paul alludes to this in 1 Corinthians 3:21, 22; 6:2.
    Jesus speaks of it in Matthew 5:3-10, where receiving the
    kingdom of heaven (v. 3, 10) is the same as inheriting the
    earth (v. 5); his followers will rule the new heavens and new
    earth, the new creation. So it's a big promise and the future
    of the universe depends upon it!

3. **The recipients of the promise** are 'Abraham and his
    offspring [literally, '*his seed*']' (v. 13). Who is, or are, his
    'offspring'? In Galatians 3:16 Paul makes the point that
    this verse, 'does not say 'and to seeds', meaning many
    people, but 'and to your seed', meaning one person, who
    is Christ.' So Abraham's 'offspring', the heir of the world,
    is not a collection of individuals. But on the other hand,
    it is not just Jesus as one individual; for in v. 16 of this
    passage Paul refers to 'all Abraham's offspring', which
    clearly means all Christian believers, Jew and Gentile,
    who have Abraham as their spiritual father (vv. 11, 12).
    So Abraham's 'offspring' is:

    +   neither singular and individual (just Jesus Christ);

    +   nor plural and individual (all Christians);

    +   rather it is singular and '*corporate*', the whole family
        of God in Christ. We shall see in 5:12-21 that this
        corporate identity 'in Christ' is very important.

Abraham's offspring

4. **The big question is whether or not God is able to fulfil his promise.** Will it prove 'worthless' (v. 14) or 'be guaranteed' (v. 16)? Was Abraham right to be 'fully persuaded that God had power to do what he had promised' (v. 21)?

5. **The promise is fulfilled by the imputation of righteousness to wicked people.** Throughout chapter 4 Paul's main text is Genesis 15:6 (quoted in vv. 3, 9, 22 and alluded to in several places). The important verb 'counted' (reckoned, credited, imputed) dominated in verses 1-11 (vv. 2, 3, 4, 6, 8, 9, 10, 11) and returns in verses 22, 23 and 24.

Stage 1. The promise of God: 'What God says, God does' (4:13-17a)

Paul begins with a two-sided statement about the promise of God, and then expands each side in turn.

The statement: how the promise is and is not going to be fulfilled (v. 13)

> ¹³It was not through law
>   that Abraham and his offspring received the promise
>   that he would be [*to be*] heir of the world,
> but through the righteousness that comes by [*on the basis of*] faith.

Verse 13 makes a strong contrast. How will God keep his great universe-renewing promise? Answer: the new creation will not be inherited 'through law', but 'through the righteousness on the basis of faith'. Paul expands each side of this in turn.

The promise is not going to be fulfilled through the law (vv. 14, 15)

> ¹⁴For if those who live by the law [*who are of the law*] are heirs,
>> faith has no value and the promise is worthless,
>>> ¹⁵because law brings wrath.
>>>> And where there is no law there is no transgression.

(The phrase 'those who are of the law' means 'Jews'. It does not mean 'those who live by law' as NIV has it, for in verse 16 an almost identical expression is used of Jewish *Christians*).

Why is it not possible for Jews to inherit the world by virtue of being Jews? Why would it make faith pointless and the promise 'worthless' ('just a piece of paper' as we say of an untrustworthy promise) if the promise was to be inherited just by Jews, who have the Law of Moses? The reason is that law on its own (without the promised Christ) just 'brings wrath'. Paul has proved this in 2:12. Indeed, in one sense unconverted people are actually worse off when they have a Bible, because, 'where there is no law there is no transgression'. There is sin without law (c.f. 5:13). But the law puts a clearly-labelled boundary in place between right and wrong, and when I knowingly cross that line I not only sin but also transgress (for transgression means crossing a line). To use a simple illustration from walking in the countryside: I am always wrong to trespass on someone's

land, but I am doubly guilty if I walk straight past a clear
'No Trespassing' sign to do so. To know the law without
having my sin covered by the sacrifice of Christ and my
heart changed by the Spirit of Christ, simply makes me
even more guilty than I was before.

Suppose God had said to Abraham, 'I would like
your family to inherit the world. So now go away and
do your best to be faithful to me, and then I'll be able
to keep my promise'. The promise would fail. Human
unfaithfulness would indeed have frustrated the faithfulness of God (3:3). This is why Mr X is in such an insecure place, for he is beginning to think that his part in
the new creation (his share of the inheritance) depends
on his own 'works of the law'. If it does, God's promise
to him is just a scrap of worthless paper and he has no
hope. If this was how it worked, then God's promise
would express nothing more than his good intentions.
This is how it would be if our motto was, 'What God
says, *we* have to make sure *we* do.'

The promise is going to be fulfilled by grace (vv. 16, 17a)

> [16]Therefore, the promise comes by faith [*This is why it is
> on the basis of faith*],
>> so that it may be by grace
>>> and may be [*so as to be*] guaranteed to all Abraham's
>>>> offspring
>>>> - not only to those who are of the law
>>>> but also to those who are of the faith of Abraham.
>>>> He is the father of us all.
>>>>> [17]As it is written:
>>>>> 'I have made you a father of many
>>>>> nations.' (Gen. 17:5)

The reason we may be sure the promise will happen ('so as to be guaranteed') is that it depends not at all on human initiative, privilege, religion, morality, knowledge or response but entirely on grace. Note that this means that 'faith' cannot be a virtuous disposition or something we do by our own unaided decision. To say that 'the promise comes by faith' is to say that it comes 'by grace'. Faith itself is a gracious gift of God. If it were something we decided, unaided, to do, then the promise would still not be secure, for it would depend on enough of us being sensible enough to do it – which we would never do. Our faith does not trigger his responsive grace; his prior decision of grace enables us to believe.

But because the promise rests 100 per cent on grace it really is guaranteed both to Jewish believers ('those who are of the law' in this context must refer to Jewish Christians) and to Gentile Christians ('also to those who are of the faith of Abraham', which in this context refers to believers who are not Jews). Abraham 'is the father of us all', as Paul has already told us in verses 11, 12. This is why God can make him, 'a father of many nations' rather than just one.

So it is not a case of, 'What God says, we have to make sure we do'; rather it is, 'What God says, God does' and therefore we can know for sure that he will do what he has promised to do.

Stage 2. The God of promise: 'What God says, God does, because he can raise the dead' (4:17b-22)

17b(He is our father) in the sight of God, in whom he believed – the God who gives life to the dead and calls things that are not as though they were.

18Against all hope, Abraham in hope believed and so became [*believed that he should become*] the father

of many nations,
just as it had been said to him, 'So shall your
offspring be.' (Gen. 15:5)

[19]Without weakening in his faith,
he faced the fact that his body was as good as dead
—since he was about a hundred years old
—and that Sarah's womb was also dead.

[20]Yet he did not waver through unbelief regarding
the promise of God,
but was strengthened in his faith and gave glory to God,

[21]being fully persuaded that God had power to do what
he had promised.

[22]This is why 'it was credited to him as righteousness.'
(Gen. 15:6)

We ought still to be puzzled by the time we reach verse 17. It is all very well to insist that God will fulfil his promise because it depends on him and not on us. But then how is God going to make Abraham's offspring into people who are fit to rule the world? How, in the face of human unfaithfulness, will he find a faithful people? The answer is that he does not find them; he creates them. He does what he has promised by creating out of nothing a people to whom he gives the obedience of faith.

Although the passage does not naturally start a new section half way through verse 17 (Paul is still expounding Gen. 15:6), there does seem to be a shift in emphasis from the promise of God to the nature of the God who makes the promise. He is 'the God who gives life to the dead and calls things that are not as though they were.' The expression 'as though they were' does not mean he plays 'make believe', pretending things exist when they don't; it means that by his voice (c.f. 9:12 'by him who calls') he brings into existence things that do not exist. He speaks to non-existent things as though they existed, and then they come into being and do exist! This is the power of the voice that was heard on earth saying to a dead 12-year-old girl, 'It's time to get up' (Mark 5:41), to a widow's son at his funeral, 'Young man, get up' (Luke 7:14) and to a man dead for four days, 'Lazarus, come out!' (John 11:43).

Right at the start of the promise of God, this voice brought Isaac into existence (vv. 18-22). The God who brings non-existent things into being spoke to an old man married to a barren woman (v. 19) and called into existence a son. When Abraham and Sarah asked for the maternity unit, the hospital reception would have redirected them to the geriatric ward (or the psychiatric ward when they insisted on maternity!). What happened to them was like a resurrection or a creation *ex nihilo*.

It is important to notice that the central focus in this passage is not on Abraham and his heroic faith, but on God and his life-giving promise. It is God, not Abraham, 'who gives life to the dead' (v. 17); it is God who makes the promise (vv. 18, 20); it is God who 'had power to do what he had promised' (v. 21). The passage is bracketed by the strength of God (vv. 17, 21) and at its centre is the utter helplessness of Abraham and Sarah (v. 19).

The connection between the power of God and the weakness of Abraham is Abraham's faith. 'Against all hope' (that is, against all humanly plausible reason to hope), 'Abraham in hope believed'; that is, he based his hope on the God of promise (v. 18). When Paul says, 'Without weakening in his faith' (v. 19) and 'he did not waver through unbelief' (v. 20) we must remember that both Paul and his hearers knew the Genesis story, how Abraham had some pretty big wobbles (e.g. Gen. 16, the conception of Ishmael, and Gen. 17:17, apparent disbelief)! If Paul wanted to air-brush Abraham as an unblemished hero of faith it would be neither honest (for he wasn't) nor persuasive (for Paul's hearers knew this). Presumably Paul is painting a broad-brush picture: by the grace of God Abraham proved to be a believer. For all the ups and downs of his experience, the fundamental direction of his life was to trust the God of promise. Indeed, the time came when he was willing to offer Isaac as a sacrifice because he believed in the God who can raise the dead (Gen. 22; Heb. 11:17-19).

Paul's aim is to point us to the creative power of the God of promise, and to encourage us that faith means that, in our helplessness, we take this life-giving God at his word. Paul now brings all this into the present tense of Christian experience.

3. Conclusion and application to us (4:23-25)

> [23]The words 'it was credited [*counted*] to him' (Gen. 15:6) were written
>> not for him alone,
> [24]but also for us,
>> to whom God will credit [*count*] righteousness
> —for us who believe in him who raised Jesus our Lord from the dead.
>
> [25]He was delivered over to death for our sins and was raised to life for our justification.

What happened when Abraham believed the promise of God shows the shape of the gospel. The imputation of righteousness to Abraham shows how God imputes right-eousness to the believer of every age. But for us it is even more sure. The conception of Isaac was the work of the God 'who gives life to the dead' and in that way fulfilled his promise. This God is the one 'who raised Jesus our Lord from the dead' (v. 24). The people who are raised to life by union with Jesus Christ are those who will inherit the promise. Paul moves from foreshadowing or 'type' (Isaac) to fulfilment or 'antitype' (Jesus).

But in Jesus it is real and final, because he 'was delivered over to death for our sins' (an echo of the Greek translation of Isa. 53:12; c.f. 1 Cor. 15:3), as the propitiatory sacrifice on whom the wrath was poured out (3:25). And he 'was raised to life for our justification'. The resurrection proves that Jesus' propitiation was accepted and therefore assures us of our justification. Just as the birth of Isaac assured Abraham and Sarah of the power and faithfulness of the God of promise, so the resurrection of Jesus proves to us that God is able to do what he has promised to do, to give us new life in Jesus.

From text to teaching
Getting the message clear: the theme

The first section (3:27–4:12) focuses on the exclusion of boasting. We cannot boast, because we are justified by grace alone through faith alone. The God of the whole earth is 'one', and therefore there has only ever been one way to be right with him. This is how it was for Abraham and for every Old Testament believer: their sin was not counted against them, but a free gift of righteousness was counted to them. The reason God did it this way was that there might be one united people of God, humbled together under grace. The free gift of righteousness makes all believers equal.

The second section (4:13-25) focuses on the assurance that God can and will keep his promise by grace alone. The theme is that what God says, God himself does, and he is able to do this because he has the Creator's power to raise the dead. To put it another way, we may be confident that Christ's people will inherit the earth because God raised Christ for our justification.

We may put the whole of 3:27–4:25 together as a series of contrasts between grace and works.

given to the wicked
as a free gift
because of what Jesus did
received by faith
boasting excluded
assurance guaranteed

done by the wicked
to earn God's favour
because of what we do
earned by works
boasting allowed
assurance excluded

Getting the purpose clear: the aim

Romans 3:27–4:12 addresses the first problem of Mr X and Mrs Y, their divisive sense of superiority. Paul wants to humble every Christian, and especially the Jewish Christians who may think they are in some way superior. When a religion or political movement claim to have absolute truth, their truth claims divide and lead to war. This is a valid observation and explains why those called 'post-moderns' are so sceptical of claims to the possession of truth. A truth claim may indeed be a veiled power play. In general, it is correct to say that doctrine divides. However, the doctrine of justification by grace alone through faith alone is the glorious exception. This doctrine alone is able to unite warring human beings, because this truth alone humbles us all under the free generosity of God.

It is often suggested that because doctrine divides, the best way to unite a church (or churches) is to dumb down and de-emphasize doctrine, because doctrinal distinctives will exclude some who cannot subscribe to them. This is true when the doctrinal distinctive is secondary. It is untrue when the doctrine is justification by grace alone. Other distinctives create privileged or exclusive ghetto religion. But grace alone fashions a community from which boasting is excluded. By definition, this is a community which has no pride in its history, its privileges, its morality, its Bible knowledge, or anything that comes from within itself. It is, therefore, a community that can live together in harmony and reach out with the barrier-breaking message of grace to a needy world.

Romans 4:13-25 addresses their second problem, which is the insecurity and lack of assurance that bedevils anyone who trusts even 1 per cent in their own goodness. Paul's aim is that we should grasp the life-giving and therefore promise-keeping power of the God who raised Jesus from the dead. We ought to emerge from 4:13-25 with a strong confidence in God's power to do what he has promised to do, and to do it entirely by grace. We ought to let go of even the 1 per cent of our works in which we have put our trust. Only in a Christianity that is 100 per cent grace can we rest secure and know we have nothing to prove and nothing to hide. Because I am 'a debtor to mercy *alone*' I know that, 'my name from the palms of his hands, eternity will not erase; impressed on his heart it remains, in marks of indelible grace' (from the hymn, 'A debtor to mercy alone'). We may sum up Paul's aim in this section by saying that we should understand that only 100 per cent grace makes our status secure in Jesus.

These two sections, therefore, connect closely to Paul's aim of creating harmony between unlikely people in the church in Rome.

Pointers to application

+ No boasting (3:27). Expose the things we might boast about, such as Bible knowledge, outward moral success, association with Christian people, church membership.

+ Preach for understanding of imputed righteousness, that this is absolute, instantaneous, undeserved and forever. It may be worth having a separate teaching meeting on this.

+ Preach 4:9-12 to emphasize that justification by grace alone is far more important than all external markers of being a Christian.

+ Preach 4:17 to press home that by nature we are spiritual corpses, and only the life-giving, dead-raising word of God can give us life.

+ Make the point that God's declarative word of justification is not just a legal fiction (God saying we're innocent when we're guilty), but is a life-giving word that achieves what it declares. When God declares us righteous he gives us life in Christ, so that on the Last Day we will be righteous. This is no legal fiction but life-changing reality. (God's word is very different from our words, because it always achieves what it declares.)

+ Preach the law (4:14, 15) so that we feel how much worse the law makes things, until we are given life by Christ.

+ Address the 'free will objection', that God has given us free will and cannot therefore guarantee to fulfil his promise. This objection pictures God rather like a chess grandmaster taking on a roomful of amateurs. He is very skilled, and usually he wins all his games and achieves his objectives. But we can never be entirely sure he will win them all. On this model, God's promise expresses his best intentions, and no more. On the contrary, God's promise is guaranteed, because it rests entirely on his grace. Even our faith is his gift and initiative (c.f. Phil. 1:29 'it has been granted you… to believe on him…'; 2 Tim. 2:25 'in the hope that God will grant them repentance').

+ It may be worth explaining that because his grace works in us at the level of the human spirit, what he does in us, we also do. 1 Corinthians 15:10 illustrates this well. Paul's work as an apostle was at the same time entirely the grace of God and entirely his own work. It was not some combination of the two (perhaps 98 per cent grace and 2 per cent Paul) but 100 per cent of each, as the grace of God worked in Paul so that Paul worked.

+ Show how it is the gospel of grace that builds the church, because only the gospel humbles human pride and excludes boasting. So we need to go on and on preaching the gospel of grace to Christians just as much as we preach it to non-Christians.

+ Address the person who says, 'I can't join your church because I'm not good enough. I'm a single mother, or a homosexual, or whatever other kind of moral failure, and you're bound to look down on me. I'm not good enough to join you.' Show how the gospel of grace undermines that excuse. Churches that proclaim free grace ought to be magnets for the modern equivalents of the tax collectors, prostitutes, and notorious sinners.

+ Show the danger of allowing our self-esteem or sense of identity to be bound up with our Christian ministries. Perhaps take the example of someone who serves energetically and faithfully in the church, and then is asked to give up some cherished ministry (for whatever reason), and reacts with surprising hostility and defensiveness. Why? Because they have allowed their identity to be built on this ministry rather than on the free grace of God. In a way, the test of grace is how we react when a ministry is taken away from us, including by illness. To the extent that our security is 100 per cent built on grace, our identity will not be threatened.

+ Show how our practices of prayer can undermine grace if we are not careful. If we begin to think that our prayers will be heard better in a 'sacred place', or with the aid of a cross or candles, or even with the aid of quietness, then we forget that God does not hear our prayers because of where we are, because of how hard we are concentrating, or because of anything in us. He hears them because of his 100 per cent grace given us in Christ.

+ Show how the assurance that rests entirely on grace removes the insecure tendencies of Christians towards self-promotion (because there is no need), towards a thirst for novelty (for we have been given all we need), and towards party spirit (because we are all on the same level)

Suggestions for preaching and teaching the text
It is probably best to preach this section in its two main parts.

Sermon 1 (3:27–4:12)
We might begin by asking how a church can be at the same time united and outward-looking, not united as an introspective club. We might introduce Mr X, Mrs Y and their

families (adapted for the church culture of our hearers), and show how they were there in the Jewish Christian mentality back in first century Rome.

Our teaching points might be as follows:

Main point:
All boasting is excluded in church because all Christians are justified by grace alone through faith alone (3:27, 28). We need to stress how vital this is both to harmony within the church and mission outwards from the church.

We move on to Paul's four supporting arguments:

Supporting argument 1:
There is only one God and he justifies people in only one way, by grace alone (3:29-31) OR 'If I think God makes a special case for me/us, then I am a polytheist!'

Supporting arguments 2 and 3 (we may put these together):
We are justified by a great exchange, as our sin is counted to Jesus and Jesus' righteousness counted to us (4:1-8). (And no-one has ever been justified in any other way).
Supporting argument 4:
What unites Christians is not knowing about God, religious privilege, or good behaviour, but experiencing the free grace of God (4:9-12).

Sermon 2 (4:13-25)
Again, we may begin with Mr X and his family, remind our hearers how in 3:27–4:12 Paul has excluded his boasting, and then move on to his second problem of assurance.

Our teaching points might be as follows:

1. The promise of God: what God says, *God* does (vv. 13-17).
2. The God of promise: what God says, God does, *because he can raise the dead* (vv. 17-22).

Conclusion: God keeps his promise by the death and resurrection of Christ (vv. 23-25).

Leading a Bible study on 3:27-4:25
To clarify understanding

1. What is the main conclusion Paul draws from the doctrine of justification by grace (3:27, 28)?

2. Why does he think this is so important for the church in Rome?

3. Why does 'God is one' mean that justification must be by grace for everyone (3:29-31)?

4. What did Abraham discover about boasting and getting right with God (4:1-5)?

5. What did David say about being forgiven (4:6-8)?

6. Why was Abraham justified by faith *before* he was circumcised (4:9-12)?

7. What was the promise God made to Abraham and his offspring (4:13)?

8. Why will this promise not be fulfilled by law (4:14, 15)?

9. How does grace guarantee that the promise will be fulfilled (4:16, 17)?

10. What does Paul tell us about the God in whom Abraham believed (4:17-22)?

11. How does the gospel of Jesus give us even more assurance that God has kept his promise (4:23-25)?

To encourage honest response

1. What makes us cheer/cheerful about ourselves and our church? How does this doctrine rule all such reasons for cheerfulness out of order?

2. Are there ways in which our church has begun to worship a little 'godlet' rather than the God of all the earth?

3. How can we remind one another in daily life of the truth of imputed righteousness?

4. What difference does the assurance of 4:13-25 make to our daily lives? And to our attitudes to having jobs/posts/ministries in church?

5. What difference does justification by grace make to our prayer lives both individually and as a church?

SECTION THREE:

Living Under Grace

Romans 5–8

11

INTRODUCTION TO ROMANS 5–8

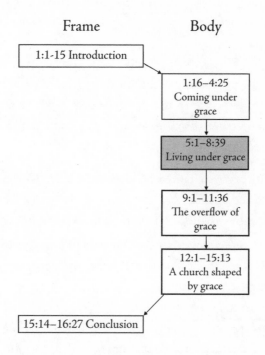

Frame

Body

1:1-15 Introduction

1:16–4:25
Coming under
grace

5:1–8:39
Living under grace

9:1–11:36
The overflow of
grace

12:1–15:13
A church shaped
by grace

15:14–16:27 Conclusion

In the first major section of the letter ('Coming under grace') Paul teaches justification by grace alone received empty-handed by faith alone, through the propitiatory death of Jesus, by which our sin is counted to him and his righteousness counted to us. This is the only way for men and women to be brought into the saving righteousness of God. He taught this truth because it excludes boasting (3:27) and guarantees assurance. It is the only basis upon which a united people of God can be forged, because we are humbled to the same level (no boasting) and have nothing to prove (because of assurance). Further, only a people humbled under this 100 per cent grace will reach out in humble evangelism to 'unlikely people' in the rest of the world, because we understand that we too are 'unlikely people'.

We now begin the second major section, which I have called, 'Living under grace'. Paul shifts from the foundations of life under grace to the present tense living of life under grace. There are three reasons for treating chapters 5-8 as a new section.

1. Paul begins chapter 5, 'Therefore, since we have been justified by faith …'. (The alternative reading, 'Therefore, let us be justified by faith…' is unlikely to be correct.)

2. The tone changes. In the first section he has made much use of what is called the 'diatribe' style, arguing with an imaginary objector (2:1-5, 17-27; 3:1-8, 9). He still does this in the second section (e.g. 6:1, 15; 7:7), but there is a greater emphasis on inclusive language ('We …') as Paul writes pastorally to those justified by grace, about what it is like to live the Christian life.

3. The dominant vocabulary changes from that of faith ('faith', 'believe') to that of life. Paul quoted Hab. 2:4 in 1:17 ('The righteous will live by faith'). We may perhaps say he majors on 'by faith' in section 1, and moves to 'will live' in section 2.

The structure and themes of chapters 5-8

There are strong links between chapter 5 and chapter 8. Indeed, this whole section has a kind of sandwich structure.

5:1-11   Suffering with assurance of future glory

    5:12-21   The basis for assurance in the work of Christ

        6:1-23   Slavery to sin

        7:1-25   The weakness of law

    8:1-17   The basis for assurance in the ministry of the Spirit

8:18-39   Suffering with assurance of future glory

Suffering is a new theme in this section. We shall see in 12:9-21 that suffering can either threaten or strengthen the unity of a church. Paul wants the church to understand suffering in the context of assurance, so that it does not cause division.

As we embark on this second section it will be helpful to bear in mind three distinct but complementary parts of the doctrine of salvation.

1. **Justification** is God's declaration that the believer is in right relationship with him. It is a forensic (i.e. law court) statement, and it is made by God at the start of the Christian life. It brings about an instantaneous and absolute change of status at conversion. It happens 100 per cent by the free grace of God; it is given because the wrath of God against sinners was poured out on Jesus on the cross (that is to say, it is based on the truth of penal substitution, that Jesus bore the penalty we deserved); and it is received empty-handed by faith, with no contribution from human works.

2. **Incorporation into union** with Christ happens at the same time as justification. A man or woman is brought into vital relationship with Christ, so that what happened to Christ is reckoned to have happened to us. We are transferred from Adam's fallen humanity into Christ's redeemed humanity. Christ is the representative Head of this new humanity, which is Abraham's 'offspring' in Christ. Like justification, this is a definite change of status: we are transferred from being 'in Adam' to being 'in Christ'.

3. **The Spirit of God** is given to every believer to begin to effect a real inward change. His work in us is not an instantaneous change of status but a gradual change inside.

These three truths (justification, incorporation into Christ, the gift of the Spirit) are distinct but inseparable. When God says something (justification, his declaration about us in Christ), what he says comes to pass. He never justifies without incorporating into Christ and giving his Spirit, and he never gives his Spirit without justifying and incorporating into Christ.

12

LIVING UNDER GRACE

ROMANS 5

What does God think of you? And does it matter? Every human being has 'significant others' (as we call them) whose opinion of us matters deeply. Whether it be a father or mother whose affirmation we crave, or a husband or wife whose unconditional love means more than the world to us, or some other significant relationship, all of us mind what somebody thinks. But what about God, the most 'Significant Other' in the universe? What does he think of me? He holds my destiny in his hands. But does he smile, or does he frown?

We learned from Romans 3 that God is very very angry with me; he is right to be angry with me; and there is nothing I can do about it. So what has changed by the time we come to Romans 5?

Attentive listening to the text
Context and structure
(see Introduction to Romans 5-8)

Structure of 5:1-21
Chapter 5 (like 3:21-26) is dauntingly full of wonderful truth. Justification, peace with God, grace, joy, hope, glory, suffering,

the Holy Spirit, the cross, the love of God, the wrath of God, final salvation, reconciliation, eternal life, all come tumbling out of the page. The danger is that we fail to see the logic, and just pick some great truths almost at random and make doctrinal points from them. So how can we get a grasp of the logical flow and main themes of the passage?

The theme of building on the foundation of justification is signalled four times by the phrase 'how much more' (vv. 9, 10, 15, 17), by the expression 'not only... but also' (vv. 3, 11), and by verbs like 'overflow' (v. 15) and 'increased all the more' (lit. 'hyper-overflowed') (v. 20). We might almost call chapter 5 'the rich overflow of grace'; in some ways it anticipates the theme of overflowing grace we shall find in chapters 9-11.

Verses 1-11 are bracketed by a restored relationship with God. This is called 'peace with God' in verse 1 and 'reconciliation with God' in verses 10 and 11. This is Paul's main point (in vv. 1-11), that the legal declaration of justification creates a restored relationship. Everything else follows from this. Justification is a legal declaration, a verdict. If that sounds a little cold, legal, forensic – the stuff of wigs and law-courts – peace and reconciliation remind us that what justification does is to restore a personal relationship. Further, the passage is bracketed by a joyful boasting (vv. 2, 11) in this restored relationship.

The main division markers in verses 1-11 are as follows:

v 1   'Therefore ...' (vv. 1, 2 state Paul's main point)
v. 3   'Not only ..., but ... also ...' (vv. 3-8 develop the main
           point)
v. 9   '... how much more ...' (these words come first in the Greek and
           are repeated in v. 10; vv. 9, 10 state two very similar truths in
           parallel)
v. 11   'Not only ... but ... also' (v. 11 restates the truth of vv. 1, 2)

Verses 12-21 focus on comparisons and contrasts between the humanity headed by Adam and the new humanity headed by Christ. The structure is as follows:

vv. 12-14	humanity in Adam ('just as…')
vv. 15-17	contrasts between Adam and Christ
vv. 18-21	humanity in Adam and the new humanity in Christ ('just as … so also …')

Working through the text
A. Peace with God (vv. 1-11)
1. *Past justification, present peace and future glory are inseparable (vv. 1, 2)*

> ¹Therefore, since we have been justified through faith,
> we have peace with God through our Lord Jesus Christ,
> ²through whom we have gained access by faith
> into this grace in which we now stand.
> And we rejoice [*boast*] in the hope of the glory of God.

Paul builds from the foundation he has painstakingly laid in 1:16–4:25, the past tense of the Christian life ('we have been justified'). From now on he builds on this foundation to the present and future tenses.

1. Past event: 'we have been justified through faith'. The definite declaration has been made.

2. Present state: 'we have peace with God' and 'have gained access … into … grace'.
   a) 'Peace with God' is not a subjective experience, as when people say, 'I feel at peace with God, I feel an inner sense of calm before God' in a 'religious building' or a quiet place ('I am nearer to God in a garden than any place else on earth'). It is an objective statement: a state of war has ended. What is more, this war was

not ended by anything I did. It is not that I sensibly decided to become a decent person and be friends with God. It is that the God who was rightly at war with me (he was rightly angry with me and there was nothing I could do about it), has made peace with me. The peace-making is all on his side. This peace comes 'through our Lord Jesus Christ' by his death (3:25). (Every section of chapters 5-8 ends with a reference to the Lord Jesus Christ, see 5:11, 21; 6:23; 7:25; 8:39). Before I was justified I might have some kind of spiritual hunger; but the objective fact was that the God I sought was at war with me. And until his right anger was satisfied and the penalty paid I could not safely get near him. But now I can.

b) 'Through Jesus' (because of the cross) 'we have gained access by faith' (empty-handed receiving) 'into this grace in which we now stand.' We have gone through a door ('access') from the realm where sin enslaves (3:9 'under sin') to the realm where grace rules (6:14 'under grace'). Before, I stood under law, which always hung over me accusing me. No matter how hard I tried, no matter how religious I might be, I could not escape my guilt. But now I stand in grace. I have been taken by the hand into the throne room (1 Pet. 3:18) and brought into grace, undeserved blessing without limit or condition. The human race is not divided by floors (very good people at the top, terrible people at the bottom, most of us in the middle thanking God we are not as bad as the people lower down), but by a door, the door of 'access … to grace' which is entered 'by faith'. To 'stand' in grace is to be a citizen of heaven (Phil. 3:20). This 'standing' is a definite status, not an experience that comes and goes with our feelings. We do not wander to and fro between being under grace and under sin.

3. Future: 'we boast in the hope of the glory of God'. We no longer boast in our own privilege, knowledge or moral achievements (2:17, 23), for all such boasting is excluded (3:27). What puts a spring in our step now is not what we have done for God, but what he has done for us, which is to give us the sure and certain hope of sharing again in the glory of God. This is the glory we forfeited in that terrible exchange (1:23); the glory we long for and seek (2:7); the glory we lack by nature (3:23); but the glory we shall one day again share (8:18), when people will be able to look at us and say, 'Now I see what God is like!' and the creation will be governed properly at last (8:19-21).

To connect these three tenses is the key to the Christian life. But what does it feel like to live this life in the present? Here is the surprise.

2. *The present tense of the Christian life is joy in suffering (vv. 3-8)*

> ³Not only so, but we also rejoice [*boast*] in our sufferings,
>> because we know that suffering produces perseverance;
>>> ⁴perseverance, character;
>>>> and character, hope.

> ⁵And hope does not disappoint us [*put us to shame*],
>> because God has poured out his love into our hearts
>>> by the Holy Spirit, whom he has given us.

> ⁶*For* you see, at just the right time, when we were still powerless,
>> Christ died for the ungodly [*for the ungodly Christ **died**.*]
>>> ⁷*For* very rarely will anyone die for a righteous man,

[*for a righteous man will anyone* **die**]
though for a good man someone might possibly
dare to **die**.
⁸But God demonstrates his own love for us in this:
While we were still sinners, Christ died for us [*for us
Christ* **died**]

It is one thing to boast in the hope of the glory of God, quite another to boast in sufferings. Or is it? Paul fills in the gap between present grace and future glory. What happens between the present and the future is 'sufferings'; this was the pattern for the Lord Jesus, and it must be the pattern for his followers (8:17). This includes explicitly Christian suffering (persecution, c.f. 12:14) but also all the trials that afflict the believer in this age (as Job discovered, these may include natural disasters, violent crime, terrorism, sickness, infirmity and bereavement).

We will only cheer about suffering if we grasp that suffering is the tie between present grace and future glory. Paul does this first by showing us what God is doing in us (vv. 3b, 4) and then what God proves to us (vv. 5-8).

What God is doing in us (vv. 3b, 4)
We 'boast in our sufferings because we know…'

1. '… that suffering produces perseverance.' 'Perseverance' means 'patient endurance', the quality of people who keep going under pressure. The word is used of the believer in 2:7 (NIV 'persistence') and 8:25 (NIV 'patiently' = 'with patient endurance'). It is the purpose of the Scriptures to give us this quality (15:4, 5 NIV 'endurance'). We learn it only through suffering.

2. '…perseverance produces character'. 'Character' means 'character that is tested and found to be trustworthy and

true'. Until we suffer, we are untested. Only suffering can stamp us with the hallmark of authentic faith (c.f. 1 Pet. 1:7; James 1:2-4).

3. '...character produces hope'. In one sense the newest Christian possesses the sure and certain hope of glory. But subjectively that experience of hope can be shallow, almost a theoretical thing, a box to be ticked on the doctrinal statement. But when believers have suffered, they hope with every fibre of their being. They have nothing else to hold on to except the hope of future glory. This is what Abraham discovered as he held on to the bare promise of God (4:18, 19).

What God proves to us (vv. 5-8)

How do we know that the experience of hope that keeps us going under pressure is not wishful thinking, make-believe, the kind of thing that secular undertakers offer the bereaved with fanciful poems about the after-life? How do we know that 'hope does not put us to shame', that it will not prove illusory at the last? The same word 'put...to shame' is used in 9:33 and 10:11 in a quotation from Isaiah 28:16 (NIV 'never be dismayed').

Paul's answer holds together the subjective and the objective in a way that is important for Christian pastoral care. Subjectively (v. 5), 'because God has poured out his love' (vv. 6-8 suggest that this is his love for us, rather than our love for him) 'into our hearts' (that is, into our present experience) 'by the Holy Spirit, whom he has given us.' One of the ministries of the Spirit to the believer is to give us a present experience and assurance that God loves us. This pouring happens at conversion (8:9) and goes on happening day by day. The words 'pour out' suggest a generous abundance (c.f. Tit. 3:6; Acts 2:17; from Joel 2:28-32).

This experience is a subjective feeling of the love of God that is firmly anchored in objective truth, as verses 6-8 make clear. (Verses 6-8 are tied to verse 5 by the word 'for'.) The objective truth is that Christ died for us.

The four sentences of verses 6-8 all end with the verb 'to die', giving a particular emphasis on the *death* of Christ. In verses 6-8 Paul teaches five things about the cross.

1. The time: Christ died 'at just the right time, when we were still powerless'. This may be a historical comment; the stability of the Roman Empire enabled the message to spread quickly. But the phrase 'at the right time' is closely parallel to 'when we were still powerless' and it seems better to take 'the right time' to be 'when we were still powerless'. That is to say, he died when we needed to be rescued - for people in dire straits - which is the appropriate time for a rescuer to mount his rescue.

2. The exchange: Christ died 'for the ungodly' (v. 6), 'for us' (v. 8 twice), which means 'in our place, as our substitute'. He was the sacrifice of propitiation upon whose innocent person the wrath we deserved was poured out (1:18; 3:25).

3. The recipients: we are 'powerless', 'ungodly', 'sinners' and 'enemies'. We were 'powerless' because we were 'under sin' (3:9) and unable to do anything to save ourselves. We were 'ungodly' like Abraham (the same word is translated 'wicked' in 4:5 NIV) because, by our ungodliness, we suppress the truth (1:18). We were 'sinners' because we had inherited a sinful nature from Adam (5:19). And we were 'God's enemies' because we refused to bow the knee in submission

to God's King (10:3, 4). God was very angry with us and there was nothing we could do about it.

4. The magnitude: verse 7 may say more or less the same thing in both halves of the verse (for emphasis); or there may be a progression from the 'righteous' person (who is worthy and virtuous) to the 'good' person (for whom we perhaps also have personal affection). It doesn't really matter. The point is that to die for unrighteous and bad people shows a love that goes beyond the best and deepest sacrifice known to human beings.

5. The proof: the cross 'demonstrates God's own love for us'. It is the past tense proof of the love God has for us. The Spirit (v. 5) takes this past tense proof and brings it home to our hearts in the present tense, so that we know here and now that God loves us.

How do I know that my subjective experience of hope in suffering will not prove to be wishful thinking and let me down? I know, because the Spirit of God pours into my heart in present tense experience the love God has for me. He does this by sealing to my heart the objective truth of the cross. We may say that the love of God is poured out by the Spirit and proved at the cross. To have subjective feelings without the objective anchor of the cross will deprive my assurance of any stability; for I will be at the mercy of my feelings. But to have the objective truth without the subjective ministry of the Spirit will leave the cross as a theoretical truth. We need the objective demonstration of God's love at the cross poured into our hearts by the Spirit in the present.

3. We have been reconciled, and so we will be saved (vv. 9, 10)

> [9]Since we have now been justified by his blood,
>> how much more shall we be saved from God's wrath
>> through him!
>
> [10]For if, when we were God's enemies,
> we were reconciled to him through the death of his Son,
>> how much more, having been reconciled, shall we
>> be saved through his life!

Verses 9 and 10 are in parallel. Verse 9 starts with the past truth of justification (as in v. 1). We 'have been justified by his blood' (3:25). Because God has made the legal declaration that we are justified (the opposite of being condemned, 5:18), we know for certain that in the Final Judgment God's wrath will not fall on us, because it has fallen on Jesus. This wrath is visible in a partial way in the moral disorder of society (1:18-32), but it will finally be poured out on all the impenitent at the end (2:5).

Verse 10 begins with reconciliation (just as v. 2 moves from justification to peace with God). Because we have been justified, we 'were reconciled' and have peace with God 'through the death of his Son'. And therefore we know for sure that on the Last Day we 'shall…be saved through his life', that is, through his resurrection, which guarantees the effectiveness of his death (c.f. 4:25).

Notice that being saved is in the future (c.f. 13:11). Although we are safe and have been justified and reconciled, we long for that great day when our bodies will be redeemed (8:23). Only then will our rescue be complete. Paul's point in these verses is that past justification and present reconciliation absolutely guarantee future salvation.

4. Summary

> [11]Not only is this so,
>> but we also rejoice [*boast*] in God through our Lord Jesus Christ,
>>> through whom we have now received reconciliation.

Verse 11 sums up the passage, repeating the joyful boasting of verse 2 and focusing it very personally on God himself and the Lord Jesus, the agent of our reconciliation.

B. Humanity in Adam, new humanity in Christ (vv. 12-21)

The trouble with being a sinner and being told that God has justified me by grace alone, is that it is often hard to believe. After all, my sin stares me in the face every day. My slavery to sin is the pressing existential reality of my life, and its consequence of death overshadows even the brightest days of life.

By nature I can understand a religion of works, because this says to me that I must try harder, that by my own initiative, I have some hope of surviving Judgment Day. But a religion that simply declares to me that I have instantaneously been vindicated before God by grace? It is hard to feel confident this is true. And if I don't feel confident this is true, I will behave in church as someone who has something to prove, or who despises those who have made less progress than me. Before I can be safely humbled under grace, I need to know that grace is strong enough to make me safe and change me.

In verses 9 and 10 Paul has said that present justification and reconciliation guarantee 'how much more' certain and wonderful it is that we shall be saved from God's wrath on Judgment Day by the blood and life of Jesus. He now develops the 'how much more' of grace, by painting a picture of two humanities.

1.   *Humanity in Adam (vv. 12-14)*

> [12]Therefore, just as
> > sin entered the world through one man,
> > > and death through sin,
> > > > and in this way death came to all men
> > > > [*people*],
> > > > > because all sinned—
>
> [13]for before the law was given, sin was in the world.
> > But sin is not taken into account when there is no
> > law.
>
> [14]Nevertheless, death reigned from the time of
> Adam to the time of Moses,
> even over those who did not sin by breaking
> a command, as did Adam,
> > who was a pattern [*type*] of the one to come.

Paul's main statement is in verse 12, where he gives the first half of a comparison ('just as …'). He does not complete the comparison until verse 18 ('just as … so also …'). The main statement is of one event with three consequences.

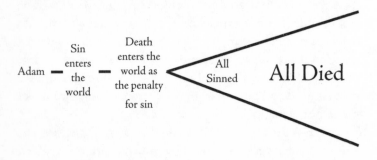

1. The event: 'sin entered the world through one man'. The
    first man ('Adam' means 'man' in Hebrew) sinned (Gen. 3)
    and when he sinned he didn't just do something wrong.
    He invited into the world an enslaving power that reigns
    (5:21; 6:13, 14) and must be obeyed (6:16, 17). This is
    the paradox of sin: Adam thought he was in control, but
    in reality he was surrendering control to a slave-master.

2. The immediate consequence: 'death' entered the world
    'through sin' (through the sin of the first man). God did
    what he said he would do (Gen. 2:17 'when you eat of
    it you will surely die'). Adam died spiritually as he was
    expelled from the presence of God; and so in due course
    he died physically. The mortality of human beings is an
    alien intrusion into the world. It entered the world on
    the coat-tails of sin.

3. The first universal consequence: 'all sinned.' Because the
    first man sinned, all human beings sinned.

    a)   This cannot simply mean that we happen to follow
    Adam's bad example; for in verse 19 Paul says we 'were
    made sinners' (established as, given the constitution of,
    sinners) rather than good people who happen from
    time to time to sin. There was a change in us. Also,
    when we come to the other half of the comparison, we
    are not 'made righteous' (v. 19) by following Christ's
    good example. This shallow idea that our sin is just
    following Adam's bad example is an old heresy called
    Pelagianism.

    b)   It includes the truth that we are reckoned or
    counted as sinners because of Adam, that Adam's
    sin is imputed to us. Adam is the head of our natural
    humanity, and what is true of him is true of us.

c)   It also includes the truth that we actually sin
because we inherit Adam's sinful nature. Our sinning
is related to Adam's neither just externally (following
his example) nor just legally (his sin reckoned to our
account), but internally and actually. We are actually
'made sinners' by the nature we inherit from him.
This is the doctrine of Original Sin.

4.   The final universal consequence:'in this way' (i.e. because
Adam sinned, and therefore all sinned) 'death came to
all people.' Adam sinned; Adam died. All the rest of
us sinned; all the rest of us came under the power of
death.

In verses 13 and 14 Paul takes a step sideways to ask what
difference the Law of Moses made to all this. As so often
in Romans he has the religious unbeliever in his sights
more than the irreligious unbeliever (because the religious
unbeliever is more likely to be listening!) What difference
does it make to know the Bible (2:18), to belong to a church
and claim a relationship with God (2:17), to disapprove of
wrong (1:32–2:1, 18), to be a 'Jew'? The answer is sad but
important.

To understand Paul's answer we need to be clear about
the distinction between sin and transgression. To sin is to
forfeit the unspoiled image of God (the glory of God) by
worshipping anything or anyone other than God (1:18-23;
3:23). To transgress is to break a command of God.
Adam did both. He sinned by desiring the fruit rather
than desiring to please God (Gen. 3:6). He transgressed
by breaking the command of God not to eat that fruit
(Gen. 2:16, 17). Since Adam, all human beings sin (v. 12);
but human beings only transgress when they have been
given the command of God in God's law.

So, 'before the law was given' (at Mount Sinai, Exod. 19, 20), 'sin was in the world' (as it had been since it entered the world with the first man, v. 12). 'But sin is not taken into account' (lit. 'reckoned, counted, imputed') 'when there is no law'. That is to say, sin is not clearly ticked off on the policeman's charge-sheet, although it is still sin, and still made them guilty. And so (v. 14), 'death reigned from the time of Adam to the time of Moses, even over those who did not sin by breaking a command'. The event of verse 12 led to all the consequences of verse 12 even without the law.

And yet Adam sinned 'by breaking a command'. The command of Genesis 2:16, 17 was a foreshadowing of the Law of Moses that did not come until many years later. This means that Adam is, in a way, the spiritual father both of those who sin without knowing the law (like the people from Adam to Moses), and also of all who both sin and transgress, because they do know the law. Just as Abraham became the spiritual father of one united church (4:11b, 12), so Adam is the terrible head of one fallen humanity, Jew and Gentile.

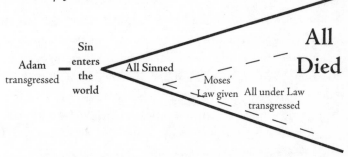

2. *Contrasts between Adam and Christ (vv. 14b-17)*

    [14b] … Adam, who was a pattern [*type*] of the one to come.

    [15] But the gift [*grace gift*] is not like the trespass.
    >   a) For if the many died by the trespass of the one man,
    >   b) how much more did God's grace
    >   and the gift that came by the grace of the one
    >   man, Jesus Christ,
    >   overflow to the many!

    [16] Again, the gift (of God) is not like (the result of) the one man's sin:
    >   a) The judgment followed one sin and brought condemnation,
    >   b) but the gift [*grace gift*] followed many trespasses and brought justification.
    [17]
    >   a) For if, by the trespass of the one man, death reigned through that one man,
    >   b) how much more will those who receive
    >   God's abundant provision of grace
    >   and of the gift of righteousness
    >   reign in life through the one man, Jesus Christ.

At the end of verse 14 Paul calls Adam 'a *type* of the one to come.' The word 'type' originally meant an impression made by a moulding, perhaps in a wax seal. It means a person or event that shows in some way the shape of someone or something else. The reality to which the 'type' corresponds is called the 'antitype'. Here Adam is a 'type' of Christ (the 'antitype') because – although there are many differences! – Adam did one action that had consequences for many people.

Having said that Adam is a 'type' of Christ, Paul spends most of his time showing us what a poor 'type' he was! He contrasts Adam's 'trespass' (vv. 15, 17, 18), 'sin' (v. 16), and 'disobedience' (v. 19) with Jesus Christ's 'grace gift' or 'gift'

(Paul uses two Greek words in each of verses 15 and 16), his one 'act of righteousness' (v. 18), and 'obedience' (v. 19). Twice, emphatically, he says that what Jesus did is 'not like' what Adam did (v. 15a, v. 16a).

First (v. 15) there is a contrast between the death of many and the overflow of grace to many. It is not just that grace and death are opposites, but that the overflow of grace is more powerful than death ('how much more'), and that the grace of God comes 'by the grace of the one man, Jesus Christ'. The only source of grace to a humanity under sin and death comes through 'the one man'. His death as a propitiation (3:25) is the only way that grace breaks into the world.

Next (v. 16), the strength of grace is seen in a contrast of power. *One* sin led to judgment and inevitably to condemnation. The word 'condemnation' is an intensified version of the word 'judgment'; we might say, 'one sin led to judgment and judgment to final irreversible judgment.' But, wonderfully, 'the grace gift followed many trespasses and brought justification.' One sin did massive damage; one grace gift in Jesus can undo all that damage. Notice that 'justification' is the exact opposite of 'condemnation'.

Verse 17 contains a surprising contrast. Part (a) is no surprise: 'by the trespass of the one man, death reigned through that one man'. This restates verse 12, but emphasizing the *rule* of death. We might expect part (b) to read, 'how much more will *life* reign … through Jesus'. Instead, it is '*those who receive … grace …* reign in life'. The opposite of the reign of death is the reign of Christians, who do what Adam was supposed to do. In Christ, as Abraham's corporate offspring, they will rule the world (c.f. 4:13).

This disabling of death's rule happens because of 'God's *abundant* provision of grace', the overflowing grace of verse 15, the 'how much more' of verses 16 and 17, the 'all the more' of verse 20. And the grace comes to us by 'the gift of righteousness', the saving righteousness of God (1:17), which is received through Jesus.

3. Humanity in Adam and the new humanity in Christ (vv. 18-21)
In verses 18 and 19 Paul completes the contrast he began in verse 12, before giving a postscript about the law in verse 20 (much as he followed v. 12 with vv. 13, 14).

> [18]Consequently,
>> a) just as the result of one trespass
>>> was condemnation for all men,
>> b) so also the result of one act of righteousness
>>> was justification that brings life for all men.
>
> [19]For
>> a) just as through the disobedience of the one man
>>> the many were made sinners,
>> b) so also through the obedience of the one man
>>> the many will be made righteous.
>
> [20]The law was added
>> so that the trespass might increase.
>> But where sin increased,
>>> grace increased all the more,
>>>> [21]so that, just as sin reigned in death,
>>>> so also grace might reign through righteousness
>>>>> to bring eternal life through Jesus Christ our Lord.

The point of verse 18 is that just as one trespass led to condemnation for *all*, so *one* act of righteousness brings justification for *all*. The words 'all' (v. 12, 18) and 'many' (v. 15, 16, 19) mean the same thing, and their meanings must be taken from the context. So the 'all' or 'many' affected by Adam's sin are 'all human beings who are in Adam, all by nature, all without exception'. But the 'all' or 'many' affected by Christ's obedience are 'all human beings who are in Christ, all believers, all who are recipients of grace'. The contexts make this clear.

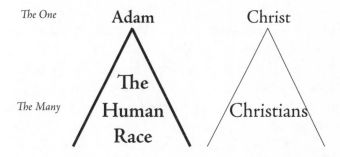

Justification does not come by many individual acts of righteousness (which would be justification by 'works of the law', 3:20); it comes by *one* act of righteousness and the benefits of that one act are credited by grace to the account of *all* who are in Christ.

Verse 19 tells us what that one 'act of righteousness' was. Just as the 'trespass' of verse 18 is 'the disobedience of the one man' (v. 19), so the 'act of righteousness' of verse 18 is 'the *obedience* of the one man' (v. 19). Both Jesus' life of obedience (sometimes called his 'active obedience') and his obedient death (sometimes called his 'passive obedience', the obedience of his passion, c.f. Phil. 2:8) make up one whole 'act of obedience' to the Father. The whole path from deity to the cross (Phil. 2:6-8) was the perfect 'obedience of faith' up to the final cry 'It is finished!' (John 19:30).

Just as Adam's disobedience 'made' us sinners, both in status (counted sinners before God) and in actuality (our sinful nature), so the one act of obedience of Jesus guarantees that all believers '*will be* made righteous', in status now (justification and union with Christ) and inwardly on the Last Day (when the Spirit's work will be complete). What God declares about us in Christ (that we are justified) he will do in us (to make us what he says we are).

In verses 20 and 21 Paul asks what difference the Law of Moses makes. In verses 13 and 14 we saw that the absence of the law did not make people innocent ('sin was in the world' and 'death reigned'). Now we see that the presence of the law makes guilty people even more obviously guilty: 'The law was added' (at Sinai) 'so that the trespass might increase.' Before Sinai, 'the trespass' was just Adam's one breaking of the commandment of Genesis 2:16, 17. Now the Law of Moses is given to all of Israel, they all start breaking it. When our sinful natures come face to face with the command of God, we immediately start breaking it. We become not only guilty sinners, but guilty trespassers. This is the effect – indeed the paradoxical *purpose* ('so that') – of the law. It was never meant to save, but only to point to the one man who could save. So Sinai only made things worse! And yet – and this is the 'how much more' of the gospel of Christ! – 'where sin increased' (it just got worse and worse, more and more blatant), 'grace increased all the more, so that, just as sin reigned in death' (v. 17a) 'so also grace might reign' (that is, *Christians* under grace might reign, v. 17) 'through righteousness' (through the gift of righteousness given to believers because of the death of Jesus) 'to bring eternal life through Jesus Christ our Lord'. Eternal life is the gift of God to believers (2:7), the result of becoming slaves of God (6:22), and the grace gift of God (6:23). Paul's point is that the free grace of God experienced in Christ transfers us into a completely new humanity, and that grace is actually more powerful than sin. Grace overflows much more than sin can spread. As one Puritan put it, 'There is more grace in Jesus than there is sin in me'.

From text to teaching

Getting the message clear: the theme

Verses 1-11 are bracketed by a cheerful boasting in God because by the death of the Lord Jesus, he has restored our relationship with him. Our justification secures our reconciliation. That reconciliation guarantees future salvation and glory. In between is suffering, through which God works in us a tested character and a deeper hope, and in which God reassures us of his love proved by the cross and applied to us by the Spirit. The central idea is therefore that our present state of grace, peace, and reconciliation is unbreakably tied to our future state of salvation and glory. What we have at present is wonderful, but it is as nothing by comparison to the 'how much more' which is to come.

It is a mistake to read verses 12-21 as a simple contrast between humanity 'in Adam' and the new humanity 'in Christ'. Paul's emphasis is on the 'how much more' of the grace that comes in Christ. His central point is that, just as one disobedience led to universal disaster, so the one obedience of Jesus Christ has the gracious power to undo all that disaster. He wants us to rest our confidence not in ourselves ('works of the law') but entirely upon the obedience of Jesus.

The grand theme of the whole chapter is assurance that comes from who Jesus is, what Jesus did, and how we are vitally united with Jesus.

Getting the purpose clear: the aim

Paul's aim in verses 1-11 is that Christians are not thrown off course by suffering. He wants us to be able to connect the three tenses of the Christian life, to know what God has said about us (justification), what is now true (reconciliation, peace with God), and therefore to be utterly confident of future glory.

Apart from the foundation of justification, the motif of boasting is the most significant connection with the first section of the letter (unfortunately disguised in NIV). If 'coming under grace' (1:16–4:25) is summed up as 'boasting excluded' (3:27), then chapter 5 tells us we can boast in God through Jesus, and even in suffering. The difference between these two boastings is that boasting in God unites, where human boasting divides. Boasting in God is a glorious shared boasting in which any human being can join. This boasting unites the nations; it is for all who believe, without discrimination of race, class, culture, education, moral achievement, or religious prowess. It is a boasting that unites the church and that reaches out in mission to others (quite the opposite of the boasting of members of a club). Paul wants the church to boast together in security under grace. We need therefore to preach this not primarily for individuals, but for the church, so that together we share in this joy. It is not just that 'I boast', but that 'we boast'.

The danger with verses 12-21 is that we teach systematic theology with no reference to why Paul wrote the passage to the church in Rome, and no connection with the flow of his argument. Paul does not tell us why he has written this section, and so we must do our best to infer it from the context. In doing this we will be guided by two factors. The first is the idea of grace being stronger than sin and death; this runs right through the passage. The second is the way Paul twice turns aside to ask how law fits into the picture (vv. 13, 14 and then again in vv. 20, 21). In summary, he says

(a) that the human race is in a terrible predicament (under sin and death); (b) that law only made it worse; but (c) that the grace that comes in Christ has power to break the power of sin and death. Law takes the portion of Adam's humanity who know it (the Jews) and makes their guilt even more clear than it was before. Grace, however, takes all kinds of people in Adam's humanity (Jew and Gentile) and transfers them to a new humanity in Christ – a humanity set free from their slavery to sin and death.

This passage is pivotal in making the link between the legal verdict of justification and the real inner change that begins in a person when he or she is vitally united with Christ. It answers the question: how can what Jesus did so long ago affect me today? When I grasp just how radical is God's grace, then – and only then – will I stand secure in grace. Then I will both begin to value the church and also reach out with the gospel of grace to others.

This passage links to the overall aims of Romans therefore in the following two ways: First, I understand that whereas distinctions of religious privilege or Bible knowledge (the law) only serve to make those who have them even more guilty (and are therefore nothing to be proud of); by contrast, all who are in Christ, without distinction, belong together to a new humanity. The local church is an expression of this new humanity, and is therefore a place of tremendous significance.

Second, I understand that this grace in Christ is, by its very nature, an overflowing grace that is reaching out all over the world. Just as Adam's sin reaches out all through the human race by our fallen human nature (Original Sin), so Christ's righteousness is reaching out by the gospel to all human beings without distinction.

Pointers to application

+ (v. 1) Make sure we understand that peace with God is objective not subjective, that it is a change of state rather than a variable feeling. It doesn't matter whether I feel close to God or far from God; if I am in Christ I have been given peace with God, brought near to God (c.f. 1 Pet. 3:18), not by anything I have done but entirely by what Christ has done.

+ (v. 1) Make sure we grasp that the fundamental problem was not that I was hostile to God (though I was) but that he was rightly hostile to me, and that there was nothing I could do about this. The peace-making had to come from him.

+ Preach the wonder of 'access' (v. 2).

+ Make clear that access comes 'through Jesus' (v. 2) and not by the mediation or ministry of any earthly priest, scholar, or worship leader. No human being on earth can 'bring us into the presence of God'. Only Jesus can do that.

+ Approach the wonder of a restored relationship with God via our human longings for affirmation from 'significant others'. If we long for a father's approval, how much more deeply do we need to be under the smile of God rather than his wrath.

+ Show how individuals' boasting in themselves always leads to strife and divides a society, but that a shared boasting in God and his 100 per cent grace unites us. Apply this to our songs (not 'me-centred' but full of wonder at his grace), and to our conversation (learning to tell one another how good and faithful God is).

+ (vv. 3, 4) Learn God's perspective on suffering. Avoid a shallow hope that we will immediately be able to 'see the point' of some suffering (usually we won't). But we will begin to grasp what God is doing in the believer through suffering.

+ (vv. 3, 4) Avoid both a shallow 'glory now' kind of Christianity (health, wealth, prosperity) and also a too-simple 'suffering now, glory later' formula. It is 'suffering now, glory later', but between suffering and glory there is a deep process of change going on in us, who are being changed inside by God. So the Christian life is not a miserable one, crawling along in pain but happy to have an entrance ticket to the new creation safely in our pockets; it is a tough life, but one in which God is daily at work in us to change us and prepare us for glory.

+ (vv. 5-8) Work hard to hold together the subjective witness of the Spirit and the objective proof of the cross. When I feel that God cannot love me (because of my sin or my suffering), the Spirit points me to the objective proof of the cross.

+ (vv. 1-11) Explore how the tenses of the passage rescue us from being imprisoned in the present. The past shapes our identity, but by justification we are granted a new identity in Christ. The future governs our security, and because past justification guarantees future glorification our future is secure. It is as if we walk on a rope bridge in a storm. Sometimes we feel very insecure. But the bridge is unbreakably tied to past justification at one end and to future glorification at the other.

+ Show how, just as the insecure child becomes the play-ground bully, so the insecure Christian causes problems in the church, because he or she always has something to prove, is always seeking affirmation. By contrast, the Christian who grasps security in grace will build others up.

+   (vv. 12-21) Address the existential question: how can
    what Jesus did so long ago and so far away really affect
    me today? Show how Paul's argument points us first
    to the experienced consequences of what one man did
    even longer ago. Teach Original Sin as an experienced
    reality (illustrated from the sinful tendencies of the
    youngest baby).

+   (vv. 12-14) Feel the misery of living in a world under
    sin and death; the paradox of a world with such wonder
    and beauty and yet so strangely marred by sin and
    overshadowed by death.

+   (v. 20) Illustrate how the clear law of God only makes
    things worse, by shining the light of truth on what we
    might otherwise have persuaded ourselves were morally
    justifiable actions.

+   (vv. 12-21) Show how fundamental is our identity in
    Christ. We can do this by going through successively
    deeper answers to the question, 'Who are you?' These
    answers might begin by occupation or role (job, husband,
    mother, etc), through nationality, culture, education and
    race. The most fundamental answer is, 'I am a human
    being' or – in Paul's terms – 'I am in Adam's humanity'.
    So our transfer into Christ's humanity changes us at
    a deeper level than occupation, role, nationality or race.
    It is the deepest change possible for a human being, to
    be transferred from one humanity to another.

+   (vv. 12-21) Press home the supremacy and wonder of the
    overflow of grace. The main emphasis of verses 12-21 is on
    this, to bring assurance that the obedience of Jesus really is
    stronger than the terrible powers of sin and death.

Suggestions for preaching and teaching the text

A. *Two sermons on Romans 5*

It is probably best to preach two sermons on this chapter, following the division between verses 1-11 and verses 12-21.

Sermon 1 on 5:1-11

We might begin as we began this chapter, by asking what God thinks of us, and whether it matters.

Our teaching points might be as follows:

1. One foundation: We are justified by faith (v. 1). How much we say about this will depend on whether or not we have just preached chapters 1–4. It is vital, but it is not the main point of this passage.

2. First consequence: We have peace with God and stand in grace (vv. 1, 2).

3. Second consequence: We boast in suffering because suffering ties us to a glorious future (vv. 3, 4).

4. Third consequence: The Spirit pours the love of the cross into our hearts (vv. 5-8).

5. Fourth consequence: We will be saved from wrath (vv. 9-10).

Conclusion: We boast in God (v. 11)!

OR we might use these 3 teaching points:

1. We have access to grace (vv. 1, 2).
2. We are filled with love (vv. 3-8).
3. We will be saved from wrath (vv. 9-11).

Sermon 2 on 5:12-21

We might lead in by looking at ways we might divide the human race – by language, race, nationality, class, education, culture, and perhaps most important, by religious knowledge and privilege. This will lead in to the idea that there is only one division that ultimately matters, that between humanity in Adam and the new humanity in Christ.

Alternatively, we might begin by considering examples in life where the action of one leader has consequences for all his followers, or the action of parents feeds into consequences for succeeding generations in their family. This will lead into the idea of Adam and Christ as the influential heads of their respective families.

Our teaching points might be as follows:

1. Adam's human race: by Adam's disobedience we are all under the reign of death-dealing sin (vv. 12-14). (And having a clear moral framework only makes it worse, because it shows up our guilt more clearly.) We need to feel the awful predicament we are all in, and that the shadow of death is the consequence of our sinful nature in Adam.

2. Christ's human race: by Christ's obedience we reign through life-giving grace (vv. 15-21). We want to focus on all the ways in which Christ's one act and life of obedience impact us, so that we respond with wonder, praise, and assurance in him.

In conclusion, we press home the way this impacts members of a church (as for the church in Rome). We understand that our church is the local expression of a new humanity in Christ. And we rejoice that this new humanity has in its DNA a powerful overflow of grace to others. It cannot remain authentic and stay introspective as a cosy club.

B.   One sermon on Romans 5

To preach one sermon on the whole chapter means we will have to focus ruthlessly on the main theme, which is the 'how much more' of grace; that what God has already done for us in Christ points certainly to a 'much more' in the future, an overflow of grace. Our teaching points might be as follows:

1. Because we have peace with God now, we are certain of an even more wonderful rescue in the end (vv. 1-11).
2. Because of Jesus' one act of obedience, we are transferred from a condemned humanity into a new humanity who will rule the world (vv. 12-21).

C.   A short series from 5:1-11

We might take verses 1-11 more slowly and expound the logic and sequence of truths as follows:

Sermon 1: Justification by grace (v. 1)—including recap from 1:16–4:25, focusing on 1:16, 17 and 3:21-26.

Sermon 2: Peace with God and standing in grace (vv. 1, 2).

Sermon 3: Suffering—what God does in us and where it leads (vv. 3, 4).

Sermon 4: The double proof that God loves us (vv. 5-8).

Sermon 5: Full salvation—when it will come and how we may be sure of it (vv. 9-11).

Leading a Bible study on 5:1-11

To clarify understanding

1. What has happened to every Christian, and what does it mean (v. 1a)?

2. What three consequences are there of being justified (vv. 1b, 2)?

3. Why do we boast in sufferings (vv. 3, 4)?

4. How can we be sure our hope will not disappoint us (vv. 5-8)?

5. When did Christ die and for whom (vv. 6-8)?

6. How is God's love in Jesus deeper than any human love (v. 7)?

7. When will be saved, from what, and how can we be sure (vv. 9, 10)?

8. What can we boast/rejoice about together (v. 11)?

To encourage honest response

1. What relationships matter a lot to us in our lives? How much does it matter to us to know we are in right relationship with God? How can we help one another to care about this relationship as much as we ought?

2. How does a shared boasting/rejoicing in God affect a church, and how does it differ from lots of individuals 'boasting' (vying for position, trying to get one up on others, etc)?

3. How will a shared boasting in God express itself in the life of a church, in our meetings, in our conversations and sharing of news?

4. How can we hold together the subjective witness of the Spirit with the objective proof of the cross, when we need reassurance that God loves us?

Leading a Bible study on 5:12-21

To clarify understanding

1. What are the consequences of the first man's sin (v. 12)?
2. What difference does it make whether or not people know God's commands (vv. 13, 14)?
3. In what way was Adam 'a pattern' of Jesus (v. 14)?
4. What words are used (in the whole passage) to describe the one thing Adam did, and the one thing Jesus did?
5. How does Paul signal (in the whole passage) that the grace of Jesus is stronger than the sin of Adam?
6. How does the one thing Jesus did affect all Christians?
7. In verse 17, who or what are the two alternative rulers of the world?
8. How did God's law make things worse (v. 20)?

To encourage honest response

1. In what ways do we feel the pain of a world under death?
2. The Bible teaches that all this pain is the result of being in a world under sin. How do our responses to pain and death often ignore this, and how can we help one another to respond in a way that takes account of needing rescue from sin?
3. How is it different to say, 'I sometimes commit sins' from saying, 'I am a sinner'? Why is the latter so much deeper and more serious?
4. Why do we find it hard to believe that Jesus' one act of obedience can change us from sinners to righteous? Why would our pride prefer this change to be done in some other way?
5. What difference does this teaching about a new humanity make to the way we treat one another in a church?
6. How does overflowing grace change the way we think about those outside of church?

13
LIVING UNDER GRACE
ROMANS 6

It is a scandal when an evil person is forgiven. In the 1970s Comrade Duch was one of Pol Pot's chief executioners in the Killing Fields of Cambodia. Those who have visited the school which he used as his prison (now a museum) will have been rendered speechless with grief and anger at what he did. Two decades later he was baptized as a Christian believer. Isn't that a scandal, that Comrade Duch should become my brother and be forgiven by God?

Attentive listening to the text
Context and structure
At the end of chapter 5, Paul has said something that must seem perverse to morally serious people. He has said (5:20) that, (a) knowing God's commands just makes sin worse, as sinful people *knowingly* disobey him; and yet, (b) even though sin goes on increasing, 'grace increased all the more', to bring eternal life to all sorts of guilty people (like Comrade Duch). Morally serious people (e.g. the Jewish

Christians in Rome) know that sin is sin, and we ought not to do it. They understand that any religion worth its salt ought to make bad people good, or at least less bad. It seems to them that Paul is in danger of preaching an immoral religion that encourages bad people to go on being just as bad. They cannot understand a religion that releases people from the penalty of sin, but doesn't seem to do anything about its power. Paul seems to them careless about sin and unduly negative about the law. Chapter 6 addresses the first objection and chapter 7 the second.

The structure of chapter 6 is as follows. Note the movement between objections, doctrinal answers, and exhortation based on doctrine.

Objection stated (v. 1)
>   Objection answered by main doctrine (vv. 2-11) – Christians have died to sin
>>   Exhortation on the basis of the doctrine (vv. 12-14) – Do not let sin reign

Objection restated (v. 15)
>   Supplementary argument 1 (v. 16)
>   Supplementary argument 2 (vv. 17-19a)
>>   Exhortation renewed (v. 19b)
>   Supplementary argument 3 (vv. 20-23)

Working through the text
A. *The objection stated (v. 1): is grace an immoral religion?*

[1]What shall we say, then?
Shall we go on sinning [*continue in sin*] so that grace may increase?

This is not a suggestion (let's go on sinning) but an accusation (this is the absurd conclusion to which your teaching of grace leads). The idea is not just that we go on sinning

(NIV), but that we continue doing what people do when they are under the power of sin. (Paul has mentioned a similar objection in 3:5, where he dismissed it out of hand. Here he answers it more fully.)

B. *The objection answered (v. 2): Christians died to sin*

²By no means! We died to sin; how can we live in it any longer?

Paul's answer is that Christians 'died to sin' and therefore it would be absurd to suggest that they go on living under its rule. (To 'live in it' refers to a whole direction of life controlled by sin. There is a similar idea in 1 John 3:6, 9). This answer is not an exhortation, that we ought to 'die to sin'; it is a plain statement of fact that is true for every Christian. He expounds this in verses 3-11. Exhortation does not begin until verse 12.

C. *The answer expounded (vv. 3-11): what does it mean to have 'died to sin'?*

What does 'we died to sin' mean? Before working through verses 3-11, it is helpful to be clear about three points.

1. The singular word 'sin' is not just something we do ('sins'); it is a power to which we are enslaved. We are 'under sin' (3:9); sin 'reigned in death' (5:21). It needs to be 'rendered powerless' (6:6), not to be allowed to 'reign' (6:12) or to 'be our master' (6:14). The one who commits sin is a slave of sin (John 8:34). Sin is like a monster waiting to pounce (c.f. Gen. 4:7). A famous World War II cartoon shows a diminutive Hitler embracing (and being embraced by) a huge Russian bear.

The caption has Hitler saying, 'I have caught a bear, and he won't let go.' Sin is like that, as we know from every experience of addictive behaviour or destructive habit.

2. Death is sin's weapon of mass destruction, the last and worst thing that sin can do to the sinner, sin's final reckoning (5:12). When sin has killed us, it can do no more.

3. Christians were united with Christ from the moment of their conversion. We were 'baptized into Christ Jesus' (v. 3). And therefore what happened to him is reckoned to have happened to us, whether it be his death (vv. 3, 5, 8), burial or resurrection (vv. 4, 5). We have been transferred to his new humanity (5:12-21). This is not an experience attained by some Christians, but how God sees every Christian. And if God sees us like this, then it is true.

   Individualistic cultures claim to find this corporate belonging hard to understand, although we know what it is to say, '*We* won' when our football team or army won, even if we ourselves were not on the field or in the battle. This can apply to things that happened before we began supporting a team. '*We* won the cup in 1925' can be true, even though the young supporter was not even born then. The team's story has become our story. Israelites of every generation could say '*We* won' when David killed Goliath. So the Christian is caught up into the career of our champion, the Lord Jesus Christ.

   [3]Or don't you know that all of us
       who were baptized into Christ Jesus
       were baptized into his death?

Christian baptism is 'into Christ Jesus', which means 'into vital union with Christ Jesus', transferring from Adam's humanity into Christ's (5:12-21). Water baptism is shorthand for everything God does when he makes someone a Christian. (Paul's aim is not to teach a particular doctrine of baptism here. He uses baptism as a picture of union with Christ. Indeed he doesn't talk about baptism again after verse 4. So it would be a mistake to rest any strong views on the mode or time of baptism on this passage). Union with Christ means that what happened to him is reckoned to have happened to us. He died, so we died; sin punished us in Christ with its last and worst penalty. It can do no more; the penalty is paid. It is important to be clear about the timings. We do not die at the time of our conversion. The death Paul is speaking of took place 2000 years ago. What happens at conversion is that our story becomes his story, and we died with him 2000 years ago.

> [4]We were therefore buried with him through baptism into death
>> in order that,
>>> just as Christ was raised from the dead through the glory of the Father,
>>> we too may live a new life [*walk in newness of life*].

Burial seals the finality of death. In Christ, we really did die to sin. The purpose was that 'just as Christ was raised from the dead through the glory of the Father' (i.e. to show the Father's character and justice), so 'we too may walk in newness of life'. Although our bodies are not yet redeemed (8:23), the way we 'walk' (i.e. live) is to be a resurrection life; this was why we were 'buried with him'.

> ⁵If we have been united with him   like this in his death
>   [*in the shape of his death*],
>   we will certainly also be united with him   in his resurrection

'If' (as is true – there is no uncertainty here) 'we have been united with Christ in the shape of his death' (i.e. in his death as a death that pays the penalty of sin), then in the future (though not yet) 'we will certainly also be united with him in his resurrection' (i.e. in the 'shape' of his resurrection, as a new life free from the reign of sin and death). We 'walk in newness of life' (v. 4) now, because in the future our bodies will be raised (v. 5).

> ⁶For we know that our old self was crucified with him
>   so that the body of sin might be done away with
>   [*rendered powerless*],
>   that we should no longer be slaves to sin—
>   ⁷because anyone who has died has been freed
>   [*justified*] from sin.

My 'old self' does not mean a bad part of me that exists along-side the new part of me (as in Eph. 4:22-24; Col. 3:9-11). It means all of me as I was 'BC' (before I came to Christ). This old self 'was crucified with Christ'. This is a statement, not an exhortation: I am not being told to crucify my old self, but that my old self has been crucified with Christ.

The purpose was 'so that the body of sin' (all of me under the power of sin) might be 'rendered powerless', which means that sin's authority is broken, 'that we should no longer be slaves to sin'. The reason sin's authority is broken is that 'anyone who has died has been *justified* from sin'. Sin has played its trump card, used its final weapon. The declaration of justification not only releases me from the penalty of sin; it also breaks the slave-power of sin over me.

Before being joined to Christ, when I resisted sin I was like a prisoner who tries to escape over the prison wall before his sentence is paid. When sin the jailer catches up with me and tells me to come back into prison, I have no choice but to go, because I am guilty and the penalty is not paid. But when the Christian resists sin he is like a prisoner who is released through the prison gate after serving his sentence. When the jailer threatens him and tells him to return to prison, he need not go. The only power that sin has over the Christian is the power of bluff.

All this is objective truth from the moment of conversion; it is not a gradual experiential process or something only attained by a spiritual elite. We are tempted by sin until the day we die. We are not corpses unresponsive to the stimulus of sin (as has sometimes been taught). But sin has no right to enslave us any more. Volume 1 of our biography has been completed ('Enslaved to sin'), and volume 2 has begun ('Justified from sin by Christ'). We are not free from sin's ability to tempt us; but we are free from its right to kill us.

> [8]Now if we died with Christ, we believe that we will also
> live with him.
> [9]For we know that since Christ was raised from the dead,
> he cannot die again;
>> death no longer has mastery over him.
>>> [10]*For* the death he died, he died to sin once for all;
>>> but the life he lives, he lives to God.

Verse 8 restates verse 5: 'Now if we died with Christ' (which we did), 'we believe we will also live with him'. This points to the resurrection morning when our present status (having died with Christ) will lead to a future bodily reality (living with him in the new creation). We may be sure of this because (v. 9) 'we know that since Christ was raised from the dead, he cannot die again' (and therefore we will rise, never to die again); 'death no longer has mastery over him' (as it did when he was identified with sinners and lived under the curse of death). 'For the death he died, he died to sin' (i.e. to pay the penalty for sin) 'once for all' (once for all time, once for all people), 'but the life he lives, he lives to God' (in the presence of God, and therefore for eternity). Just as Jesus' death was once for all time and his resurrection irreversible, so for us in him.

> [11]In the same way, count yourselves dead to sin but alive to God in Christ Jesus.

Just as Jesus now 'lives to God' (v. 10, in his resurrection body, free from the shadow of sin), so we also are to 'count' ('reckon') that we ourselves are 'alive to God in' (i.e. in union with) 'Christ Jesus'. This is not an exercise in make-believe (believing impossible things before breakfast, like the Red Queen in *Through the Looking-Glass*). It is an exercise in subjectively believing something to be true because it is objectively true. It is lining up our thinking with truth. God imputes our sin to Christ and his righteousness to us (4:1-8), and what God reckons is true, is *true*! In our spiritual status, we are now alive in Jesus; in our bodily reality, we will one day live with him, in the resurrection.

Notice again that there is no moral exhortation so far. We are not told to 'die to sin' or to 'crucify' ourselves. We are simply told to bring our thinking into line with God-given reality.

D. *The appeal of grace (vv. 12-14): do not let sin reign*
Only after detailed exposition of the truth does Paul move to moral exhortation (a warning to the preacher not to exhort until our hearers understand the basis of exhortation!).

¹²Therefore do not let sin reign in your mortal body so that you obey its evil desires.

¹³Do not offer the parts of your body [*your members*]
to sin,
as instruments of wickedness,
but rather offer yourselves to God,
as those who have been brought from death to life;
and offer the parts of your body [*your members*] to him
as instruments of righteousness.

¹⁴For sin shall not be your master, because you are not under law, but under grace.

The 'mortal body' is all of me as I am in this age, under the shadow of death, subject to weakness and decay. My 'members' (NIV 'the parts of your body') do not just mean my physical limbs; they include all my faculties: powers of reasoning and imagination, the ambition or desire of the eye, feet to take me to places of my choice, the hand as an expression of abilities, energies, influence over others, the heart with capacity to love, money as an extension of my power, 'all your heart, mind, soul and strength'. The picture is of soldiers presenting arms before a general, offering all the weapons they have as 'instruments' in his service.

The appeal is not that we must try to break free from sin, for such a moralistic appeal (so common in school assemblies) would be pointless; unconverted people 'under sin' cannot break free; this is just the point. If we could break free, we would have no need of a Saviour. Paul first tells us that the power of sin has been broken by the cross and then appeals to us to make joyful use of the freedom won for us by Christ. We offer ourselves 'as those who *have been brought* from death to life' (v. 13). It is because we are no longer 'under law' but 'under grace' that the decision to offer ourselves to God is possible (v. 14). We are to enter into a freedom that has been won for us.

The fact that the appeal is necessary reminds us that no Christian this side of the resurrection reaches a state of sinless perfection. Every day we need to hear the exhortation not to let sin reign, to offer all that we are to God for righteousness. We cannot say, 'I will never sin again'. But we can say, 'I need not sin now. At this moment I am free not to sin. Before my conversion, I made choices every day. But every choice I made was a choice about how to sin. I had the terrible freedom to choose to do wrong. Every choice I made had me at the centre. Now at last I am free to offer myself to God'.

The story is told of a great eagle tethered to a post, walking sadly round and round. One day a new owner announced he would release the bird. A crowd gathered, the rope was removed—and the eagle continued walking round and round in the same old rut. He was free to fly and yet did not. The sad absurdity of that scene is like the Christian who continues in sin.

E. *The objection restated (v. 15): isn't law necessary to safeguard morality?*

> [15]What then? Shall we sin because we are not under law but under grace? By no means!

Paul restates the objection of verse 1 in a slightly different form. Verse 14 says we are 'not under law' when we might have expected it to say 'not under sin'. Paul will return to law in chapter 7, but the objection restated says, 'Dear Paul, it seems to me that the law of God is necessary to safeguard morality in religion. If we are released from the authority of law, what is to stop our religion becoming a licence to sin?'

Paul develops his basic point that 'we died to sin' (v. 2) with three supplementary arguments.

Supplementary argument 1 (v. 16): you've got to serve either sin or God

¹⁶Don't you know that when you offer yourselves to someone to obey him as slaves,

> you are slaves to the one whom you obey—
>> whether you are slaves to sin, which leads to death,
>> or to obedience, which leads to righteousness?

There are two parts to this argument. The first one seems obvious: 'when you offer yourselves to someone to obey him as slaves, you are slaves to the one whom you obey'. My obedience is the litmus test of my slavery: I am a slave of the one whom I actually obey. I may call myself a slave of someone else (e.g. of Christ), but if I actually obey sin (an unchanged life) then it shows I am still the slave of sin. One path 'leads to death'; the other 'leads to righteousness' (that is, right living).

The second part is that there are only two possible slaveries open to me, 'whether … slaves to sin … or to obedience' (that is, the obedience of faith, 1:5; 16:26; c.f. 15:18). What I cannot be is slave to no-one, my own autonomous self. This is because sin is by nature the service of myself. The moment I decide to serve myself (and to be a slave of no-one), I sin and – by definition – become a slave to sin! Sin is everything other than the worship of God with heart, mind, soul, and strength. So there is no such thing as human autonomy. I cannot avoid some kind of slavery. There is no place of neutrality; to use an analogy from World War II, there is no spiritual Switzerland.

Supplementary argument 2 (vv. 17-19a): the message of grace has set you free to serve God

> [17]But thanks be to God that,
>> though you used to be slaves to sin,
>>> you wholeheartedly obeyed the form of teaching
>>> to which you were entrusted.
>
> [18]You have been set free from sin
>> and have become slaves to righteousness.
>>> [19]I put this in human terms because you
>>> are weak in your natural selves [*because of
>>> the weakness of your flesh*].

How is the transfer effected from slavery to sin into slavery to God? It happens when I am 'entrusted', placed into the charge of, a particular 'form of teaching' and submit to this teaching from the heart ('you wholeheartedly obeyed'). This 'form' (or pattern or shape) 'of teaching' is justification by grace through the one act of obedience of Jesus.

This teaching is not entrusted to the care of the Christian; rather, the Christian is entrusted into the care of this teaching. That is to say, he hears (and goes on hearing) the declaration of God about him in Christ, that he is justified not condemned, that he has died to sin in Christ, and that he is set free from slavery to sin. Just as in Cognitive Behavioural Therapy our behaviour is changed by first reshaping our thinking, so with the gospel of grace. We hear what God says about us, and receive it with a whole heart as true. This changes our behaviour.

When Paul uses the expression 'slaves to righteousness' he immediately qualifies it by saying, 'I put this in human terms' (i.e. I have used an inadequate metaphor) 'because of the weakness of your flesh' (to help you to grasp my main point). Speaking of two slaveries helps us understand the transfer, but they are very different slaveries. We are transferred from a cruel slavery to a gracious slavery, from a closed slavery to an open slavery, from a forced response to a free response, from a slavery that leads to death into a slavery that leads to life.

The appeal of grace renewed (v. 19b)

19bJust as you used to offer the parts of your body [*your members*]
> in slavery to impurity
>> and to ever-increasing wickedness,
>> [*and to lawlessness leading to lawlessness,*]
> so now offer them [*your members*]
>> in slavery to righteousness
>>> leading to holiness.

Paul renews the appeal of verses 12-14. He sets before us two masters ('impurity' and 'righteousness', shorthand for 'the God of righteousness'), and two roads. One is a vicious downward spiral ('lawlessness leading to lawlessness' c.f. 1:19-32), the other a growth in grace ('righteousness leading to holiness'). Paul's focus is not on the final destinations (see vv. 20-23), but on the processes unleashed by the two surrenders.

Paul's appeals (vv. 12-14, 19) are not really commands. He does not speak as one wielding a big stick ('Offer yourself in slavery to God or else!'), but with the voice of warm appeal based upon the reality of what God has done for us in Christ. These are not one-off appeals, as if we could respond with wholehearted obedience today and never need to do the same again because our Christian life has gone up to a new level (the higher spiritual life). The appeals need to be heeded again and again. We shall return to this in 12:1.

Supplementary argument 3 (vv. 20-23): only slavery to God leads to eternal life

[20]When you were slaves to sin,

you were free from the control of [*with regard to*] righteousness.

> [21]What benefit did you reap [*What fruit did you have*] at that time

> from the things you are now ashamed of?

>> Those things result in death!

[22]But now that you have been set free from sin and have become slaves to God,

> the benefit you reap [*the fruit you have*] leads to holiness,

>> and the result is eternal life.

[23]For the wages of sin is death,

but the gift [*grace gift*] of God is eternal life in Christ Jesus our Lord.

The focus here is 'fruit' (NIV 'benefit reaped') and 'wages'. Paul contrasts one slavery and its consequences (vv. 20, 21) with another slavery and its consequences.

Slavery to…	Freedom from…	Present experience	Future destiny
Sin	Righteousness	Shame	Death
God	Sin	Holiness	Eternal life

First, there *was* a kind of freedom under slavery to sin (v. 20): we were 'free with regard to righteousness'. Righteousness exercised no control over us. That freedom is enticing and we are tempted to return to it. But we are ashamed of those things, because we know in our hearts they 'result in death'. Death is the proper penalty for that slavery, and our sense of shame shows we know it. Even if we twist our consciences to persuade ourselves that these behaviours are alright, if they come into the open we will blush. Sin leads to both guilt and shame (and different cultures emphasize one more than the other).

It is very different with the freedom from sin and slavery to God (v. 22). Instead of shame in the present there is 'holiness'. And instead of death in the future there is 'eternal life'.

So, to sum up (v. 23):

1. 'the wages of sin is death'. Paul changes the metaphor from a harvest ('fruit') to the pay, probably of a soldier (the word is used of a soldier's pay in Luke 3:14 and 1 Cor. 9:7). General Sin never fails to pay his army. Every soldier is paid his wages, and those wages are death. This is what we deserve.
2. 'the grace gift of God is eternal life in Christ Jesus our Lord' (that is, in vital union with Christ Jesus). This is not what we have earned (as Paul says of Abraham, using a different word for 'wages', in 4:4). It comes only from union with Christ Jesus our Lord.

From text to teaching
Getting the message clear: the theme
The theme of the chapter is the objective doctrinal truth that Christians died with Christ to the slave-driving bullying power of sin. This is an indicative (a doctrine that is taught) rather than an imperative (a response that is commanded). This objective truth comes from our vital union with Christ by faith. It means that because he died to pay the penalty for sin, we too have died and our penalty has been paid in Christ. It means that because he was raised, we can now walk in newness of life knowing that one day we too will

be raised. The authority of sin has been broken because the penalty for sin has been paid. Having been enslaved to sin, now at last we are free to offer ourselves to God. Because we died with Christ, we are free in Christ. This is a glorious and life-changing truth.

Getting the purpose clear: the aim

Paul shows his immediate aim in the exhortations of verses 12-14 and verse 19. It is that freed people should exercise the freedom that has been won for them in Christ. We've been set free: so act free! His aim is to change behaviour through doctrinal understanding, that people who have been placed in the care of the doctrine of grace should respond by offering themselves to the God of grace. He wants us to offer ourselves afresh to God today! Our preaching ought to keep Paul's balance of the didactic and the hortatory.

Paul will come back to this appeal to 'offer' or 'present' ourselves to God in 12:1. He is not aiming just for a collection of individual responses; he wants men and women in the church in Rome to respond in this way as a church humbled under grace together.

Alongside this, Paul clearly aims to answer the objections voiced in verses 1 and 15, that a religion of grace doesn't actually work, doesn't change bad people, and that law is necessary to safeguard morality. He doesn't backpedal at all from his insistence on grace alone, but rather sets out to prove that of the two strategies available to religion (law and grace), only grace actually sets people free not to sin. Law shows them they ought not to sin, and makes their sin clearer than ever (5:13, 20), but it cannot set them free from slavery to sin. Only grace does that.

Pointers to application

+ Make sure we understand the force of the objection (vv. 1, 15), and that it results from the 'ticket in the pocket' misunderstanding of grace. This teaches 'Christ for us' without teaching 'us in Christ'. It teaches that when the declaration of justification is made, God as it were gives us an entrance ticket to the new creation and tells us to keep it safely in our pockets, or file it away, until we need to present it to St. Peter at the pearly gates. It is a piece of paper that does not affect us now, but will benefit us then. But, as Calvin put it, 'Those who imagine that God bestows free justification upon us without imparting newness of life, shamefully rend Christ asunder.' Christ died for us, and now lives in us by his Spirit.

+ Explain 'the law strategy' for changing people. This is the strategy, one way or another, of every religion, government and political philosophy. Its message is, 'Do bad things and you'll be punished; do good things and you'll be rewarded'. These incentives are the strategy of law. They lie behind everything except biblical religion.

+ Expose the inability of law to make bad people good. (Paul expands on this in ch. 7).

+ Help us feel the terrible slavery to sin and our utter inability to break free. Expose the shallowness of the idea that we are autonomous ('born free' as Rousseau put it), perhaps illustrating from the Existentialist philosophers (for whom our identity is defined by our autonomy, our making choices), or from Luther's debates with Erasmus (especially Luther's *The Bondage of the Will*).

- Expose sin's bluff, when it threatens us and cajoles us to go back into its ways, telling us we cannot escape, accusing us of our past failures, convincing us we must sin now. Hold imaginary conversations with 'sin, the jailor' and tell him our sentence has been paid and he has no hold over us.

- Help us to get status and feelings in their proper relation, to understand that our status changes instantaneously and our awareness of status follows. Paul calls us to live in the light of a change of status that has already happened.

- Expose the absurdity of the Christian continuing to live in sin. Those who have visited the Checkpoint Charlie museum by the old Berlin wall will have read of many who sought to escape from the slavery of East Berlin to the freedom of the West. But there is no example of anyone trying to climb the wall from West to East!

- Challenge us to take the definite step of offering ourselves to live in freedom for God—and then to take that step again tomorrow and the next day … (to make clear it is a definite step, but one which can never be taken too often). Avoid raising false hopes of achieving perfection, but don't blunt the challenge.

- Be specific about the facets and faculties of our humanness that we ought to offer day by day, our minds (so that we think and reason in the service of God), our feet (to take us to the places where we serve God), our eyes (so that our ambitions and desires are to serve God),

our hands (so that we use our ability to make a difference in the world, for the glory of God), our capacity to
love (giving ourselves in friendship to the unlovely), our
capacity for sexual love (so that if we marry we marry to
serve God), our money (used to serve God) ...

✦ Warn against the danger of beginning the Christian
life with grace and then living it by law. We can never
teach grace too often, because it is not natural. Our
default position will always be law, and only the regular
teaching and reminders of grace will guard us from this
danger.

Suggestions for preaching and teaching the text

A. *Two sermons from chapter 6*

There are two ways to divide the chapter in two. Perhaps the
more obvious is to take verses 1-14 and then verses 15-23,
each section starting with a statement of the objection
(the questions of vv. 1, 15). Alternatively, we might start
with the main doctrine of verses 1-11 and then move to
exhortation in verses 12-23. Neither division is really tidy,
because the chapter holds together as a unit and mixes
doctrine with exhortation. It is probably simpler to divide
it into verses 1-14 and verses 15-23.

Sermon 1: 6:1-14

We might lead in by the scandal of grace (as in my example
of Comrade Duch). We want people to feel the force of
the objection and not to dismiss it as absurd. Let us listen to the morally serious non-Christian who cannot see
how grace works, and the morally serious Christian who is

tempted to live under law because she wants to live a moral life (and her life is marked by ongoing guilt and a joyless sense of moral obligation).

Only when we feel the force of their objections will we feel the power of Paul's arguments of grace. It is worth exploring what a religion of law can and cannot do. It can restrain evil, and is needed for that (e.g. 13:1-7). But it cannot change the heart.

Our teaching points need to follow the structure and balance of doctrine followed by exhortation. Most of our time will need to be spent teaching the truth of verses 1-11.

1. All of us as Christians died to sin because we are united with Christ (vv. 1-11).
2. Now we are freed from sin's slavery, offer ourselves freely to God (vv. 12-14).

Sermon 2: 6:15-23
We might begin with a strong challenge to offer ourselves to God today, and to explain that this is the aim of the sermon. We want ourselves and our hearers to say at the end, 'Lord, here we are. All that we are, and all that we have, and all that we will be, we offer and present to you today. Take us as your willing slaves'.

Our teaching points might be as follows:

1. Offer yourselves as willing slaves to God, because it is the only alternative to slavery to sin (v. 16).
2. Offer yourselves as willing slaves to God, because he has set you free by the word of his grace (vv. 17-19a).
3. Offer yourselves as willing slaves to God in the pathway of holiness (v. 19b).

4. Offer yourselves as willing slaves to God because these slaves are given eternal life (vv. 20-23).

B. *One sermon on chapter 6*

If we have to preach Romans 6 in one sermon, we shall have to focus ruthlessly on the central points. We might have the following teaching points:

1. All Christians died to sin because we are united with Christ (vv. 1-11).
2. So we are set free to offer ourselves to God, and ought to do so (vv. 12-14, with 19).
3. We should choose this slavery because this slavery alone leads to life (vv. 15-23).

Leading a Bible study on 6:1-23

It is important for the leader to be able clearly to take the group through the doctrine, so that the group time can be more profitably used for helping one another realistically and practically to respond in offering all our faculties to God. Unless we respond like this, we have failed to achieve the aim of the passage.

To clarify understanding

1. Put the objections of verse 1 and verse 15 into your own words in as sympathetic a way as possible. How is the objector responding to what Paul has just said at the end of chapter 5?

2. Find all the places in verses 1-11 where Paul speaks of the Christian as being united with Christ in some way, so that what happened to him is reckoned to have happened to us. Are there examples in ordinary life where what happens to someone else is reckoned to have happened to us?

3. Paul speaks of 'sin' not just as something we do, but as a power over us. Find the places in the chapter where Paul speaks in this way.

4. What is the connection between sin and death (look back at 5:12, 16, 21)?

5. What two things does Jesus' resurrection mean for us, according to verses 4, 5, and 8?

6. What does it mean (and not mean) for the Christian to have 'died to sin'?

7. What does Paul mean by telling us to 'count yourselves dead to sin but alive to God in Christ Jesus' (v. 11)?

8. What response does Paul call for in verses 12-14? How is this different from telling people to do their best and turn over a new leaf?

9. What are the two slaveries on offer (e.g. v. 16)? Why do I have to be a slave to anybody? Why can't I just serve myself?

10. How were Christians transferred out of slavery to sin, according to verses 17, 18?

11. Where do the two slaveries lead (vv. 19-23)?

To encourage honest response

1. How do we experience the power of sin over us?

2. What 'members' (faculties, parts of our humanness) can and ought we to offer to God, and how practically can we do this, both as individuals and as a church?

3. How does this chapter show us that we are free to offer ourselves to God, and what incentives does it give us actually to offer ourselves, again and again? How can we encourage one another with these truths and incentives?

14
LIVING UNDER GRACE
ROMANS 7

Is your home a mess? Is your life a mess? Some years ago there was a TV series called 'Life Laundry'. It was pop-psychology about how to make both your home and your life more ordered. The best-selling book was called How to de-junk your life. My attention was caught when my wife borrowed the sequel, How to de-junk your life forever. I thought that sounded a wonderful idea. I had thought it was going to be a week by week struggle. But maybe there was some secret of the higher tidy life, some step of de-junking which would end the struggle forever?

In a similar way any serious Christian longs to 'de-sin' their life. We know how destructive sin is and long to be free of it. Sin spoils lives, spreads to other lives, and separates people from one another and from God. We long to be rid of it, but it seems such a struggle. Perhaps there is some secret, some way to 'de-sin your life forever'? Christian history has been full of people who have claimed this secret to reach the Higher Life, a Second Blessing, the Baptism of the Holy

Spirit, or whatever it may be. A leader of something called the 'Victorious Life Movement' claimed, 'It is the privilege of every Christian to live every day of his life without breaking the laws of God either in thought, word or deed.' It would be wonderful if this were true. But is it?

Attentive listening to the text
Context and structure

Romans 7 is closely tied to Romans 6. Romans 6 is mainly about the tyranny of sin. But in 6:14, 15 there is—rather to our surprise—a reference to not being 'under *law*'. In 6:19 sin is described as 'lawlessness'. Romans 7 deals with some very similar issues to Romans 6, but shifts the focus from the tyranny of sin to the powerlessness of law. So in 6:2, 'We died to sin' and in 7:4 we 'died to the law'. In 6:21, 22 we considered the 'harvests' (lit. 'fruit') of living under sin or with Christ, and in 7:4, 5 we again consider the possibility of 'bearing fruit' for God.

The central theme of chapter 7 is the law. The words 'law' or 'commandment' appear 29 times in 25 verses. In addition the law is called 'the written code' (v. 6) and 'the good thing' or 'that which is good' in several verses (e.g. v13).

Chapter 7 divides naturally into three parts:

1. (vv. 1-6) The Christian has died to the law so as to be set free for a new and fruitful relationship with Christ.
2. (vv. 7-12/13) A first-person story in the past tense (e.g. 'I died ... I found ... sin produced ...).
3. (vv. 13/14-25) A first-person story in the present tense (e.g. 'I am ... I do ... I agree ... I know ...').

(V. 13 may be taken either with vv. 7-12 or with vv. 14-25.)

Working through the text

A. The believer is set free from the law so as to be united with Christ by the Spirit (vv. 1-6)

Paul states a principle in verse 1, illustrates it in verses 2 and 3, applies it to believers in verse 4, and then teaches the need for this application in verse 5 and the consequences in verse 6.

1. *The principle (v. 1): the law rules a person only while they live*

> ¹Do you not know, brothers—for I am speaking to men [*those*] who know the law—that the law has authority over a man [*has mastery over a person*] only as long as he lives?

The principle is that the Law of Moses ceases to bind a person when they die. The verb 'has mastery over' (NIV 'has authority over') echoes the same verb in 6:9, 14 where it is used of the mastery or dominion of sin and death.

2. *The illustration (vv. 2, 3): death breaks one relationship and enables the start of another*

> ²For example,
>> by law a married woman is bound to her husband
>>> as long as he is alive,
>>> but if her husband dies,
>> she is released from the law of marriage
>> [*the law of the husband*].
>
> ³So then, if she marries [*is joined to*] another man
>> while her husband is still alive,
> she is called an adulteress.
>> But if her husband dies,
> she is released from that law

and is not an adulteress, even though she marries [*is joined to*] another man.

Paul takes one part of the Law of Moses, the seventh commandment. His point is simple: death ends the obligation of the woman to her husband (lit. 'the law of the husband', i.e. the law as it governs her marriage relationship) and frees her to enter another marriage relationship. One relationship is terminated that another may begin.

(It is doubtful if this illustration settles the difficult questions of remarriage after divorce. Paul states a well-known general truth to illustrate a doctrinal point. Other texts help us more clearly with remarriage after divorce.)

3. *The application of the principle to the believer (v. 4): now we are no longer 'married' to the law, we can be 'married' to Christ*

> ⁴So, my brothers, you also died [*have been put to death*] to the law
>> through the body of Christ,
>>> that you might belong to [*be joined to*] another,
>>>> to him who was raised from the dead,
>>>>> in order that we might bear fruit to God.

Notice that the same verb 'joined to' is used in verse 4 (NIV 'belong to') and verse 3 (NIV 'married to').

Verse 4 teaches four truths:

1. Christians 'have been put to death to the law' (the passive shows that God has done it; we could not do it for ourselves). In a narrow sense this meant that the Jewish believer was released from the obligation to keep the Law of Moses, including food laws, male circumcision, the Passover and other festivals. But in a deeper sense

it means that all believers have been released both from the law's authority to condemn us (the curse of the law, as in Gal. 3:13) and from the powerlessness of the law to change us (8:3 'what the law was powerless to do …').

2. God did this 'through the body of Christ', which means his death as a propitiation for us on the cross (3:21-26). (The idea that 'the body of Christ' here means the church is alien to the context and should be rejected).

3. The reason God did this was 'that you might be joined to another, to him who was raised from the dead'. There is a slight complication between the illustration (vv. 2, 3) and the reality (v. 4). In Paul's illustration the husband dies and the wife (who is still alive) remarries. In the reality which Paul is illustrating, the believer is like a wife who dies and then, as a resurrected wife, marries a resurrected husband.

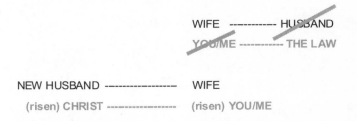

The key point is that death ends the first relationship and makes possible the second.

Because this new husband has been raised from the dead, this new marriage will last forever. There is no 'till death us do part' in the marriage of the church to Christ.

4. God's goal was 'in order that you might bear fruit for God', a contrast to the shameful 'fruit' of the first marriage (6:21; 7:5).

It is worth asking what all this meant for the many believers before Christ (such as Abraham in chapter 4, and all spoken about in the Psalms quoted in 3:9-20, as well as the believers blessed by David in 4:6-8). In one sense they were under the dominion of the Law of Moses. That is to say, they had to live under that system, to take part in the sacrifices at the Temple, and so on. And yet in a deeper sense, as they trusted the promises of God (following in Abraham's footsteps), they too knew in anticipation the blessings that would become clearly available after Christ. And they too bore fruit for God in changed lives. To these believers before Christ the law became a delight, and they could even speak of it being written on their hearts (e.g. Ps. 37:31). The tragedy was that most of the Jews experienced the law simply as bringing condemnation, because they separated it from the Christ to whom it bore witness.

4. The need for this new relationship (v. 5)

> [5]For when we were controlled by the sinful nature [*when we were still in the flesh*],
>
>> the sinful passions aroused by the law [*through the law*]
>>> were at work in our bodies [*members*],
>>>> so that we bore fruit for death.

The death, resurrection, and new marriage of verse 4 is vitally necessary when we consider what the first marriage was like (v. 6). When we were 'in the flesh' (i.e. before our death and resurrection with Christ, while we were in the old realm controlled by sin), 'sinful passions ... were at work in our members' (all the faculties of our humanness, as in 6:13, 19). These overwhelming appetites, with self at the centre, meant that the harvest of our lives was one of death. Everything we thought, said and did spoke of a world under the curse, a divided world, a world that ought to be justly governed by human beings but is in fact oppressed by them.

The shock is that these sinful passions were 'through the law'; the law was the agent through whom these sinful passions were stirred up in us (NIV 'aroused by the law' gets the meaning well). Our old husband just made us behave worse! To bear a better fruit we had to marry a better husband.

5. The consequences of this new relationship (v. 6)

> ⁶But now, by dying to what once bound us,
>> we have been released from the law
>>> so that we serve in the new way of the Spirit
>>> [*newness of Spirit*],
>>> and not in the old way of the written code
>>> [*oldness of letter*].

What a relief to be released from marriage to the first husband! To make this possible, God had to kill us with Christ, raise us from the dead, and release us from our bondage to the law. We used to 'serve' (that is, serve God) 'in oldness of letter', in which the law stood outside us as a dead letter, as it were coming down to us from the top of Mt. Sinai, speaking words that condemned. But now we serve God 'in newness of Spirit', in which the Spirit has written the letter in our hearts. This is what happens when we are joined to our resurrected husband by union with Christ.

So what is life going to be like now, in 'newness of Spirit'? And what about the law? After all, Paul has said so many negative things about the law, that we must wonder whether he is rejecting it altogether. Paul now turns to this question.

B.   *When law outside meets sin inside: utterly sinful sin exploits the good law, and the good law exposes utterly sinful sin (vv. 7-13)*

The main point: the law is good.

Paul has said some very negative things about the Law of Moses:

+   Law shows us sin, but cannot save (3:20).
+   Law makes us even more guilty than we were before, because it shows us the boundary which we deliberately cross (4:15).
+   Before the law came, there were many sinners but only one trespasser (Adam). When law came, a whole lot of sinners became trespassers as well (5:20).
+   The best thing that can happen to us is to be released from the law: (6:14).
+   Law actually stirs us up to sin more (7:5).

We may imagine an objector writing,

> 'Dear Paul, you seem to think the Law of Moses is a very bad thing. But I thought it was given by God to Moses. Since when has God changed his mind and decided it is bad when he originally told us it was good?'

If this objection were sustained, it would be very serious, for it would mean that Paul's doctrine of grace was immoral, so much so that it made a good thing into an evil. Although there are puzzles, the central point of verses 7-13 is crystal clear at the start (v. 7a) and the end (vv. 12, 13): God's law is not a bad thing but a good thing.

In between (vv. 7b-11) Paul tells a story in the first person singular ('I') and mostly past tenses. We will look first at the point of the story, and then ask who is the 'I' who is telling it. The purpose of the story is to explore the relationship between law and sin, to prove that, although sin is bad, law is good.

1. The law exposes sin (v. 7b)

> ^{7b}Indeed I would not have known what sin was
>   except through the law.
> For I would not have known what coveting really was
>   if the law had not said, 'Do not covet.' (the tenth
>   commandment,   Exod. 20:17).

Paul begins by developing what he had trailed in 3:20b. There was sin in the world even without law (5:13) and men and women without the law are still 'without excuse' (1:20). But the law exposes sin, shines the light of God's truth on sin, unmasks sin, strips off the deceptive veneer and shows it up for the ugly rebellion that it is. When I do something selfish, it is selfish even if no-one has told me not to be selfish. But when God tells me it's wrong to be selfish and I go ahead and am selfish, my selfishness is clearly seen to be wrong. Paul takes covetousness as his example, probably because covetousness is the root of sin. As James says, 'after desire (lit. covetousness) has conceived, it gives birth to sin' (James 1:15).

2. Sin exploits law (vv. 8-11)

> ⁸But sin, seizing the opportunity afforded by the commandment,
>   produced in me every kind of covetous desire.
> For apart from law, sin is dead.
>
> ⁹Once I was alive apart from law;
>   but when the commandment came,

> sin sprang to life
> and I died.

[10]I found that

> the very commandment that was intended to bring
> life [*that was into life*]
> actually brought death [*the same, into death*].

[11]For sin, seizing the opportunity afforded by the
commandment,

> deceived me,

> > and through the commandment put me to death.

Verses 8-11 are bracketed by the verb 'seize the opportunity',
which means that sin uses the law as its base of military
operations. The good law gets kidnapped and used for bad
purposes. Verse 8 states the principle, verse 9 tells a story to
illustrate the principle, verse 10 gives Paul's conclusion, and
verse 11 restates the principle.

The principle (v. 8) is that sin seizes the opportunity
provided by the commandment of God. The law is called
'the commandment' (singular) because it is essentially uni-
tary: it commands one thing, wholehearted loyalty to God
(c.f. Deut. 6:4, 5). All the detail was practical expression of
that one command. Such is the perversity of the human
heart ruled by sin, that the command to love God immediately stirs up in us rebellion. When the commandment
comes from outside, to a stubborn heart, it makes rebellion
spring into life. 'For apart from law, sin is dead', that is to say,
dormant. An occupied territory might be sullenly hostile;
but when the occupying power send their tax-collectors
round with the command to pay taxes, then passive hostility springs into life as active rebellion. When the command
of God comes, announcing that we should worship and love

him, then the human heart is seen in its true colours and is stirred up to active rebellion.

Verse 9 is like a line drawing or cartoon, telling a story with a few brushstrokes. A man sits in a room tied to a sleeping monster called 'sin'. He is, in a precarious sense, 'alive' while the monster dozes. But then 'the commandment' enters the room and says in a loud voice to the man that he must kill the monster 'sin'. What happens? Surprise, surprise, the monster wakes and doesn't want to be killed! If it's your life or mine, says the monster, that's an easy choice. And so the man dies, killed by his own monster, awakened by the law.

Verse 10 draws the moral from the story. To his surprise, the man finds that 'the commandment that was into life actually brought death'. That is, the law the man thought could bring him life (as he did 'works of the law'), proved to have exactly the opposite effect. The NIV paraphrase, 'the commandment that was *intended* to bring life', may give the wrong impression that the Law of Moses was ever intended *by God* to give people life by their own efforts; it never was, but always pointed to the need for a Saviour. But many thought it was the way to life, as we shall see in 9:31, 32 and 10:3. The man thought the authoritative voice telling him to kill the monster 'sin' could actually kill it and enable him to live free from sin. Instead, it just served to wake up the monster who showed him who was boss. It needs more than the voice of the law to set a person free from slavery to sin.

Verse 11 reiterates the point of verse 8, adding the element of deception ('sin ... deceived me').

Conclusion (vv. 12, 13)

> [12]So then, the law is holy, and the commandment is holy, righteous and good.

¹³Did that which is good, then, become death to me? By
no means!
But in order that sin might be recognized as sin,
it produced death in me through what was good,
so that through the commandment sin might become
utterly sinful.

Verse 12 is the positive conclusion: 'the law is holy' or, to
put it another way, 'the commandment' (which sums up the
law) 'is holy, righteous and good.' The law is not sin. The
question of verse 7a has been answered.

Verse 13 comes back to the role of law in exposing sin.
It is not the voice of the law that kills; it is the monster
'sin' that kills. But sin uses the law 'in order that sin might
be recognized as sin' and so 'become' (i.e. be clearly seen to
be) 'utterly sinful'. The sinfulness of sin is supremely seen in
its ability to take something as purely good as the law and
make it the base of operations that kill.

We may sum up Paul's two points about how the good
law is related to evil sin, in a diagram.

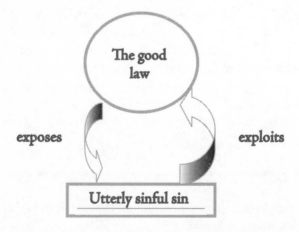

Who is telling the story?

Much ink has been spilled trying to answer this. We will build up a composite answer in stages.

1. Our natural assumption is that 'I' is Paul. After all, he is writing the letter! The puzzle is how he can say, 'Once I was alive' (v. 9). In what sense could Paul have ever been 'alive', indeed ever have been 'apart from law' (e.g. Phil. 3:5). He had no period of childhood innocence! No, if it is Paul's story, there must be a degree of flexibility in the story-telling.

2. The only human beings who could precisely say they 'were alive ... apart from law' would be Adam and Eve. They were very much 'alive' as they walked with God in the garden, until the commandment came to them (Gen. 2:16, 17), and then sin (in the form of the serpent) sprang to life (we might picture a slumbering serpent up until then), 'deceived' them, and they died, expelled from the garden. Indeed, Paul's use of the tenth commandment fits well, for Eve coveted the fruit (Gen. 3:6) before she took it. The story certainly reminds us of Adam and Eve. However, the puzzle now is that 'the law' in this passage refers most naturally to the Law of Moses, which was given not to Adam and Eve, but to Israel, and not until many years later.

3. So perhaps 'I' is Israel? Paul has given us a vital clue to the connection between Adam and Israel, in 5:12-14. When Adam 'broke the command' he did what Israel would later do. So the story of Adam anticipates the story of Israel. When the commandment came to Adam, sin sprang to life and he died. When the law came to Israel, their stubborn hearts were more clearly seen, and they came under the curse. The stories are essentially the same.

4. This brings us back to reading it as Paul's own story. This is the way we most naturally read it. If Paul was pretending to tell someone else's story, it was rather a cryptic way of doing it! Because it is Israel's story, and Israel's story is essentially Adam's story, this is the story of Everyman, including Paul. Paul tells his story in a way that reminds us of Adam's story and Israel's story, to make the point that whenever and wherever God's perfect standards come into contact with sinful human beings, two things happen: God's commandment exposes sin as utterly sinful, and sin proves its utter sinfulness by exploiting the good law to stir us up to sin more. This is true for the Jew, for whom the commandment comes as the Law of Moses; but it is equally true when any human being knows right and wrong and chooses wrong (as in 1:18-32). In whatever way God's standards come to us, their coming to us does not in itself do us any good.

C. When law inside meets sin inside: when the Spirit writes the law on our hearts, a desperate struggle begins in a believer, which will not end until the resurrection (vv. 14-25)

Because law is powerless to change us, we desperately and urgently need the grace of God working in us by the Spirit day by day—and even then it's a wretched struggle! (vv. 14-25). Verses 14-25 defy simple interpretation. Hardly any two commentators agree about precisely how to read these paradoxical verses. The problem is that Paul says strongly negative things and emphatically positive things in the same breath.

On the negative side, he says:
+   he is 'fleshly, sold under sin' (v. 14);
+   that he doesn't do the good things he wishes he did (vv. 15-20);

+ that 'the good thing' (i.e. the law, v. 12) 'does not live in' him, that is, in his flesh (v. 18);
+ that 'sin' lives 'in' him (vv. 17, 20);
+ that 'evil is right there with' him (v. 21);
+ that he is 'a prisoner of the law of sin at work within (his) members' (v. 23);
+ that he is 'a wretched man' (v. 24).

And yet in the same passage he says:
+ that he really does want to do what God wants (vv. 15, 16, 18, 19, 20, 21);
+ indeed that, 'in (his) inner being (he delights) in God's law' (v. 22);
+ that he expresses heartfelt thanks through, 'Jesus Christ *our* Lord' (v. 25);
+ and that, he himself in his mind is 'a slave to God's law' (v. 25).

So the question is, who is speaking? Is this:
1. Paul the Christian?
2. Paul speaking dramatically on behalf of the unconverted person?
3. Paul speaking dramatically on behalf of some kind of half-converted person, perhaps the Christian still relying on the law to make him good, or the Christian needing to move into the higher life of the Spirit in Romans 8?

Four factors persuade me that this is Paul the Christian portraying for us one aspect of the normal Christian life (although we need Romans 8 to complete the picture).

1. The natural flow of the chapter. Paul shifts from his story in the past (vv. 7-13) into his present tense story of Christian experience. Just as his past tense (unconverted)

story is the story of every human being, so his present tense (converted) story is the story of every Christian. It is hard to avoid the impression that other ways of reading this make the passage a bit cryptic.

2. His heart desire to do God's will, which is a mark of the Spirit of God. It is true that all human beings sometimes want to do good things and fail (c.f. Ovid, 'I see and approve better things, but I pursue the worse'). But Paul speaks of wanting to do the will of God at a deeper level than this, indeed with his 'inner being' (v. 22, an expression used elsewhere only in 2 Cor. 4:16 and Eph. 3:16, in both cases of the Christian believer), (c.f. the similar expression 'new man' in Col. 3:10). The unbeliever does not have this heart desire (e.g. 3:11, 18). Some argue from Paul's silence about the Spirit between 7:6 ('newness of Spirit') and chapter 8 (the great chapter of the Spirit), that 7:7-25 portrays some spiritually subnormal life. I think this is mistaken; although the Spirit is not named in verses 7-25, he is present every time a heart desire to do God's will is mentioned (and supremely in v. 22).

3. The distinction he makes between himself and his 'flesh'. He distances himself from his negative actions. His delight in God's will comes from his 'inner being' (it expresses who he truly is); but of his wrong actions he says, '…it is no longer I myself who do it, but it is sin living in me' (vv. 17, 20). He does not say that 'the good thing' (the law) does not live in him, but that it does not live 'in my flesh' (v. 18). So it looks as though the 'I' of verse 14, who is 'unspiritual, sold as a slave under sin' is his 'flesh', rather than the totality of who he now is.

4. The order of words in verse 25, and the flow into chapter 8. The argument that Paul speaks as an unbeliever or some kind of half-converted believer usually rests

partly on the movement from Romans 7 to Romans 8. In 7:24, 25a he laments his wretched state, calls out for a rescuer, and then gives thanks that 'through Jesus Christ our Lord' God will rescue him. If he is moving from an unspiritual or semi-spiritual life, we might expect him now to rise into the sunlit uplands of Romans 8. He doesn't. In 7:25b he simply summarizes the struggle he has been describing all alone. What is more, the spiritual weather in Romans 8 is not as sunny as we might hope, for it includes a deep groaning and longing for 'the redemption of our bodies' (8:23).

We will read these verses therefore as a present tense description of the normal Christian life, portrayed as a life in urgent day by day need of the grace of God.

> [14]We know that the law is spiritual;
> but I am unspiritual, sold as a slave to sin [*fleshly, sold under sin*].

The problem is that the 'spiritual' law, which is so good (v. 12) has only partially invaded the converted person. There is still a 'fleshly' part of me, which will remain until resurrection morning.

> [15]I do not understand what I do.
>> For what I want to do I do not do,
>> but what I hate I do.
> [16]And if I do what I do not want to do,
>> I agree that the law is good.

'I do not understand what I do', that is, I cannot make head or tail of the bundle of moral contradictions that I seem to be. My heart desire and my actions so often just don't line up. But 'I agree that the law is good', that is, I accept the conclusion of verse 12. I know that the problem is not a bad law, but a sinful me.

¹⁷As it is, it is no longer I myself who do it, but it is sin living in me.

> ¹⁸I know that nothing good lives in me
> [*I know that the good thing does not live in me*],
>   that is, in my sinful nature [*my flesh*].
> For I have the desire to do what is good,
> but I cannot carry it out.
> ¹⁹For what I do is not the good I want to do;
> no, the evil I do not want to do—this I keep on doing.
> ²⁰Now if I do what I do not want to do,
> it is no longer I who do it, but it is sin living in me that does it.

> ²¹So I find this law at work: When I want to do good, evil is right there with me.

Verses 17-20 are bracketed by, '… it is no longer I who do it, but it is sin living in me'. It used to be me as a whole who did evil. No longer. Now it is me wanting to go God's way, but struggling against indwelling sin. God has invaded but not completed his conquest of me. 'The good thing' (i.e. the law, v. 12) has not taken over my flesh (v. 18). And so (v. 21) in the parliament of my life, whenever I am planning to do good, 'evil is right there'. There is no nature reserve within the human person (even the converted person) that is untouched by indwelling sin.

> ²²For in my inner being I delight in God's law;
> ²³but I see another law at work in the members of my body,
>   waging war against the law of my mind
>   and making me a prisoner of the law of sin at work within my members.

I struggle between two laws. God's law has been written on my heart, so that at the very deepest level of my being I really do 'delight in God's law'. But 'the law of sin' is still at work and there is a war being waged within me. I feel like a prisoner who has been set free and has crossed into friendly territory, but the enemy troops keep coming over the border and kidnapping me back into my old prison.

> 24What a wretched man I am! Who will rescue me from this body of death?
> 25Thanks be to God—through Jesus Christ our Lord!

> So then,
>   I myself in my mind am a slave to God's law,
>   but in the sinful nature [*the flesh*] a slave to the law
>   of sin.

It feels a 'wretched' struggle. I cry desperately for a rescuer, longing for 'the redemption of my body' (8:23) on resurrection morning. And thank God that 'through Jesus Christ our Lord' that morning will come! In the meantime the struggle is summed up by verse 25b:

1.   '…in my mind' (that is, here, not just my cognitive faculties, but my inner being) I am a willing 'slave to God's law' (having offered myself to him, as in 6:12-14, 19).

2.   '…in the *flesh*' I remain 'a slave to the law of sin.'

It is important to read on into chapter 8, where Paul says that 'what the law was powerless to do in that it was weakened by the flesh, God did …'. One of the things chapter 7 does for us is to press home forcibly the fact that the law alone cannot do us any good. The law outside ('oldness of letter' 7:6) can neither forgive nor empower to resist sin.

But I doubt if chapter 8 is the remedy for the struggle of chapter 7. Chapter 7 shows that even walking 'in

newness of Spirit' (7:6), with a heart delight in God's law
(7:22), it is still going to be a painful struggle (7:24) until resurrection morning (7:25a). The struggle is a sign of
spiritual life. Before I was converted, my pathetic attempts
to turn over a new leaf cost little, and lasted less. As the
Spirit gives me strength to struggle, it hurts much more.
Two spies are captured: the one who resists torture suf-
fers far more than the one who tells all at the first turn
of the screw. When a child begins to walk, the wonder is
not that they sometimes fall, but that they have begun to
take their first steps. The parents don't say, 'Oh look! She's
fallen over. Come and see.' They say, 'Come quickly. She's
walking!' The wonder is not that we fail, but that we mind
about failing and get up to walk again.

We may picture the relationships between sin, law, the
Spirit and a human being by three diagrams.

A. *The unbeliever is characterised by REBELLION against
    God's law (7:7-13).*

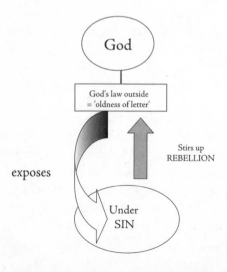

B. *The invasion begins: the believer is characterised by STRUGGLE between desire to do God's law and indwelling sin resisting this desire (7:14-25).*

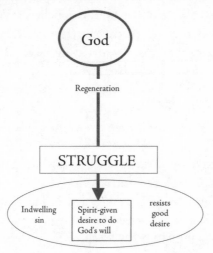

C. *The invasion is complete: at the RESURRECTION sin surrenders and the struggle ends (7:25a).*

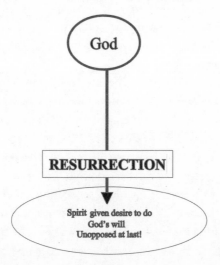

From text to teaching

Getting the message clear: the theme

To be set free from slavery to sin we must also be set free from the negative effects of law on the unbeliever. We need to be released from that destructive marriage by dying with Christ, to be raised to marry our resurrected husband (7:1-6). This is vitally necessary, because law outside the human heart and sin within the human heart make an explosive mixture. Law exposes sin, but sin exploits the clarity of law to stir up the human heart to sin even more blatantly (7:7-13). Without the presence of the Spirit writing the law on the human heart, the effect of law is entirely negative. And even with the Spirit, in the normal Christian life, it is a terrible struggle. But that struggle is a sign of life, and a pointer to resurrection morning when the struggle will end.

We might sum up the chapter by saying its burden is to press home to us the inescapable need for the grace of God by the Spirit writing the law in the heart. We need this grace day by day, and even then it will be a struggle.

Getting the purpose clear: the aim

Don't rely even 1 per cent on the law to change you: cry daily for the gracious work of the indwelling Spirit of God. Paul writes to those who 'know the law' (v. 1); it may be he has the Jewish believer especially in his sights, the one who will especially be tempted to see the law as a supplement to the grace of God in Christ. He wants to make sure this person grasps that it was never the purpose of the law to make bad people good; only the gospel can ever do that. He wants us not to be surprised at the struggle, and to see it as a sign of life, so that we do not get discouraged by the presence of indwelling sin, but rather long more deeply for the work of the Spirit day by day, and above all for the resurrection morning.

A church that does not understand this will not persevere in living under grace, in harmony. They will revert to a divisive reliance on human initiative and merit, letting some kind of external laws supplement the perceived insufficiency of the grace of God.

Pointers to application

+ Use the imagery of our being 'married' (joined to) the law to show what a miserable marriage moralism makes, however good the morals. Explore the cycles of sin, guilt, condemnation, more sin, more guilt, more condemnation etc. Look at the 'fruit' of that marriage.

+ With specific examples (e.g. from the Ten Commandments) show how the law of God exposes and shines a searchlight on our sin, showing it up clearly for the horrible thing it is.

+ Again with specific examples, show how the presence of clear law teaching stirs us up to more sin. (How much more tempting it is to take a look inside a letter labelled 'private and confidential' than any old letter!)

+ Encourage realistic expectations of the normal Christian life, both as individuals in our struggles with sin, and as churches struggling with sin in the way we relate to one another. Show us we need not be discouraged by these struggles, which will generally be fiercer now we are converted. Indeed, the fiercer struggle may well be a sign of spiritual life.

+ If there are perfectionist or 'higher life' teachings around, correct them using this chapter.

+ Look at heart delight in the law of God, how the Spirit of God enables us deeply to delight in the sheer beauty and goodness of God's way of living.

+ Expose the inability of the law to make us good, and guard us against thinking we need a dose of law to change us and help us on in our Christian lives. Demonstrate the proper uses of the law to show us how we ought to live to please God and to convict us of our failure to live as we ought, but not to be an instrument to make us good.

+ Show that while the whole human person has been invaded by the Spirit of God, no single part or facet has been fully subdued, this side of the resurrection. We must be realistic about this and never think we have ever won the battle in any area. The enemy can attack any facet of our personhood at any time. Be specific, and warn, for example; the respectable and happily married business traveller against sexual temptations (internet porn, prostitutes, an affair with a work colleague); the generous donor against becoming complacent and thinking he or she has their giving 'sewn up'; the hard-working person approaching retirement and not suspecting that laziness may be lurking around the corner; the prayer warrior beginning to feel they have their prayer life under control; or the melancholy believer prone to self-pity thinking she has got over that and has it under control. Sin within us is like one of those trick birthday candles that keeps reigniting when we think we've blown it out.

+ Perhaps the deepest application is that we ought to end this chapter crying deeply and daily for the ongoing ministry of the Spirit of God in our hearts. A heart-cry for grace is the proper response to the weakness of law.

Suggestions for preaching and teaching the text

A. *One sermon on chapter 7*

We might lead in by our longings for short-cuts to sanctification, for some kind of higher life, to see that it is natural and right to have these longings, but important to have a realistic understanding of what life under grace will feel like in practice.

Our teaching points might be as follows:

1. The believer is set free from the law so as to be united with Christ by the Spirit (vv. 1-6).

2. When law outside meets sin inside: utterly sinful sin exploits the good law, and the good law exposes utterly sinful sin (vv. 7-13).

3. When law inside meets sin inside: when the Spirit writes the law on our hearts, a desperate struggle begins in a believer, which will not end until the resurrection (vv. 14-25).

B. *Three sermons on Romans 7*

We could expand each of these three teaching points into a sermon.

Sermon 1. When is it right to end a marriage? (vv. 1-6)
This provocative title uses the imagery of the passage.

1. We begin by portraying that a marriage of a human being with an unchanged heart to the law is very destructive.

2. We then teach how that marriage is ended by God, by the drastic step of killing us in Christ, and raising us so that we may marry a resurrected husband for ever.

3. Finally, we look at the good fruit of that new marriage.

Sermon 2. When law outside meets sin inside (vv. 7-13)
We explore more fully the dynamics of our 'marriage' to the law when we are unconverted.

1.   Law exposes sin. We teach the distinction between sin and transgression and show how the preaching of the law shines God's searchlight on human sin.
2.   Sin exploits law. We show how, paradoxically, the good commandment to love God stirs up human rebellion.

Sermon 3. When law inside meets sin inside (vv. 14-25)
1.   The believer wants to go God's way from the heart.
2.   The believer still has indwelling sin which resists this desire fiercely.
3.   The struggle is a sign of life and points to resurrection morning.

Leading a Bible study
To clarify understanding
1.   What illustration does Paul use in verses 1-3? What is the main point of the illustration?
2.   How is it different in verse 4?
3.   How did our law 'husband' affect us? So why was it necessary that this marriage be ended (v. 5)?
4.   How is our new 'marriage' different (v. 6)?
5.   What is the main point Paul is making in verses 7-13 (see vv. 7, 12, 13)?
6.   How does he picture himself, sin and law in the story he tells about his non-Christian past in verses 7b-11? How does this help us understand the effect of law on an unbeliever?
7.   What two things happen when the law comes into contact with an unbeliever, someone 'under sin' (vv. 7-13)?

8. In verses 14-25 he moves from the past tense into the present. What positive things does he say about himself as a Christian?
9. What negative things does he say?
10. How can these both be true at the same time?
11. What is he looking forward to in verse 25a (see 5:9, 10; 8:23; 13:11)?

To encourage honest response
1. Think of examples in our experience of how the law of God exposes sin in our lives.
2. How does the law stir us up to sin more?
3. What does it feel like to be a Christian with the heart desire to do the will of God? Compare our experiences before and after we became Christians.
4. Have we ever been discouraged by sin and failure in our lives? How does this chapter encourage us to respond?
5. Have we ever felt that we need both grace and a few external rules to help us live the Christian life? How does this chapter help?

15

LIVING UNDER GRACE
ROMANS 8

How safe do you feel living under grace? How sure of the future? To entrust ourselves to the free grace of God in Jesus can feel like falling backwards into the arms of a friend who may or may not be there, and may or may not catch us even if he is. Is it safe to entrust ourselves entirely to the God of grace? We feel this acutely when two things happen: when we fail and fall in the struggle with sin from within, and when we are afflicted by suffering from without. Both of these experiences threaten our confidence that grace works. Just as the person falling backwards is tempted to move a foot back to save themselves, so we are tempted to add a proportion of self-reliance to our Christian lives.

Attentive listening to the text

Context and structure

Romans 8 and Romans 5

Romans 8 concludes the second main section of the body of the letter, 'Living under grace'. We have seen that chapters 5–8 have a kind of sandwich structure.

5:1-11   Suffering with assurance of future glory

    5:12-21   The basis for assurance in the work of Christ

        6:1-23   The broken slavery of sin

        7:1-25   The weakness of the law

    8:1-17   The basis for assurance in the ministry of the Spirit

8:18-39   Suffering with assurance of future glory

So in reading chapter 8, we will notice a number of themes picked up again from chapter 5.

Romans 8 and Romans 7

It is important also to read chapter 8 as following closely on chapter 7. But we need to decide how the two chapters work together. Broadly speaking, we may divide approaches to this as follows, the difference being in how we read 7:14-25.

1. 7:1-6 introduces 'newness of Spirit'. Our 'marriage' to law has been ended and now we are 'married' to Christ by the Spirit.

2. 7:7-12 takes a step back (signalled by the past tenses) to how law and sin interacted in Paul's (and everyman's) life as an unbeliever. Law exposes sin, but sin exploits law to stir us up to more blatant sin. Law cannot and does not rescue us from slavery to sin.

3. 7:14-25 is either:
   a) a present tense description of the struggle with sin that characterises life in the Spirit, and this life in the Spirit continues with Romans 8; or
   b) a continuation from 7:7-13 of the life of the unbeliever (or the half-converted believer) whose struggle against sin is unavailing and whose hopes that the law will help are disappointed.

4. 8:1-39 describes (or continues to describe) life in the Spirit.

The two approaches may be represented in these diagrams.

Approach 1.

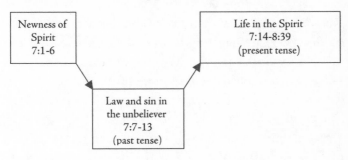

Approach 2.

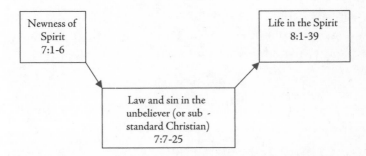

I have suggested (introduction to Rom. 7:14-25) that it is more natural to adopt approach (1). The reason it is a struggle to live under grace is that the Christian is a part-rescued person. We have been justified and reconciled to God, but we are not yet saved (5:9, 10; c.f. 13:11). We live in 'newness of Spirit' with a delight in God's law in the innermost depths of our being (7:22) and yet God's invasion of us is not complete, for we struggle with indwelling sin

(7:17, 20). When Paul shifts from the past tenses of 7:7-13 into the present tenses of 7:14-25, he moves from his life as an unbeliever into the normal Christian life. No Christian is ever more than part-rescued this side of the resurrection.

The structure of Romans 8
Romans 8 begins with 'no condemnation' by the wrath of God (v. 1) and ends with 'no separation' from the love of God in Christ (v. 39). The overarching theme is assurance. Between these end markers two other themes dominate: first (and mostly in vv. 1-17) there is life in the Spirit, who is named 15 times in verses 1-17 and then 4 more times later in the chapter; second (vv. 17-39) there is suffering. Verse 17 is the hinge between these two ('… children … heirs … if indeed we share in his sufferings …'). Verse 31 ('What, then, shall we say …?') signals Paul's great conclusion.

It is probably best to divide the chapter in three, including verse 17 in both first and second sections.

1. (vv. 1-17) Life in the Spirit (continued from 7:14-25)
2. (vv. 17-30) Suffering and glory
3. (vv. 31-39) Unbreakable ties to Christ

Working through the text
A. Life in the Spirit (8:1-17, continued from 7:6 and 7:14-25)
Paul begins with a statement (v. 1), which he explains (v. 2) and expands (v. 3) before going on to God's purpose (vv. 4-11).

The statement (v. 1)

> [1]Therefore, there is now no condemnation for those who are in Christ Jesus,

This is a summary of the letter so far. 'Now' refers not to individual conversion or some supposed change of gear into the higher Christian life, but to the gospel events which have brought into the open (1:17 'revealed'; 3:21 'made known') the justification by faith by which believers of every age have been rescued from condemnation.

'Therefore' refers back generally to the argument so far, but very specifically to 5:12-21. Paul uses this word 'condemnation' only here and in 5:16, 18 in all his letters. It is the opposite of 'justification' (5:16). The words 'through Jesus Christ our Lord' (7:25) and 'in Christ Jesus' (8:1) tie us back to Paul's exposition of life in union with Christ in 5:12-21 (developed in 6:1-11).

The explanation (v. 2)

> [2]...because through Christ Jesus the law of the Spirit of
> life set me free from the law of sin and death.
>
> [...*because the law of the Spirit of life in Christ Jesus set you/
> me free from the law of sin and death.*]

(We are not certain whether Paul wrote 'me' or 'you', but it doesn't matter.)

This very compressed verse needs unpacking.

1. The phrase 'in Christ Jesus' is repeated from verse 1 (disguised in NIV). The word 'in' carries the senses both of 'in union with' and 'through the work of'. What has happened to us, has happened because of what Jesus did (NIV 'through Christ Jesus') and because we have been united by faith with him ('in Christ Jesus'), and therefore we benefit from what he did.

2. It is most natural to take 'the law' to refer to 'the Law of Moses' in both phrases.

3. The 'law of sin and death' is a compressed way of summing up what the Law of Moses does to the unregenerate sinner (7:7-12). The law when it comes from the outside into contact with sin, exposes sin, condemns sin, and results in the death of the sinner (7:7-10). This terrible 'marriage' was always heading for the rocks (7:1-5). This is what someone has called 'the law on the wall', like the Ten Commandments written on a church wall, true and good but outside of our sinful hearts.

4. 'The law of the Spirit of life' is a shorthand for what happens when the Spirit of Christ takes the obedience of Christ (5:19), imputes the righteousness of Christ to us, and writes the fundamental demand of the good law on the cleansed heart of the believer, changing us from the inside, and so leading to eternal life (6:23). The 'law on the wall' becomes the 'law in the heart'.

Paul has 'trailed' the ministry of the Spirit in 2:15 (probably); 2:29; 5:5; and 7:6. Now he begins to expound this theme.

The explanation expanded (v. 3)

³For

>   what the law was powerless to do [*the weakness of the law*]
>> in that it was weakened by the sinful nature [*the flesh*],
>   God did
>> by sending his own Son
>>> in the likeness of sinful man [*sinful flesh*]
>>> to be a sin offering [*and for sin*].
>   And so he condemned sin in sinful man, [*in the flesh*]

How were we 'set free' (v. 2)? Paul takes each part in turn. Negatively, he speaks of '*the weakness of the law*, in that it was weakened by the flesh'. He has shown in 7:7-12 (and

3:20; 4:15; 7:5) that law is powerless to save. When the law remains outside of us, it is just a dead 'letter' (2:29; 7:6).

The law cannot save. But God can! 'the weakness of the law ... God did ...' (i.e. God did what the law was too weak to do). How did God do it?

'By sending his own Son ...':

1. '...in the likeness of sinful flesh' taking our human nature upon him with all its weakness, being really tempted and fully identified with sinners, and yet without sin (the word 'likeness' guards this difference).

2. '... for sin' an expression which usually refers in the Greek Old Testament to a sacrifice for sin.

As an old hymn puts it, 'Because the sinless Saviour died ... the wrath of God is satisfied', and that terrible slave-master sin has been 'condemned ... in the flesh', that is, in the flesh of Jesus on the cross. This is why we may be sure 'there is no condemnation for those who are in Christ Jesus'.

Notice that the basis of our rescue is the death of the Son on the cross, and the application of that rescue to our lifestyle is by the ministry of the Spirit. Both are necessary. No one benefits from the Cross without receiving the Spirit, and no one receives the Spirit who is not justified by the blood of the Son.

God's purpose: why did God set us free? (vv. 4-6)

> ³ᵇ... he condemned sin in sinful man, [*in the flesh*] ⁴in order that
>   the righteous requirements [*requirement (singular)*]
>   of the law
>   might be fully met[*fulfilled*] in us,
>   who do not live according to the sinful nature [*flesh*]
>   but according to the Spirit.

> [5]Those who live according to the sinful nature
> [*Those who are according to the flesh*]
>> have their minds set on what that nature [*the flesh*]
>> desires;
> but those who live in accordance with the Spirit
>> have their minds set on what the Spirit desires.
>
>> [6]The mind of sinful man [*the flesh*] is death,
>> but the mind controlled by the Spirit is life and peace;

Why did God 'condemn sin in the flesh' of Jesus? Why the cross, and why the gift of the Spirit to apply the benefits of the cross to the believer? Answer: 'in order that' something might happen that could not happen through the law: 'the righteous requirement (singular) of the law' is now 'fulfilled in us ...'.

What does this mean? We need to hold together two parts of the answer.

1. By his death Jesus fulfils the law *for* us. This links back to verse 3b, about the cross.
2. By the Spirit we fulfil the law *in union with* Jesus. This links forward to verses 4b-6, which speak of how we actually 'live' (lit. 'walk').

The word translated 'righteous requirement' is used in the singular only four times by Paul in his letters, all in Romans (1:32; 5:16, 18; 8:4). (He also uses the plural in 2:26). In the singular, the word means something like 'what the law says is *the right thing*'. So in 1:32 it is the 'righteous decree' of God that sinners deserve to die. In 5:16 it is translated 'justification' with the sense of 'fulfilled law', 'what the law says is the right thing has been done'. In 5:18 it is 'the one act of righteousness' of Jesus, his one 'fulfilment of the law', which is also called his 'obedience' (v. 19).

The key is to hold together the doctrines of the work of Christ *for* us and the person of Christ *in* us. Although these are distinct they are inseparable.

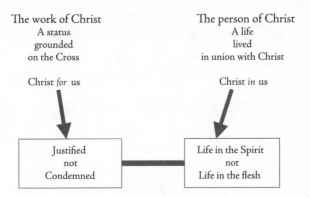

The law says that 'the right thing' is for sinners to die (1:32). This 'right thing' happened when Jesus died; he did 'the right thing' by his perfect obedience to death (5:18, 19). So he won for us a status not of 'condemnation' ('wrong thing'), but of justification ('right thing') (5:16). This is part (a) of the truth: Christ fulfilled the law *for* us, on our behalf.

But we must not stop with part (a). For by the Spirit we are vitally united with Christ, transferred from Adam's condemned humanity into Christ's justified humanity (5:12-21). And therefore in union with Christ we begin to do 'the right thing', to 'fulfil the right thing of the law' by actually walking according to the Spirit.

So in verses 4-6 Paul moves from the basis of our justification (Christ for us, verse 3) to the application of our justification to life (Christ in us, verses 4-6)—how we walk. He fulfilled the law for us, and therefore in him we begin to fulfil the law by walking according to the Spirit. Paul contrasts two ways to 'walk', according to the flesh (the unconverted life), where the 'mind' (control centre, inner being) is set on the flesh, heading for death; or according to the Spirit, with the inner being invaded by the Spirit, and therefore heading for 'life and peace'.

Paul now expands on each of these two ways in turn.

The first way: life in the flesh (vv. 7, 8)

> ⁷the sinful mind [*the mind-set of the flesh*]
>> is hostile to God.
>> It does not submit to God's law,
>> nor can it do so.
>
>> ⁸Those controlled by the sinful nature [*Those in the flesh*]
>>> cannot please God.

The 'mind-set of the flesh' (the life governed by an unconverted control-centre):

1. '… is hostile to God' (5:10) because it worships idols rather than God (1:18-32);

2. '… does not submit to God's law' but rebels against its demands;

3. '… cannot please God' (c.f. Heb. 11:6 'Without faith it is impossible to please God') because it is trapped in slavery to sin (3:9) and cannot escape.

The second way: life in the Spirit leading to resurrection (vv. 9-11)

> ⁹You, however,   are controlled not by the sinful
>   nature but by the Spirit
>   [*are not in the flesh but in the Spirit*],
>> if the Spirit of God lives in you.
>>> And if anyone does not have the Spirit of Christ,
>>> he does not belong to Christ.

¹⁰But if Christ is in you,

> (a) your body is dead because of sin,
>
> (b) yet your spirit is alive [*the S/spirit is life*] because
> of righteousness.

¹¹And if the Spirit of him who raised Jesus from the
dead

> is living in you,
>
>> he who raised Christ from the dead
>>
>> will also give life to your mortal bodies
>
> through his Spirit,
>
>> who lives in you.

Verse 9 clarifies that life in the Spirit is not some kind of
higher Christian life; it is the normal and only authentic
Christian life. Those 'in the flesh' are those without Christ.
Those 'in the Spirit' are those in whom 'the Spirit of God'
dwells. And because 'the Spirit of God' is also 'the Spirit of
Christ' (there is no authentic spirituality outside of Christ),
all who 'belong to Christ' have the Spirit.

Verse 10 explains to us the 'so what?' of having the Spirit,
and verse 11 expands on this. 'But if Christ is in you' (which
he is, if you have the Spirit of Christ, whom you have if you
belong to Christ, v. 9), then although (a) 'your body is dead
because of sin' (indwelling sin means your body is decay-
ing and will die), nevertheless you may be sure (b) that 'the
S/spirit is life because of righteousness'. It doesn't matter
whether this is 'the Spirit' (the indwelling Spirit of Christ)
or our 'spirit' (our inner being); the point is that the Spirit
of God has invaded our spirit, and his presence there points
to a future of eternal life because of 'righteousness', the justification won for us by Christ.

Verse 11 clarifies the truth of verse 10. 'And if the Spirit
of him who raised Jesus from the dead is living in you' (which

he is, if you belong to Christ, v. 9), then we may draw the following wonderful conclusion: 'he who raised Christ from the dead will also give life to your mortal bodies'. How? Paul repeats the beginning of the verse, for emphasis: 'through his Spirit, who lives in you.' The indwelling Spirit is the Spirit of the one who raised Christ from the dead; this is what he did for Christ, and this is what he will do for anyone whom he indwells. He cannot live in a person without guaranteeing bodily resurrection to that person. So although we struggle now with the 'body … dead because of sin' we know that this same 'mortal body' will be raised at the end. (Similarly, in 6:5 Paul makes the point that because we are now 'united with Jesus in a death like his', we know that in the future 'we will certainly also be united with him in his resurrection').

Conclusion (1): the Christian's obligation (vv. 12, 13)

> [12]Therefore, brothers, we have an obligation—
> > but it is not to the sinful nature [*flesh*], to live according to it.
>
> [13]For if you live according to the sinful nature [*flesh*],
> > you will die;
> but if by the Spirit you put to death the misdeeds of the body,
> > you will live,

'Therefore', because the indwelling Spirit of Christ guarantees future bodily resurrection, 'we have an obligation'. We don't owe our sinful nature anything, because that nature is just heading for death. That nature has not given us any benefit for which we ought to thank it and respond by serving its desires. But (by implication) our obligation is 'by the Spirit' to 'put to death the misdeeds of the body', because this is the path to life. Notice that (a) we have to 'put to death the misdeeds of the body' (we do not just 'let go and let God' do it for us), but that (b) we do not do this in our own strength ('works of the law') but 'by the Spirit'. It is by the grace of God working in us that we put to death that old way of living. Notice also that we 'put to death' in the present continuous tense, indicating ongoing activity; this mortification of the old life cannot be done in one go, but needs a daily taking up of the cross and denial of self (Luke 9:23). This is the appeal of 6:12, 13, 19, but now stated with explicit reference to the Spirit.

Conclusion (2): the Christian's privilege (vv. 14-17)

> [14]…because those who are led by the Spirit of God, *these* are sons of God.

> [15]For you did not receive a spirit that makes you a slave again to fear,
>> but you received the Spirit of sonship [*of adoption*].

>> And by him we cry, 'Abba, Father.'
> [16]The Spirit himself testifies with our spirit that we are God's children.

> [17]Now if we are children, then we are heirs—heirs of God and co-heirs with Christ,
>> if indeed we share in his sufferings [*we suffer with him*]
>> in order that we may also share in his glory [*we may be glorified with him*].

Why will we 'live' (v. 13)? 'Because those who are led by the Spirit of God,' these same people 'are sons of God.' Adoption guarantees eternal life. To be a 'son' of God (v. 14) is to be a 'child' of God (v. 16). The word 'son' is used because in Paul's culture the son came into the inheritance. Men and women in Christ are together 'co-heirs with Christ' (v. 17).

To be 'led by the Spirit of God' does not mean what we sometimes call 'guidance' (What job should I do? Whom should I marry? Where should I live?, etc); it means living 'according to the Spirit' rather than 'according to the flesh'. It is to live rightly, freed from 'slavery' to sin (6:14 'Sin shall not be your master'). That slavery carried with it 'fear', the terror of the condemned sinner under the wrath of God (2:5). The indwelling Spirit is 'the Spirit of adoption', by whom 'we cry, "Abba, Father"', who bears witness internally, in our experience, that we really are 'God's children'. The cry, 'Father!' encompasses all the trust and all the security it is both necessary and possible for a human being to have on earth. The apostles treasured the memory of the original Aramaic word 'Abba' used by Jesus (e.g. Mark 14:36). The point of verse 16 is not that the Spirit makes us children of God, but that he makes us *aware* that we are children of God.

Verse 17 draws the conclusion, that 'if we are children' (which we are, if we belong to Christ), 'then we are heirs':

1. 'heirs of God'. This does not mean that God will die (!) but rather that we will receive all that God has promised, i.e. 'the world' (4:13);

2. 'and co-heirs with Christ'. We inherit the promises not as individuals, but as Christ's new humanity, Abraham's corporate 'offspring' (see on 4:13).

As we experience the wretched struggle with indwelling sin (7:24), we are to know that the Spirit of Christ within us guarantees that one day we will inherit the world with Christ in a resurrection body in which sin will be no more. Far from despairing, this gives us confidence to press on with the battle against sin day by day.

But there is a sting in the tail of verse 17. To be a 'co-heir' with Christ means to be united with Christ (to be 'in Christ'), which means that the shape of his career must be the shape of our career—'if indeed we suffer with him in order that we may be glorified with him'. Paul now turns to that suffering.

B. Suffering and glory (8:17-30)
Paul makes a daring claim (v. 18) and follows it with a three-part proof (vv. 19-27) before his conclusion (vv. 28-30).

The claim (v. 18)

> [17b]*if indeed we suffer with him in order that we may be glorified with him.*
> [18]For I consider that
> > our present sufferings [*the sufferings of this present time*]
> > > are not worth comparing
> > with the glory that will be revealed in us.

In verse 17b Paul says that the pathway to future glory —for us, as it was for Jesus—must lie through present suffering. To which the obvious question is: Is it worth it? Does future glory outweigh present suffering? Is it worth following this costly path? Paul 'considers' (indicating a measured thoughtful conclusion) that it is worth it (c.f. 2 Cor. 4:17).

1. On the one hand there are 'the sufferings of this present time'. The New Testament speaks not primarily of two places (earth and heaven) but of two ages (this age and the age to come). The 'sufferings of this present time' include all the pain of living in a broken world, but – for the Christian – suffered 'with him' (v. 17). Paul knows how heavy this is. He does not make this statement lightly, but writes as one who has suffered deeply and

feels the sufferings of others (e.g. 2 Cor. 11:23-28). Verses 35-39 paint suffering in very strong terms.

2. On the other side of the scales there is 'the glory that will be revealed in us' (v18), to be 'glorified with him' (v17). This is not just that we will see *his* glory; it is that his glory will be seen in *us*. Glory is the outward shining of God's inward being, the invisible God made visible, not least through human beings who are his 'image and likeness'. We exchanged this glory for worthless idols (1:23) and so we lack this glory (3:23). The believer seeks the restoration of this glory and will be given it (2:7, 10) - we have a sure hope of this glory (5:2). Paul begins and ends verses 17-30 with this glory, which is the final destiny of the children of God (8:30). At present the true nature of the children of God is hidden (c.f. Col. 3:3); one day it will be revealed for the universe to see. On that day we will rule the world in Christ, restored to the unblemished likeness of God, perfectly Christlike (1 John 3:2).

Paul says that the sum total of human suffering in this age is like dust in the scales by comparison with that future glory. This claim is so massive that he embarks on a cosmic proof in three stages. He takes men and women mired in the maze of incomprehensible suffering and gives us an aerial view, so that we see where it leads.

Proof part A: This glory is so great that the whole creation groans in longing for it (vv. 19-22)

> [19]*For* the creation waits in eager expectation for the sons of God to be revealed.
>
> > [20]For the creation was subjected to frustration [*futility*],
> > not by its own choice,
> > > but by the will of the one who subjected it, in hope
> > > [21]that the creation itself will be liberated

> from its bondage [*slavery*] to decay
> and brought into
> > the glorious freedom of the children of God
> > [*the freedom of the glory of the children of God*].

²²We know that the whole creation has been groaning as in the pains of childbirth right up to the present time.

How do we know future glory outweighs present suffering? 'For' (omitted in NIV) 'the creation' (that is, the universe, with particular emphasis on the sub-human created order) 'waits in eager expectation' (the word suggests craning the neck to see, as one might do in a crowd watching for a coming king) 'for the sons of God to be revealed'. Christians are God's children now (v. 16), but only on that great day will they be seen as such by all.

Why is creation so eager for this?

1. Because it 'was subjected to futility' (everything Ecclesiastes laments about a messed-up world);

2. 'not by its own choice' (of course it didn't want that!);

3. 'but by the will of the one who subjected it' (that is, God) 'in hope' (that is, looking forward with sure and certain hope);

4. 'that the creation itself will be liberated from its slavery to decay' (a world under sin and death, 5:12);

5. 'and brought into the freedom of glory of the children of God'. Creation was meant to be the theatre of God's glory, singing his praises and showing his beauty. It will never be 'free' to be this as it ought until it is governed as it needs to be, by human beings in the image of God (Gen. 1:26-28; 2:15). Rebellious human beings ruin not only their own lives, but the order of all creation

(Gen. 3:14-19). Like a play in which the lead actors are drunk, or an orchestra whose conductor has not bothered to do his job, creation is malfunctioning because we human beings don't run it properly. The 'freedom of the glory of the children of God' is the freedom creation will enjoy when the children of God run it properly at last.

We may show how a universe of glory differs from a universe of decay in two diagrams.

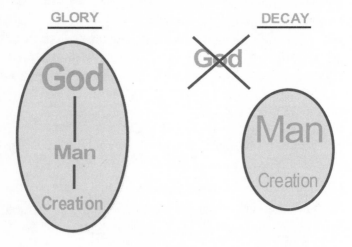

No wonder creation longs for that great day! And that day will come (v. 22)! The 'groaning' of creation is not its death-throes, but the birth-pangs of a renewed and restored creation in which all things will be made new (Rev. 21:5). Paul's point is that the glory we anticipate is a very big thing. It is the restoration of the universe under redeemed humanity in Christ. It is much bigger than a collection of individual places in 'heaven'. Present suffering is terrible; but it is outweighed by this cosmic vision of glory to come.

Proof part B: Christians groan in longing for this glory to be revealed (vv. 23-25)

> [23]Not only so, but we ourselves,
>> who have the firstfruits of the Spirit,
>>> groan inwardly
>>>> as we wait eagerly for
>>>>> adoption, the redemption of our bodies.

> [24]For in this hope we were saved.
>> But hope that is seen is no hope at all.
>> Who hopes for what he already has [*sees*]?
>>> [25]But if we hope for what we do not yet have [*see*],
>>>> we wait for it patiently [*with patient endurance*].

Within the groaning creation there cries a groaning church. (The same word 'groan' is used of Christians in 2 Cor. 5:2, 4). The three stages of Paul's proof have been called 'a symphony of sighs'. Creation waits in hope; Christians wait in hope (the same word 'wait' is used in verses 19, 23, and 25). Paul teaches here the origin, the object, and the implication of this groaning.

1. The origin of Christian groaning is the Spirit of God. All human beings groan under the pain of a world under sin. But Christian groaning is different, and comes because we 'have the firstfruits of the Spirit'. This does not mean we have part of the Spirit (the first bit of the Spirit, as opposed to the fullness of the Spirit); it means we have the Spirit (the whole of the Spirit as an indivisible person) living in us (8:9) as the firstfruits of a greater harvest to come. His gracious invasion of our hearts is the pledge and foretaste of the age to come, the guarantee of our resurrection (8:11). Christian groaning

is not therefore the shapeless cry uttered into empty space, saying, 'This is awful', grumbling and doubting; it is a cry given by the Spirit of adoption, directed to our Father, longing for his promised future. It is the cry, 'Come, O Lord' (Maranatha, 1 Cor. 16:22); 'Come, Lord Jesus' (Rev. 22:20); 'Your kingdom come, your will be done on earth as it is in heaven' (Matt. 6:10).

2. The object of Christian groaning is for 'adoption, the redemption of our bodies'. We have 'the Spirit of adoption' (v. 15), but this new status as children of God is hidden and experienced in the context of daily struggle (7:14-25). We long for the day our bodies ('this body of death' 7:24) will be redeemed and our adoption complete.

3. The implication of this groaning is patient endurance. This is the point of verse 24. Our rescue is 'in … hope', which means that – by the definition of hope – it is not yet seen and experienced in full. So the implication of Christian groaning is that 'we wait for it with patient endurance' (used in 2:7 to describe the direction of the believer's life; in 5:3, 4 to describe what suffering works in the believer; and then again in 15:4, 5 to describe how the God of patient endurance uses the Scriptures to work patient endurance in believers).

Proof part C: The Spirit of God groans in longing for that glory to be revealed (vv. 26, 27)

> [26]In the same way, the Spirit helps us in our weakness.
>> *For* we do not know what we ought to pray for,
>>> but the Spirit himself intercedes for us
>>>> with groans that words cannot express

[*wordless groanings*].

> [27] And he who searches (our) hearts knows the
> mind of the Spirit,
>> because the Spirit intercedes for the saints
>> in accordance with God's will.

The Spirit helps us, because in our weakness 'we do not know what we ought to pray for' (or 'how to pray as we ought'). This is not speaking of the specifics of prayer in a particular situation (Should I pray for this illness to be healed, to get this job, or whatever?) but more deeply that if it were not for the Spirit we could not even pray in the right general direction. Only by the Spirit do we know to pray 'your kingdom come' and have the confidence that the kingdom will come. Only by the Spirit do we know that the pain of a messed-up world is labour pains rather than death-throes, that we really can pray in confident hope for the new creation and the redemption of our bodies.

The wonder is that beneath our groanings there is the groaning of God praying to God! The Spirit of God himself (who is fully God) 'intercedes for us', praying to God, 'with wordless groanings'). This is not prayer on human lips (speaking in tongues), but the prayer of God to God that is so deep it needs no words. And (v. 27) not surprisingly, God knows the mind of God and will answer the prayer of God: 'he who searches hearts'—that is, God—'knows the mind of the Spirit'—that is, God!—'because the Spirit intercedes for the saints' (for all Christians) 'in accordance with the will of God.'

Under the groaning of creation there cries the groaning of a part-rescued church. But—and this is the really wonderful thing—beneath the groaning of a part-rescued church there cries the wordless groaning of God crying to God on behalf of the saints. This prayer will most certainly be 'in accordance with the will of God' and therefore we may rest assured it will be answered. And if the groaning of God will be answered, so will the Spirit-given groaning of Christians, and so will the groaning anticipation of the whole creation.

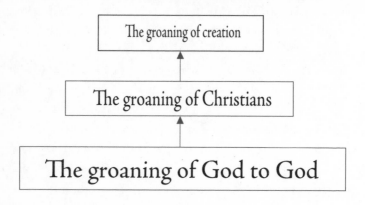

This is why we may be sure that future glory outweighs the pain of present suffering.

Conclusion (vv. 28-30)
It is important to read verses 28-30 in the context of verses 18-27. They are the conclusion to Paul's argument in support of the claim that future glory outweighs present suffering.

> [28]And we know that in all things God works for the good of those who love him, who have been called according to his purpose.
> [*And we know that*
>   *to those who love God*

> *all things work together for good,*
> *to those called according to his purpose*]

29For those God foreknew he also predestined
to be conformed to the likeness of his Son,
that he might be the firstborn among many brothers.
30And those he predestined, *these* he also called;

those he called,   *these* he also justified;

those he justified,   *these* he also glorified.

'The Spirit intercedes for the saints in accordance with God's will' (v. 27). But what is God's will? Verses 28-30 tell us. Verse 28 lays out this will, in general terms, as it is directed (a) 'to those who love God', which means, (b) 'to those called according to his purpose'. Christians are defined both by their loyalty (they love God) and by God's purpose and call. For those people, 'all things' — including the sufferings of this present time (v. 18)—'work together for good', not just the individual good of the believer, but the good of the whole creation. There is more at stake here than what is good for me personally! The working together of all things under God is the birth-pangs of the new creation, which will be perfectly good.

Paul expands the 'purpose' of God (v. 28) by four movements through five stages: foreknowledge, predestination, calling, justification, and glorification.

1. **Foreknowledge** does not just mean that God knows facts in advance, that he chooses people because he happens to know they will later believe. Knowledge here is not so much a cognitive matter (knowing facts), but a matter of personal relationship (c.f. Amos 3:2, 'You only have I *known* [NIV 'chosen'] of all the families of the earth'). Long before a Christian knows God, God

has known him or her and entered, in anticipation, into relationship.

2. **Predestination** means that God begins to put this personal foreknowledge into effect. In verse 29 we are told God's purpose:

a) that we should become perfectly Christlike ('to be conformed to the likeness of his Son'). Christ is the only human being to have perfectly shown the world the image and glory of God (2 Cor. 4:4; Col. 1:15; John 1:14). In Christ we are being 're-newed ... in the image of (the) Creator' (Col. 3:10; c.f. 2 Cor. 4:16, 17). Even 'our lowly bodies' will be transformed to be 'like his glorious body' (Phil. 3:21) and will 'bear the likeness of the man from heaven' (1 Cor. 15:49). Between now and that day there is to be a progressive change in Christian people who become gradually more and more 'conformed to the likeness of his Son'.

b) that we should be part of a large Christlike family ('that he might be the firstborn among many brothers'). The world to come will not be ruled by a whole lot of individual Christlike people, but by Christ's one Christlike family (c.f. Heb. 1:6; Rev. 1:5; 1 Cor. 15:20; Col. 1:15, 18).

3. **Calling** here means the effective call of God rather than the open invitation that calls to all humankind. This call speaks light into darkness (2 Cor. 4:6) and life to the dead (4:17). We will see this use of 'calling' in chapter 9.

4. **Justification** has been at the heart of Romans. When God calls a man or woman, he declares him or her righteous on the basis of the death of Jesus.

5. **Glorification** has been the focus throughout verses 18-30. The past tense 'glorified' is used because, although the event itself is future, it is 'as good as done' because God says it will happen.

Paul's point is that *all* those with whom God begins this process complete it. Unlike the successive years of a university course, there are no dropouts. There is no leakage. I have drawn out this sense by adding the word 'these' (a literal translation) three times in verse 30: every one of those who go through one stage, all these without exception go to the next stage. So if in the present I have been justified then, however terrible 'the suffering of this present time', I know I am unbreakably tied back to the foreknowledge, predestination and calling of God, and therefore safely secured to future glorification.

C. *Unbreakable ties to Christ (8:31-39)*

³¹What, then, shall we say in response to this?

Here is the grand 'So what?' after Romans 5-8 (or perhaps Romans 1-8). Paul's answer divides in two parts.

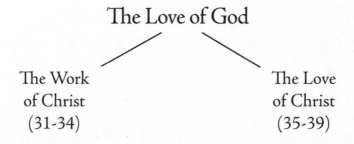

The Love of God

The Work of Christ (31-34)

The Love of Christ (35-39)

1. The love of God and the work of Christ (vv. 31b-34)
Paul begins with the work of Christ for us on the cross.

³¹ᵇIf God is for us, who (can be) against us?
    ³²He who did not spare his own Son,
        but gave him up [*handed him over*] for us all—
            how will he not also, along with him, graciously
            give us all things?

³³Who will bring any charge against those whom God
has chosen?
    It is God who justifies.
³⁴Who is he that condemns?

Christ Jesus, who died—more than that, who was raised
to life—
    is at the right hand of God and is also interceding
    for us.

Three times Paul throws down a legal challenge. Will God's declaration stand in the court of the universe, when he declares us justified and not condemned?

+   'If' (i.e. since) 'God is for us' (which he is, in Christ) 'who can be against us?'
+   'Who will bring any charge against those whom God has chosen?'
+   'Who is he that condemns?'

In each case the legal challenge is answered by the cross of Christ. When the accuser brings charges against Christians, he has to put a hand over his mouth when he sees the cross. First (v. 32), God 'handed him over' (c.f. 5:8, 9) his own Son (foreshadowed in Abraham giving up Isaac in Gen. 22:12, 16). This sacrifice guarantees that he will give us all things necessary to get us to glory. If he has made this sacrifice he will make sure the sacrifice was not in vain.

Then again (v. 33b) 'It is God who justifies'; he justifies because Jesus became our propitiation (3:21-26). Finally

(v. 34b) 'Christ Jesus, who died – more than that, who was raised to life' (his resurrection sealing the effectiveness of his death, c.f. 4:25) '- is at the right hand of God' (the place of authority where he sat down after completing the work of making purification for sins, Heb. 1:3) 'and is also interceding for us' by the mere fact of his presence there, with his pierced hands, feet, and side.

2. *The love of God and the love of Christ (vv. 35-39)*

³⁵Who shall separate us from the love of Christ?
Shall trouble or hardship or persecution or famine
or nakedness or danger or sword?

³⁶As it is written:
'For your sake we face death [*are being killed*] all day
long;
we are considered as sheep to be slaughtered.' (Ps. 44:22)

³⁷No, in all these things we are more than conquerors through him who loved us.
³⁸For I am convinced that
neither death nor life,
neither angels nor demons [or *rulers*],
neither the present nor the future,
nor any powers,
³⁹neither height nor depth,
nor anything else in all creation,
will be able to separate us from the love of God
that is in Christ Jesus our Lord.

If verses 31-34 point us to the objective truth of the cross of Christ, verses 35-39 focus on the subjective disposition of love towards us by the Father and the Son. Verses 35 and 39 use the same word 'separate'. Paul's theme is the unbreakable tie that holds us to 'the love of Christ' (i.e. his love for us,

v. 35), which is the same as 'the love of God that is in Christ Jesus our Lord' (v. 39). Paul presses home the strength of this tie in three ways.

1. In verse 35 he gives a list of sufferings: 'trouble or hardship or persecution or famine or nakedness or danger or sword'. These give a terrible feel for the range and pain of 'the sufferings of this present time' (v. 18). But none of them can separate us from the love of Christ. In verse 36 he quotes from Psalm 44. This is a Psalm of God's people suffering (probably in exile). Unlike some of the people, these are suffering 'for your sake', for the sake of God's reputation. Like sheep queuing for the abattoir ('sheep to be slaughtered') they experience deep suffering. And yet their suffering is in some way a filling up of the sufferings of Christ.

2. In verse 37 he coins a new phrase 'to be a super-conqueror' and says that because Christ loved us and died for us, we are bound to come out on the winning side, vindicated, and inheriting the world to rule (hence 'conquerors').

3. In verse 38 he uses a number of pairs to indicate totality. Just as 'heaven and earth' means 'everything —high stuff and low stuff, and everything in between', so 'death … life' means everything, and so do the other pairs. Nothing, nothing, nothing, will be able to separate us from the love of God that we know and experience in Christ Jesus our Lord.

From text to teaching
Getting the message clear: the theme
The grand theme is assurance, from 'no condemnation' at the start to 'no separation' at the end of the chapter. In

between, the argument progresses in two main stages with a conclusion. The first stage is verses 1-17, whose focus is the ministry of the Spirit. Because Christians walk by the Spirit now, they may be certain that they are heading for glory later. We must hold together the present ministry of the Spirit with his role to point us securely towards a promised future. In the second stage, verses 17-30, the focus shifts from the Spirit to suffering, but we are still being pointed to future glory. The central point is stated in verse 18 that, for the Christian, certain glory later outweighs present suffering. The conclusion in verses 31-38 needs to hold together the objective and the subjective: the objective truth of the cross guarantees that God loves us for ever in Christ.

Getting the purpose clear: the aim

The overall aim of Romans 8 must be to promote a proper, cross-based, Spirit-given, assurance for the believer who struggles with sin (7:14-25) and with suffering (8:17-39). Both failure with sin and pressures from suffering unsettle us deeply, and the only remedy is to know with equal depth the unbreakable love of God for us in Jesus.

Under this overall aim, we shall now see how the three main sections of the chapter contribute. Verses 1-17 encourage us to walk daily by the Spirit and by the Spirit to put to death the deeds of the body, motivated by an understanding of where the Spirit points (to our resurrection). We are not to give up the sometimes wretched struggle (7:24), but to persevere. We are not to fall back on a reliance on external rules ('oldness of letter' 7:6), but walk only by the Spirit who writes the law in our hearts. We want to reconnect the link that Satan loves to break, between the present tense motions of the Spirit of God in the heart and future glory.

We slip into thinking that our experience of the Spirit is just a slightly stronger version of conscience. In fact it is sure evidence that we are headed for glory.

Verses 17-30 encourage us to grasp deeply what is going on with the sufferings of this present time, so that we not only understand but feel that they are pointing both us and the whole universe towards an eternal weight of glory which outweighs present suffering. Verses 31-39 press home to us eloquently and passionately that the objective love of God for us, shown in the work of Christ on the cross, and the subjective disposition of God's love towards us, guarantee that we cannot be separated from that love.

How do the aims of Romans 5-8 relate to the aims of the letter as a whole?
This is a good point to look back on the whole section 'Living under grace' to ask how this section contributes to Paul's overarching aims in the letter, to promote harmony within the church and a zeal for missionary partnership beyond the church. Why do we need to understand our unbreakable relationship with God (5:1-12; 8:17-39), our reliance upon the work of Christ and the ministry of the Spirit (5:12-21 with 8:1-17), our freedom from slavery to sin and condemnation by the law (chapters 6 and 7), the struggle with indwelling sin (7:14-25) and so on? Of course it is a good thing to understand these things, but how will it make us a harmonious and outward-looking church?

The key is to grasp the connection between works and as-surance. We go back to our imaginary (but not unrealistic) Mr X (pp. 153-155), who begins to rest his standing before God and in the church partly on his own moral uprightness, Bible knowledge or religious privileges. Not only does this make him boast (and so destroy harmony); it also undermines his assurance. And an insecure Christian is a dangerous Christian (and an insecure pastor is an especially dangerous one!). If I am insecure, I always feel I have something to prove. So my attitude to my fellow Christians will have an element of competitiveness (however discreet). And my evangelistic involvement (if any) will never be the humility of one forgiven sinner telling other sinners where to find grace.

Pointers to application

+ The message 'no condemnation' (v. 1) only makes sense to those who have grasped that without Christ we are and must be condemned. It may therefore be necessary to recap some of the argument of the letter so far (especially 1:18–3:20). We need to feel the wonder of 'no condemnation' and never take it for granted.

+ We may also need to recap 'the law of sin and death' (v. 2). We need to understand and feel our helplessness, and the inability of moral guidance ('the law on the wall') to help us (v. 3).

+ Show how vital it is that the 'law on the wall' should become the 'law in the heart'. Previously the law bid me fly, but left me on the ground. Now the law bids me fly and the Spirit gives me wings.

+ Stress that the 'no condemnation' and the setting free (vv. 1, 2) are instantaneous, not the result of a gradual process.

+ Assurance is not arrogance, but rather a humble acknowledgement of what God has done for us.

+ Whatever our many and various needs in life, our deepest need has been wonderfully and fully met in Christ.

+   (v. 10) Help us to feel the misery of living in a body that is mortal ('the body is dead'), perhaps from the terrible experience of seeing a loved one's health decline in the face of a terminal illness. Help us to grasp that this is all the result of our human sin, of living in a world under God's righteous curse. But help us to rejoice in the fact that the indwelling Spirit guarantees that one day we will rise with resurrection bodies (v. 11).

+   (vv. 14-16) Make sure we know that only Christians are the children of God (i.e. that 'Dear Lord and Father of *mankind*' is a misleading opening line to the famous hymn).

+   Make clear that to be a disciple of Christ is to have the Spirit of God (who is a Person not an influence) and to be a child of God the Father (vv. 9-16). These are alternative descriptions of Christians. They describe exactly the same people; we are either all of these or none.

+   (vv. 15, 16) Make sure we understand that there is a subjective and experiential dimension to Christian assurance, that the Spirit of God 'testifies with our spirit that we are God's children'. A non-Christian student was quoted as saying after a gospel address, 'It doesn't seem real. It seems true, but it doesn't seem real.' We need to pray for the ministry of the Spirit testifying with our spirit that our union with Christ is both objectively true and subjectively real.

+   (vv. 17b, 18) Be realistic about the sufferings of this present age. Make sure this does not seem like some abstract theological construct, but rather engages with our hearers where they are. Be specific in preaching against the shallow untruths of the 'health, wealth and prosperity gospel' which is no gospel. This travesty of the gospel is endemic in many parts of the world. In some countries the wedding vows are changed from 'for better, for worse; for richer, for poorer' to 'for better, for best; for richer, for richest' on the grounds that for a Christian it is never going to be 'poorer' or 'worse'. These people say, 'Come to Jesus and stop suffering.' 8:17 says, 'Come to Jesus and suffer with him. Come to Jesus and your life will probably become tougher in all sorts of ways.' Satan will ask to sift you like wheat, and he will be given permission to do so (c.f. Luke 22:31; Job 1:1–2:10). Indeed, the quotation in 8:36 suggests our gospel invitation might say, 'Come to Jesus and join the queue for the abattoir!' Such a gospel may not fill our churches; but it will be a great safeguard against disillusionment. In their Christian lives people will be able to say that they experienced 'just what it said on the tin'.

+ (v. 18-27). Make sure we grasp that the glory to be revealed in us is not talking about heaven, but rather about the even more wonderful, and rock-solid real, prospect of our being made perfectly Christlike to govern the new creation.

+ (vv. 19-22) Help us to understand how human sin has ruined the world. It may help to give specific examples of how our selfishness has caused a wonderful and beautiful world to become disordered. What creation needs is not the absence of human beings (as some extreme eco-warriors may suggest), but rather the government of Christlike human beings.

+ (v. 22) Help us feel the difference between understanding the pain of the world as labour pains rather than death throes; how that crucial difference in where the pain leads can make all the difference to how we bear up under it in hope. It has been said that, 'It is not suffering that destroys a person, but suffering without purpose.'

+ (vv. 23-25) Encourage us to patient endurance as the practical outworking of understanding Paul's argument. If we really get what he is saying, then we will hang in there when it's hard.

+ Help us to look critically at our hymns and songs, to see if what drives them and energises us to sing is our present experience or our future hope. Christian prayer and song ought to be driven not by the ambiguous encouragements of present circumstances but by the unambiguous glory of future hope. We sing not because the present is enjoyable, but because the future is glorious.

+ (vv. 26-28) Help us to respond with wonder and confidence that the future for which we long is the future for which God prays to God! And therefore it could not possibly be more certain.

+ (vv. 29, 30) Make sure we understand that the purpose of these great truths is assurance rather than complacency. They are not to make us apathetic about evangelism, but humbly confident in our security when afflicted by doubts and suffering.

+ (vv. 29-31). Use the doctrine of predestination for the purpose for which it is intended, to promote and deepen assurance in the face of suffering. The entrance to the Christian life is like an archway. As we approach from the outside we see the open invitation, 'Come to me, all who labour and are heavy laden'. After we enter, we look back and see over the inside the words, 'Chosen from before the foundation of the world.' Both are equally true. All are invited to come. But those who come learn later that their coming and their subsequent perseverance are entirely by the grace of God. Were it otherwise, none of us would persevere under suffering.

+ (vv. 31-34) Perhaps dramatise the court scene in which the accuser (the Satan) says, 'God, look at (name). It is outrageous for you to declare her justified. She is a sinner … (and then add the chargesheet, all of it true)'. To which God always replies, 'Yes, every charge is true. But look at those scars on my Son. I gave up my Son for her. The penalty has been fully paid. How dare you accuse! You cannot condemn'.

+ Press home the logic of verse 32. For God to give up Jesus to death and then abandon us on the roadside on the way to glory would be like a rich man spending a vast sum on a car and then leaving it on the roadside saying he couldn't afford the petrol to run it; it would be absurd.

Suggestions for preaching and teaching the text
It is probably easiest to divide the chapter into its three main sections.

Three Sermons on Romans 8
Sermon 1: Romans 8:1-17
We might lead in by asking, 'How safe do you feel?' and explore the kinds of regrets about past failures, and anxieties about future pressures, which make us feel insecure.

Our teaching points might be as follows:

To be a real Christian means …

1. To be under new management (vv. 1-8);
2. … who gives us new hope for our bodies (vv. 9-11);
3. … and guarantees us a great inheritance (vv. 12-17).

Alternatively, we might divide the passage as follows:

To be a real Christian means…

1. No condemnation, because of the sacrifice of God the Son (vv. 1-4);
2. Resurrection hope, because of the indwelling of God the Spirit (vv. 5-11);
3. Present assurance in the security of God the Father (vv. 12-17).

Our tone is not so much exhortation ('Now be good and walk by the Spirit') as encouragement to see the connection between the Spirit's ministry in us in the present, and future resurrection.

Sermon 2: Romans 8:17-30
We might start by stating Paul's claim in verse 18 and playing 'devil's advocate' to challenge it and suggest that it is an outrageous overstatement. We want people to feel just how heavy the suffering is on one side of the scales, so that they appreciate just how massively heavy the glory has to be to outweigh it.

Our teaching points might be as follows:

1. Present suffering is bad, but future glory is far better (v. 18). We will need to explain what 'glory' means.
2. A messed-up world longs for human beings to run it properly (vv. 19-22).
3. Christian believers long for new bodies to run the world properly (vv. 23-25).
4. God himself longs for Christians to run the world properly (vv. 26, 27);
5. … and therefore he will make quite sure that they do (vv. 28-30)!

Sermon 3: Romans 8:31-39

We might begin by looking at some of the sufferings that unsettle our assurance as a church, and how we respond in ways that divide the church or make it inward-looking.

Our teaching points might be as follows:

1. Christian security rests on the already-paid penalty for sin (vv. 31-34);

2. ... and this proves the unbreakable love of God in Christ (vv. 35-39).

Leading a Bible study on Romans 8

In a chapter so rich and so long it is important for the leader to have a clear grasp of the main themes and flow, to stop the group getting stuck on points of detail, or going home with no overall sense of the clear teaching of the chapter. Don't worry if smaller issues are left to one side; make sure we go home rejoicing in the big truths!

To clarify understanding

1. Why is there no condemnation for those united with Christ Jesus (vv. 1-4)?

2. What is the connection between what Jesus did for us and what we do by the Spirit as men and women united with Jesus (vv. 1-6)?

3. What are we taught about the unbeliever's mind (control centre) in verses 6-8? Why is it impossible for them to please God (v. 8)?

4. Who lives in all Christians, according to verses 9-11? (Look at the three different ways the answer is described).

5. Why does having the Spirit guarantee our future bodily resurrection (v. 11)?

6. What is our obligation as Christians (vv. 12, 13)?

7. What does the Spirit do for and in us (vv. 14-17)?

8. What question does verse 17b raise, and how does Paul answer it in verse 18?

9. What is creation waiting for, and why (vv. 19-22)?

10. What are Christians waiting for, and how are we to wait for it (vv. 23-25)?

11. What does the Spirit do, and how does he do it (vv. 26, 27)?

12. What are the five stages by which God fulfils his great purpose in Christians (vv. 28-31)?

13. What is God's great aim (v. 29)?

14. How does Paul answer the law court challenge that asks if any charge can be made to stick against God's chosen ones (vv. 31-34)?

15. What is Paul's main point in verses 35-39?

To encourage honest response

1. How does the struggle against sin (7:14-25) make us feel? Why does it unsettle us and make us doubt the grace of God?

2. In what ways do we experience the work of the Spirit as described in this chapter?

3. How can we help one another to connect this experience with assurance of future resurrection?

4. In what ways do we actually experience 'the sufferings of this present time'?

5. In what ways do we see futility, frustration and decay in creation?

6. Are our groanings Christian groanings, or just pagan cries of misery?

7. How can we encourage one another to wait with patient endurance under pressure?

PT MEDIA

RESOURCES FOR PREACHERS AND BIBLE TEACHERS

PT Media, a ministry of The Proclamation Trust, provides a range of multimedia resources for preachers and Bible teachers.

Books

The *Teach the Bible* series, published jointly with **Christian Focus Publications**, is specifically geared to the purpose of God's Word – its proclamation as living truth. Books in this series offer practical help for preachers or teachers tackling a Bible book or doctrinal theme. Current titles are: *Teaching Matthew, Teaching John, Teaching Acts, Teaching 1 Peter, Teaching Amos* and *Teaching the Christian Hope*. Forthcoming titles include: *Teaching Mark, Teaching Daniel, Teaching Isaiah, Teaching Nehemiah, Teaching 1, 2, 3 John, Teaching Ephesians, Teaching 1&2 Samuel.*

DVD training
Preaching & Teaching the Old Testament:
                    Narrative, Prophecy, Poetry, Wisdom
Preaching & Teaching the New Testament:
                    Gospels, Letters, Acts & Revelation

This training resource is based on the core 'Principles of Exposition' material from the Cornhill Training Course. **David Jackman** has taught this material to generations of Cornhill students, as well as to countless preachers and Bible teachers in the UK and overseas.

The **Old Testament** set contains four DVDs (and workbooks) covering Narrative, Prophecy, Poetry and Wisdom. The **New Testament** set covers Gospels, Letters and Acts & Revelation.

Each DVD gives instruction on how to tackle the particular biblical genre. For example, what are the key principles in preaching or teaching Old Testament narrative stories? Or, what are the key principles in preaching the Psalms?

The resource is designed not only for preachers, but for those teaching the Bible in a variety of different contexts.

+ **Interactive** DVD-based training material
+ **Workbooks** in PDF format (downloadable)
+ Designed for **individual** or **group study**
+ Flexible format ideal for **training courses**
+ Numerous **worked examples and answers**
+ Optional **subtitles** for English as a second language

Audio

PT Media Audio Resources offer an excellent range of material for the preacher or Bible teacher, covering over twenty years of conferences. The *Instruction On...* series (how to teach a bible book) and the *Sermons On...* series (model expositions) are available as mp3 CDs and downloads.

For further information on these and other PT Media products, visit our website at **www.proctrust.org.uk** or email **media@proctrust.org.uk**

**TEACHING
AMOS**

Unlocking the Prophecy of Amos
for the Bible Teacher

BOB FYALL

SERIES EDITORS: DAVID JACKMAN & ROBIN SYDSERFF

**TEACHING
ACTS**

Unlocking the book of Acts
for the Bible Teacher

DAVID COOK

SERIES EDITORS: DAVID JACKMAN & ROBIN SYDSERFF

SPIRIT OF TRUTH

Unlocking the Bible's Teaching on the Holy Spirit

DAVID JACKMAN

**TEACHING
1 PETER**

Unlocking the book of 1 Peter
for the Bible Teacher

ANGUS MACLEAY

SERIES EDITORS: DAVID JACKMAN & ROBIN SYDSERFF

Other books from PT Media:

Teaching Acts:
Unlocking the book of Acts for the Bible Teacher
David Cook
ISBN 978-1-84550-255-3

Teaching Amos:
Unlocking the prophecy of Amos for the Bible Teacher
Bob Fyall
ISBN 978-1-84550-142-6

Teaching 1 Peter:
Unlocking the book of I Peter for the Bible Teacher
Angus MacLeay
ISBN 978-1-84550-347-5

Teaching Matthew:
Unlocking the Gospel of Matthew for the Expositor
David Jackman
ISBN 978-1-85792-877-8

Spirit of Truth:
Unlocking the Bible's Teaching on the Holy Spirit
David Jackman
ISBN 978-1-84550-057-3

TEACHING
JOHN

Unlocking the Gospel of John
for the Bible Teacher

DICK LUCAS & WILLIAM PHILIP

SERIES EDITORS: DAVID JACKMAN & ROBIN SYDSERFF

TEACHING
THE CHRISTIAN HOPE

Unlocking Biblical Eschatology
for the Bible Teacher

DAVID JACKMAN

SERIES EDITORS: DAVID JACKMAN & ROBIN SYDSERFF

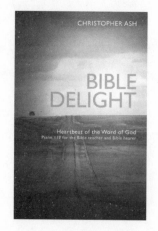

CHRISTOPHER ASH

BIBLE
DELIGHT

Heartbeat of the Word of God
Psalm 119 for the Bible teacher and Bible hearer

Christian Focus Publications

publishes books for all ages

Our mission statement –

STAYING FAITHFUL

In dependence upon God we seek to help make His infallible Word, the Bible, relevant. Our aim is to ensure that the Lord Jesus Christ is presented as the only hope to obtain forgiveness of sin, live a useful life and look forward to heaven with Him.

REACHING OUT

Christ's last command requires us to reach out to our world with His gospel. We seek to help fulfil that by publishing books that point people towards Jesus and help them develop a Christ-like maturity. We aim to equip all levels of readers for life, work, ministry and mission.

Books in our adult range are published in three imprints.

Christian Focus contains popular works including biographies, commentaries, basic doctrine and Christian living. Our children's books are also published in this imprint.

Mentor focuses on books written at a level suitable for Bible College and seminary students, pastors, and other serious readers. The imprint includes commentaries, doctrinal studies, examination of current issues and church history.

Christian Heritage contains classic writings from the past.

Christian Focus Publications Ltd
Geanies House, Fearn, Ross-shire,
IV20 1TW, Scotland, United Kingdom
info@christianfocus.com
www.christianfocus.com